SPEAKING VOLUMES

Ray Willbanks grew up in the American South and was educated at the University of Alabama and the University of Texas. His interest in Australian literature began in graduate school and in 1978 he published *Randolph Stow,* the first book-length study of that writer's work.

A founding member of the American Association of Australian Literary Studies, and fiction editor of *Antipodes,* Willbanks is active in the promotion of Australian literature in the USA. He is professor of English at Memphis State University.

Penguin Books

SPEAKING VOLUMES

AUSTRALIAN WRITERS AND THEIR WORK

RAY WILLBANKS

Penguin Books

Penguin Books Australia Ltd
487 Maroondah Highway, PO Box 257
Ringwood, Victoria 3134, Australia
Penguin Books Ltd
Harmondsworth, Middlesex, England
Viking Penguin, A Division of Penguin Books USA Inc.
375 Hudson Street, New York, New York 10014, USA
Penguin Books Canada Limited
10 Alcorn Avenue, Toronto, Ontario, Canada M4V 1E4
Penguin Books (N.Z.) Ltd
182-190 Wairau Road, Auckland 10, New Zealand
First published by the University of Texas Press, 1991
Published by Penguin Books Australia, 1992
10 9 8 7 6 5 4 3 2 1

Printed in Australia by Australian Print Group, Maryborough, Victoria.

National Library of Australia
Cataloguing-in-Publication data:

Willbanks, Ray.
Speaking Volumes: Australian writers and their work.

Includes index.
ISBN 0 14 017385 4.

1. Authors, Australian – 20th century – Interviews. 2. Australian literature – 20th century – History and criticism. I. Title.

A820.9003

CONTENTS

ACKNOWLEDGMENTS

I WISH TO THANK the Association for the Study of Australian Literature, and then President Shirley Walker, for inviting me to the ASAL meeting in Launceston, Tasmania, in 1987, which began this project, and I wish to thank the Literature Board of the Australia Council, which funded a Familiarization Tour in the same year.

My thanks go again to the Literature Board for a subsistence grant in 1989 which helped a great deal with my expenses while I was in Australia conducting interviews. According to the terms of the grant, I am happy to include the following statement: "This project was assisted by the Australia Council, the Federal Government's arts funding and advisory body."

I thank also the College of Arts and Sciences of Memphis State University for a Faculty Development Leave for the fall term 1989 which gave me the time away from teaching to work on this project. Also: "This work was supported in part by a grant from Memphis State Faculty Research Fund. This support does not necessarily imply endorsement of research conclusions by the University."

I owe a personal thanks to Brian Kiernan for putting up with me at his home in Sydney for longer than he should have had to, and to his dog Blackie, who gave up his room. I want also to thank Bill McGaw for his hospitality and his invitation to join the Commonwealth Prize festivities in Sydney. In Melbourne, thanks to B. Wongar for the trip to the country and the bush walk and to Lynda Grbin, who gave me her apartment. Thanks to Fay Zwicky and to Thea Astley, who have cooked, housed, driven, and generally fussed over me. Thanks to Mark Macleod for the sightseeing in Sydney, and to Lyla, Rosie, and Rupert Rosenblum for the lovely times at Watson's Bay.

A special thanks to Elaine Lindsay, who has made the Literature Board such a pleasure.

I am most grateful to all the writers. Of course, without them there would be no book and no reason for one.

INTRODUCTION

AT PRESENT no Concorde flies from Los Angeles to Sydney; even the daily nonstops plow their way through the night sky high above the black Pacific for an incredibly long fourteen hours, time enough for two movies, two meals, two bottles of Australian wine, two-thirds of a novel . . .

Dawn reddens the huge engines of the 747, and down thirty-seven thousand feet below shines the long, long east coast of Australia. The flight has two hours to go. Looking out and down on that mostly empty, vast continent, again conscious of the even greater surrounding sea that the plane has passed over all night, an alarm of animal fear clutches, then passes on, leaving in its wake the sudden awareness of how far one has come—the other side of the earth, the bottom of the planet. Mentally, I locate the return ticket in the bag beneath my seat, and in that instant I recall the meaning of the word "ticket" in nineteenth-century Australia. A convict, if not sentenced for life, worked for his "ticket of leave." An early settler longing for relatives and a British home saved for a ticket and a three-month passage on an uncertain sea. If on my third trip to Australia I could still feel displaced looking down on this distant island, speeding comfortably alongside it at seven hundred miles an hour, what must arriving in Australia have felt like for the convicts and the early settlers, when home was not measured in hours, but in months, or lifetimes, when Christmas came on heat waves and winter chilled July? I looked at my watch as if to check the season. It was 5 A.M., late October, and down below in Sydney it was spring.

At last—the red tiled roofs shining in the early morning sunlight, the watery coves filled with sailboats, the vast Sydney Harbor, the bridge, the white fins of the Opera House—a city—three million people after so much water and space and time. And on the ground, sitting up front with the cab driver, Australian style, another surprise—Sydney, this time, did not feel like the end of the earth; it felt solid, accommodating, another version of home.

It is people I go to literature for, for stories about what it is to be human, for versions of myself lived out in different times, in different places. Australian writers in the past have told us a great deal about the place—the wombat, the bandicoot, the Bunyip, the outback: sheep, drought, bush fires. Contemporary writers are telling us even more. They are telling us about ourselves. It is the brochured koala and the kangaroo, perhaps the blond surfer on an empty beach, that fill the tourists with a hope of finding a land unspoiled, but it was the contemporary Australian writers who had brought me here the first time and who were now bringing me back. It was the writers whose talent had supported an amazing film industry in the 1970s, and whose marvelous fiction was currently flashing in bookshop windows across America. I had chatted with a number of these writers on previous trips to Australia; now I wanted to strengthen conversation into something I could share with others who were discovering or studying Australian fiction.

While much, perhaps most, Australian fiction has been documentary during the two-hundred-year history of the country, realistically, somberly, ironically recording the perils and passage points that have altered somewhat over the decades, shifting from the bush to the city, Australian fiction of the last half of this century has become, in accordance with Western literature in general, more psychological and more complex, and to me more rewarding. My own interest in Australian writing began in 1970 when, as a graduate student studying with Joseph Jones at the University of Texas, I first read the novels of Patrick White and Randolph Stow. I found myself suddenly in a literary world which introduced me to a country I did not know and to a style of writing that in its blend of realism, poetry, myth, symbol, psychology, and metaphysics was richly satisfying and intellectually challenging. My interest in Stow led me to write a Ph.D. thesis on his fiction and to publish in 1978 a book of criticism on his poetry and fiction.

The importance of Patrick White is monumental, not only for the quality of his work and the influence he has had on younger writers, as many interviewed in this book attest, but also because his winning the Nobel Prize in 1973 inspired Australian artistic self-confidence and quite suddenly caught the attention of readers, writers, and critics around the world.

It does not take long in a discussion with Australian academics or writers to encounter the phase "cultural cringe," a reference to the Australians' lingering belief in their second-class cultural citizenship, or to be made aware of the chronic need for Australians to define themselves in terms of national identity and to prove their worth to the rest of the world. In their interviews, Fay Zwicky, Thomas Keneally, David Williamson, Peter Carey, and others speak on variations of this concern, on their own ambivalence on what it means to be Australian, what it means to be a part of a small

English-speaking country of sixteen million on a South Pacific landmass whose nearest neighbor is Asia.

It is my contention that contemporary Australian literature not only is providing Australians with a multifaceted identity at home but also is providing the country with a large measure of international recognition and esteem. In addition to the academic interest in Australian literature in Europe and Asia, there is a great deal of critical activity in the United States, with the measurement of current Australian literary success being both popular and academic. In 1986 a group of American academics from around the United States met at Columbia University and formed the American Association of Australian Literary Studies. The AAALS has grown sixfold since that time and publishes both the *Newsletter* and *Antipodes: A North American Journal of Australian Literary Studies.* In 1988 the Edward A. Clark Center for Australian Studies was founded at the University of Texas and facilitates the study of numerous Australian subjects.

It is, I think, particularly noteworthy when academic literary interests and the marketplace coincide. Though many of us knew the quality of writing that was emerging from Australia in the 1980s, I, for one, did not know how much fiction was being reviewed and thereby brought to the attention of the public. I was interested to learn from Thomas Keneally of a conversation he had in 1987 with Mitch Levitas, editor of the *New York Times Book Review.* Levitas reported that the *Times* was reviewing more fiction from Australia than from any other country outside the United States.

It was because of my own early interest and because of the growing interest in the United States in Australian literature that I became an initial member of the American Association of Australian Literary Studies and later Fiction Editor of *Antipodes.* In 1987 I was invited to Australia as a guest of the Association for the Study of Australian Literature and given a Familiarization Grant from the Literature Board of the Australia Council. During that visit I met Patrick White, Thea Astley, Jessica Anderson, Thomas Keneally, and a number of other Australian writers. From those meetings, I published several interviews in *Antipodes.* In 1988 I returned to Australia briefly with similar resulting interviews and publications. My more extensive reading in Australian fiction convinced me that I wanted to do a collection of interviews, asking questions from an American's point of view and quite a few specific questions regarding the writers' works and their attitudes toward themselves and their country. In late 1989 I returned to Australia and, with the exception of Patrick White, I reinterviewed all the writers I had talked to before and added a number of new ones.

As I began this piece, I left myself in a taxi headed toward Ward Street and a little hotel just off King's Cross, Sydney's version of Times Square, complete with hookers, girlie shows, a McDonald's, and most important for me, a subway stop. Friends kept raising an eye when I told them I was staying at King's Cross, but I had never met an Australian transvestite outside a Patrick White novel and it was fun to stroll among the varyingly sexed ladies of the evening, as well as among people from all over the world. I had first learned of the Cross through a Jessica Anderson novel, *Tirra Lirra by the River*; King's Cross was where Nora, her heroine, had lived and where Anderson herself had lived in a quieter time; so this seemed the place for me, and it was for awhile, though in the weeks which followed I lived with friends in several places in Sydney: Paddington, Watson's Bay, Balmain, and later in Melbourne and in Perth. Although a good number of writers do live in other places—Adelaide, Perth, Brisbane, the countryside, the coast, Tasmania—Sydney and Melbourne are centers of the literary life in Australia. In or near Sydney, I interviewed Jessica Anderson, Thea Astley, Peter Carey, Robert Drewe, Helen Garner, Kate Grenville, David Malouf, Frank Moorhouse, Patrick White, and David Williamson. In Melbourne, I talked to Beverley Farmer and B. Wongar; in Perth, Elizabeth Jolley, Tim Winton, and Fay Zwicky. Although Tom Keneally calls Sydney home, I caught up with him at his apartment overlooking Broadway in New York.

So, I set out first from King's Cross. Originally, I had wanted to interview thirty fiction writers, but I was given a page limitation by my publisher which cut that number almost in half. I made several considerations in choosing the resulting sixteen, including the quality of a writer's work and the availability of the work in the United States and resultant name recognition. I wanted a writer/critic for an overview commentary; I also wanted to represent theater and film. The list, at least the longer list, was affected by the availability of the writer. For example, although I tried for an aboriginal writer, the particular writer who seemed appropriate for my project never responded to my queries. Also, because of page limitations, I decided not to include any expatriate Australian writers, although in a larger book, certainly, they would be included. Although the resultant inclusion of writers in this volume was shaped in part by circumstance, the writers interviewed are representative of the best of Australian writing. I would hope that my omissions might be included in another volume. In the meantime, I would send the reader to other collections of interviews mentioned elsewhere in this book.

Again, because of space limitations I have not included a list of critical articles dealing with the works of each writer interviewed, but instead, refer the reader to two American bibliographic indexes which list recent criticism.

To avoid, as much as was practical, repeating information contained within the individual interview, I have intentionally kept the descriptive information that precedes each interview short.

Within the interviews I have tried to do several things. I hoped to give the reader a bit of biography, a bit of personality, and, by my selection of the titles for discussion, an indication of the major works by the writer. With some writers, I wanted to deal with specific technical, stylistic, thematic, or philosophical questions about their work. With some, I wanted to talk about Australian/American influence, with others about theater, film, and national issues, both literary and philosophical. Each interview is tailored to the writer. Although I had done my homework and had written out what I wanted to ask, in some instances the interview contracted or expanded according to the dynamics of the moment, which is, of course, what separates an interview from an essay. Although the writers were offered an opportunity to read and edit what they had said to me, only Helen Garner and Jessica Anderson chose to do so. Both made a few changes of a stylistic nature in their remarks.

One interview, the one with Patrick White, differs from the others. I was invited to tea by Patrick White in 1987. Feeling my way through the morning, I understood two things to be inappropriate: asking him direct questions about his work, and switching on a tape recorder. When I returned to Sydney in 1989, Patrick White was in the care of a nurse and the request for another meeting seemed inappropriate. However, I think my account of the 1987 morning visit belongs in this collection; the form is different, but the experience is revealing. Because it is a departure from my interview pattern and because of White's stature, I have placed it first in the collection.

Interviews are governed by a number of things: the rapport between interviewer and interviewee, the intrusive presence of the tape recorder, the kind of night-before that either has had, the recall of an anecdote that a question will obliquely set off, the eagerness of the author to make revelations, or the shield he or she throws up to deflect too close an encounter. Ideally, the good interview will have some of the aspects of a short story: the creation of character, bits of revelation, a sense of closure. Some interviews in this collection achieve the shape I wanted better than others; some tell a life story, as in the case of B. Wongar; some focus closely on the work, as with David Malouf; others achieve a mixture. Altogether, the interviews form a composite of conversation about contemporary writing in Australia, with certain recurring issues serving as markers of who the modern Australian is, what nags from the past, what engages the imagination.

Perhaps a partial gathering of the issues and the writers who address them is useful: (*a*) the past, including convict times, the nature of the land, the treatment of Aborigines—Astley, Keneally, White, Wongar, Zwicky; (*b*) Australia versus England, prevailing attitudes—Grenville, Jolley, White, Williamson; (*c*) national identity and/or national character flaws—Carey, Keneally, Moorhouse, White, Williamson, Zwicky; (*d*) sexuality, hippies, feminism—Drewe, Garner, Jolley, Moorhouse, Williamson; (*e*) drama and film—Keneally, Williamson; (*f*) writing, publishing, the Australian critics—almost everyone; (*g*) American influences—almost everyone.

Perhaps two final notes of explanation are useful for the American reader. These concern the Literature Board and the numerous literary prizes given in Australia. The Literature Board was established by the Australian government in 1973 to support writers through direct subsistence grants and through subsidies to publishers to bring more Australian writing into print. Between 1973 and 1974, the Literature Board supported the publication of fifty-four works of fiction; by 1986 the number had grown to over two hundred. Writers themselves will argue the mixed blessing of this government patronage, but the Literature Board has been an important factor in stimulating and disseminating creative writing in Australia. It has also provided funds for critical research and subsidized literary journals; my own grants and the subsidy for *Antipodes* are personal examples. For more information on the workings of the Literature Board, I refer the reader to Thomas Shapcott's *The Literature Board: A Brief History* (1988).

The literary prizes referred to in this book are as follows: The Miles Franklin Award, one of the most prestigious of the Australian prizes, is given for a published novel portraying some aspect of Australian life. The Miles Franklin was established in 1957 and currently is valued at $25,000. The *Australian*/Vogel Prize is a literary award for an unpublished novel by a writer under thirty-five and is valued at $15,000. The Patrick White Prize was established by the author with his 1973 Nobel Prize money and is given to an older Australian writer who has not received critical attention equal to the quality of the work; this prize most recently provided an award of $20,000. There are also prizes given by the various Australian states, such as the New South Wales Premier's Prize; by newspapers, such as the *Age* Book of the Year Award; and by other organizations, such as the National Book Council Award and the Gold Medal presented by the Association for the Study of Australian Literature. While these awards provide important recognition for achievement, they are also welcome as income supplements in a country in which the average print run for a novel is only three thousand. Beyond Australia, two prizes have been of great importance to the Australian writer, the Nobel Prize, which has gone to Patrick White, and England's Booker Prize, which has been awarded to Thomas Keneally and Peter Carey.

What remains clear in my memory after the intellectual probing and the literary questions have been laid to rest is the kindness and generosity of the writers I talked to in Australia, their genuine friendliness and warmth, which included permitting my photographs. In an age suspicious of sentiment, I suppose reticence in matters of affection is a safer course than hyperbole, but I must say how special I found these Australians, how much I learned, and how much I was nourished by being with them. I hope something of this pleasure is captured for the reader in the interviews which follow.

RAY WILLBANKS

MEMPHIS, TENNESSEE

PATRICK WHITE

was born in 1912 in London, where his parents, well-to-do fourth-generation Australians of English extraction, were living. White was brought back to Australia as a baby; then at thirteen he was sent to England for secondary schooling. At eighteen, his parents allowed him to return to Australia to work as a jackaroo; afterward, he again returned to England, this time for study at Cambridge University. While living in England, he published his first novel, *Happy Valley,* in 1939. In 1940 White was commissioned as an Air Force intelligence officer; he served in the Middle East during World War II. In 1948 he returned to Australia to live. Writing a psychological, metaphysical, sometimes mythical fiction, a fiction not subjugated to the limits of realism, White has been a tremendous influence on his contemporaries, leading the way in creating a fiction and drama experimenting in language and in form. Not only is White the most impressive of Australia's writers; his work sets him in the first rank of writers in the twentieth century. In 1973 Patrick White was awarded the Nobel Prize for Literature. Australian critics responding to a recent poll named *The Twyborn Affair* among the top three contemporary Australian novels. White died in 1990.

The Ploughman and Other Poems, 1935
Happy Valley, 1939
The Living and the Dead, 1941
The Aunt's Story, 1948
The Tree of Man, 1955
Voss, 1957
Riders in the Chariot, 1961
The Burnt Ones (stories), 1964
The Ham Funeral (drama), 1965
The Season of Sarsaparilla (drama), 1965
A Cheery Soul (drama), 1965
Night on Bald Mountain (drama), 1965
Four Plays (drama), 1965
The Solid Mandala, 1966
The Vivisector, 1970
The Eye of the Storm, 1973

The Cockatoos: Shorter Novels and Stories, 1974
A Fringe of Leaves, 1976
Big Toys (drama), 1978
The Twyborn Affair, 1979
Flaws in the Glass (self-portrait), 1981
Signal Driver (drama), 1983
Netherwood (drama), 1983
Memoirs of Many in One, 1986
Three Uneasy Pieces (stories), 1987
Shepherd on the Rocks (drama), 1987

PATRICK WHITE AT SEVENTY-FIVE

On January 24, 1988, six months after I had had tea with Patrick White at his home in Sydney, I was delighted to see him sparring in a ten-second interview on American television. Both *Good Morning, America* and the *ABC Nightly News* showed the reenactment of the arrival of the First Fleet at Sydney Harbor along with protesting Aborigines, fireworks, and an appearance by Prince Charles and Princess Diana. The report switched from a laughing Prince and Princess to Patrick White sitting in apparent ease and good health in his garden. Asked what he thought of the bicentennial celebration, White, in the softest of voices, said, "Well, I think it's shocking the way the royal goons are going to be here most of the year." He added, "I can't really see an awful lot to be proud about in our past, and certainly not in our present."

Six months earlier he had told me the same thing, citing the transportation of convicts, the treatment of the Aborigines, and the allegiance to monarchy as Australian blemishes. In a letter he had written to me, he said, "I am too ashamed of so much that has gone on in our history and can't accept the pouring of millions into a 'festival' when we do so little for the aboriginals and the many contemporary white Australians who are starving. The Queen of England will be coming to open the new and unnecessarily extravagant Parliament House and her spawn will be popping up all over the country at various moments." He intended to protest in his own way, he said. He would refuse to allow any play of his to be staged during the bicentennial year or any work of his to be published. True to his word, when it appeared that the publication date of his new book *Three Uneasy Pieces* was going to be delayed until 1988, he took it from one Melbourne publisher and gave it to another who would bring it out in 1987.

Patrick White as I saw him at seventy-five—a man of strong convictions with no timidity of expression. As we talked in July 1987 I found him angry and impatient with his fellow Australians. Though arthritic and asthmatic and needing his rest, he was not, happily, as he had pictured himself a few months earlier in his letter to me. "I am crumbling," he had written, "osteoporosis, a filling chest, glaucoma, and a hernia." He had invited me to visit him, lamenting doubtfully, "if I am still around." From his letter, I had expected to find him, if still around, decrepit and depressed. Instead of gasping his last, I found him scrappy and vituperative. The hernia had been repaired, the chest was clear, and he wasn't dependent upon the cane he carried.

When I arrived at the white frame house on Martin Road on the sunny, chilly July morning, White's longtime companion, Manoly Lascaris, in sweater and gloves, was working in the front garden among azaleas, camellias, and a few stalky red impatiens. Their Italian gardener had quit some months before, Lascaris explained to me, and he was tending the flowers. Crippled for awhile by arthritis, he had undergone six months of acupuncture, and now he was able to move without pain and to enjoy the garden.

He took me around to a side entrance to the house. Patrick White must have been watching from behind a curtain—he must have been—for he opened the door as soon as we were on the steps. And there he was—a big man, white hair, deep-set eyes, drawing me into the house with a handshake and a point of his cane. He led me through a short hall into the living room and seated himself across from me, positioning himself with a direct beam of bright light shining on his eyes. I remembered the glaucoma. As a playful put-down or a blunt truth, I never knew which, he said, "I've forgotten your name. Is it Millikin or Millbank, or something like that?" Thus began two hours of conversation, gossipy, bitchy, full of laughter and complaints and pronouncements, a roller coaster ride that touched on everything but his work. Any attempt on my part in that direction was masterfully diverted, as I had expected it would be.

In *Flaws in the Glass,* White spoke of visitors who came expecting him to be like one of the characters in his novels, or to be full of high sentence and philosophical pronouncements. They got a surprise, he said. And yet despite what he said, the depth and the presence were there. And even with all the laughter and kindness, I knew I was with the great man and was never comfortable enough to forget it.

Impatient under the bright light (too strong? not strong enough?), White soon led Manoly Lascaris and me down the hall toward the kitchen, where he proposed to make tea and take it outside. I glanced about, wanting to linger in front of walls covered with startling paintings, to inspect bold colors thick on canvas. I wanted to examine a long case filled with White's own books published in various English and foreign-language editions. I paused at a utility staircase leading to the second floor, thinking that it was nothing like the one in *The Eye of the Storm,* an elaborate affair that Sister de Santis had moved ponderously up and down as she waited on Elizabeth Hunter. I had thought White had used his home as a setting in *Eye,* but I could see nothing in it that I recognized from the novel. Obviously, I was wrong.

In the kitchen, White got the tea things together, heated water in a blue coffeepot, put brown mugs and saucers on a tray, took a box of cookies from a plastic container on a shelf. "You don't mind if I put the box on the tray, if I leave them in the box, do you?" he asked.

I carried the tray to the back door, where White angrily shouted down two little dogs, one white, one orange. I asked about cats. I'd seen cats in pictures with him. "We've always had cats," he said. "But now we're without one. Cats usually live a long time. We're too old," he said, sadly, "to start a new one."

We crossed a narrow lawn to a raised deck covered by a twiggy canopy, leafless now in the winter. Lascaris warned us to wait before sitting down. "Bird shit," he said, cleaning off the chairs.

The house and yard are on ground higher than the street. Beyond White, in the distance through the trees, I could see commercial buildings. It wouldn't be long, White complained, until all the houses along his leafy green street would be torn down for "progress." "It is sad," he had written me, "that such a beautiful world can also be so vile."

Over tea we spoke of Tasmania, where I had just been. "We were there once," White said, "to escape the Nobel Prize. It's a lonely place, isn't it? I could still hear the rattle of the convict chains. I was there once before, when I was ten years old. I could have heard the chains even better then, if I had known what I was hearing."

He spoke of Tasmanian farmer-poet Barney Roberts, who had been captured during World War II, and how much he liked his poetry. He spoke of New Zealander Janet Frame and his regard for her fiction, and told warm, comical stories of his friend Thea Astley, who had once been his neighbor when she and her family were living at Epping, a short distance from his home at Castle Hill. He remembered the time he had invited the American actress Anne Baxter to meet Thea, thinking she might want to star in a movie of Thea's novel *A Descant for Gossips.* "We all got along," he said, "but nothing ever came of the movie idea."

Had he seen David Malouf's new play, *Blood Relations,* which was then on stage in Sydney? I asked. He had, he answered. "Did you like it?" I persisted. He looked through me. "I like David," he said.

I tried to remember other questions on my list. "You met Frieda Lawrence once when you were in New Mexico. What was she like?"

He didn't pause. "Jolly," he said. "Not at all the earth mother you'd expect." His tone told me the subject did not interest him.

So I shifted again. White was wearing a gray crew neck sweater. From his neck hung an ivory-colored ink pen. On another cord hung a fat, misshapen cross. I asked him about the cross, what it meant that he was wearing it.

He smiled, as if in anticipation of his answer. "This was given to me by a nun who lives in a tree. She makes these crosses. And what I wonder is," he grinned mischievously, "if she keeps making these crosses, what's going to happen to her home?" We laughed. Manoly Lascaris poured more tea.

I remembered that I had a small present for White in my bag. Before I had left the States I had cast about for something to give him. I love his work and I was grateful that he had agreed to see me. So I wanted to hand him something, though I doubted if I could please him. I had found stuck away in a desk in my home in Memphis a small black wool, satin-lined Greek coin purse that I had bought on a whim some years before. It was a small piece, not as big as my hand, but fitted with a long black cord, if one wanted to wear it. Embroidered in white on the black wool was the outline of a wise man, Confucius perhaps, sitting on a bench. Behind him, around him, were tiny purple flowers, pinheads of color. Purple, the color of transcendence. Back at home, it had seemed the perfect gift for him. Now, as I removed it from my bag and handed it to him, I wondered if I was being silly. "I don't know why I want to give this to you," I said. "But the purple spots remind me of the purple you use so often in your novels. Particularly *The Twyborn Affair.*"

"Do I?" he said. And that was all he said.

He looked at it for a moment, then promptly put it around his neck, layering it with the pen and the wooden cross. I wondered if some day hence he would have an American story to go with that of the nun. "Some people tell me," he said, his eyes on me, "this cross looks like a piece of sucked gingerbread." His eyes widened and we burst out laughing.

Flickers of shade dappled the sun on Patrick White's face as we sat under the naked branches of the arbor, our conversation bumping into silences as it wound down. I'd been mesmerized by the eyes, hard and hostile as he raved about the growth of Sydney or the stupidity of the bicentennial, distant when I bored him, warm and laughing when he touched on something that he enjoyed. There was also pain and nastiness and impatience. I kept thinking of Milton's Satan, who had been to the heights and depths and seen it all, of Lazarus, who had come back to tell all. White was wrong if he thought that a visitor who came seeking the author found only the man. The eyes belonged to both.

I asked him if I could take his picture. He got up and stood in the sunlight in front of a shrub and said with a kind of sadness, "How many, many times I've stood in this spot and had my picture made." I focused longer than I had to, not wanting to give up those eyes.

Back in the kitchen, White got out the Yellow Pages and looked up the telephone number of the Cosmopolitan Coffee Shop, where I was to meet a friend. He insisted on dialing the number. When the arrangements were made, Lascaris got out the Fiat and drove me around Centennial Park to the coffee shop. Along the way we talked of his American mother, who had recently died in Vermont in her nineties, and of his forty-five-year relationship with Patrick White. He double-parked in front of the Cosmopolitan and continued to tell me stories about White in a gentle and loving voice until impatient traffic forced me from the Fiat and him along his way.

I would love to tell what he said, this other half of the Living Legend. But even now I can hear Patrick White's words in one of his moments of bitterness as we talked. "You'll probably go out and tell X [famous writer] just what I said about her. Everybody tells everything."

Well, I haven't told all. And with Patrick White strong enough to shout down the monarchy on round-the-world television I wouldn't dare tell it all, even if I wanted to.

JESSICA ANDERSON

Reece Scannel

An Ordinary Lunacy, 1963
The Last Man's Head, 1970
The Commandant, 1975
Tirra Lirra by the River, 1978
The Impersonators (U.S. title: *The Only Daughter*), 1980
Stories from the Warm Zone and Sydney Stories, 1987
Taking Shelter, 1989

keeps her birth date to herself, but the place was a country town near Brisbane. At eighteen she moved to Sydney, and except for a few years in the late 1930s when she lived in London, she has spent her life in Sydney. She has twice won the Miles Franklin Award, for *Tirra Lirra by the River,* and for *The Only Daughter.* Australian critics responding to a recent poll named *Tirra Lirra by the River* one of the top three contemporary Australian novels. Anderson's fiction is frequently concerned with the observation of manners, particularly those of a family or of a group as in *The Commandant* or *Taking Shelter,* and with the perception and sensitivity of its members. Our conversations in 1987 and 1989 occurred in Anderson's apartment on the eighth floor of a high rise at Darling Point overlooking Sydney Harbor.

INTERVIEW

RW: In *Stories From the Warm Zone and Sydney Stories* you go back to the beginning, to your childhood in Brisbane in the twenties. Since the inner workings of the family are often the subject of your fiction, would you describe your family and your childhood?

JA: My father was the youngest son of an Irish immigrant family. He was the only one born in Australia. They were farmers. My father was a public servant. Public service was a means by which immigrant families and the poor raised themselves to the middle class. They would become schoolteachers or clerks—my father became an inspector of agriculture and worked in that department all his life. My mother was English, but she came out when she was three. Her father was a music teacher. They were poor, too. She also joined the public service. They were interested in all the arts, my father more so than my mother, and in politics they were liberal thinkers, which at that time meant they were radical—again, my father more so than my mother. I was the youngest of four children.

RW: Was the family pretty much as you described it in *Stories?*

JA: Yes. I could have gone into more detail, but I was true to all their characters. I had to make up some dialogue, but it is amazing how much of their talk I recalled. Perhaps because I was the youngest, and had to listen more often than speak, I have remembered some of their talk all my life.

RW: Was your stuttering the problem you made it?

JA: Yes, it was.

RW: In "The Appearance of Things" you wrote that your sister Rhoda died in her forties, while you were in your thirties. What did she die of?

JA: Cancer. Both my sisters, actually. My elder sister had the grievous experience of leaving young children behind. The younger of my sisters, the counterpart of Sybil in the stories, survived until her children were grown. My brother died fairly recently.

RW: Was he like his namesake in the book, Neal?

JA: Yes. He was primarily an archivist and a collector. He had the true collector's passion. His chief interest was Australiana. He left seven hundred Australian etchings to the National Art Gallery in Canberra, and his house was absolutely crammed with books, mostly Australian. He started collecting as a young boy. Stones, minerals, stamps, medals . . .

RW: You were very close to him in recent years, I believe.

JA: We grew closer after we were the survivors of the family. He still lived in Brisbane in the house in the book. Because of the sex and age differences, we seemed to have lived in different channels in the same family, so that we recalled different aspects of it, and often amazed each other. We had many long talks about this, and then, when I came to do research for *The Commandant,* we discovered more common ground, and he was very helpful to me.

RW: What was Brisbane like in the twenties?

JA: It was a parochial place, not a bush town, but a colonial city.

But it wasn't altogether narrow and rigid. I should say that there were a lot of frustrated people. There were two very good public libraries, and the Russian writers were well read. There must have been many people with aspirations for something beyond their society, or they wouldn't have been reading Chekhov and Dostoyevski. Brisbane had a beautiful setting, a fertile hinterland, and a deep, winding river. It was subtropical and there were dramatic and memorable storms. And the skies were so beautiful. Even when you were a child, the night sky made you see how trivial all the stuff on the ground was. It made you long for something larger and more splendid that would match the sky. It's given over to the motorcar now, so it's all standardized highways, freeways, shopping malls, and strung-out suburbs. Still, if you go out of doors and look up after midnight, when the lights are out, it still has that splendid sky.

RW: At what age did you move to Sydney?

JA: Eighteen.

RW: How did you support yourself?

JA: I hardly did. I got a job painting screen slides. I had been to art school and could draw a bit. Then I got a job helping an artist who designed electric signs. I got odds and ends of jobs.

RW: Where in Sydney did you live?

JA: At King's Cross. At Bomera, actually. That's the house at Potts Point in *Tirra Lirra by the River* next to where Nora lives. That's how I knew it so well.

RW: You were living at King's Cross twenty years after Nora would have lived there?

JA: Yes. I would have been there when she returned from the suburbs, when she went back to find Ida. About 1936.

RW: What was Potts Point like then?

JA: Very nice. Quieter. Sophisticated. It attracted people from all over Australia. It was the only bohemian center in the whole of the country. It was a meeting place. People were poor, but very free. We had a good life.

RW: What was this like for you coming from Brisbane?

JA: It was lovely.

RW: At what age did you get married?

JA: Well, I lived with my first husband, an artist, for three years before we married. I was married at twenty-one.

RW: Living with a man before marriage was quite liberated for those days, wasn't it?

JA: Yes. It was indeed.

RW: What did your mother think of that?

JA: I didn't tell her.

RW: What sort of artist was your husband?

JA: He was a commercial artist who longed to be a painter. That's a sad story that I don't want to go into at the moment.

RW: But he wasn't at all like Nora's husband in *Tirra Lirra*?

JA: Not even slightly. Neither of my husbands were like that man. I have seen men like that and I've known marriages of that kind. I've talked to women who have had that sort of marriage but I haven't been one of them.

RW: Nor did you have Nora's stingy mother-in-law?

JA: No indeed.

RW: How did you get started in radio writing?

JA: It was a matter of money. Everything in those days was a matter of money. I started to do half-hour radio things for commercial radio. Gradually I became interested in technique. As time went on I did some better plays and then I started to submit them under my own name for the ABC.

RW: How did you get started doing it?

JA: Just by listening to the radio and then submitting something.

RW: How many years did you do this?

JA: Off and on for a good long while.

RW: Then you were successful at this?

JA: Not really. I've never actually been awfully successful at anything I've done.

RW: What?

JA: Apart from novels. But that was slow progress. Very slow. I began by publishing to some praise, but you can hardly call it success.

RW: Of course, one of the reasons I'm asking such autobiographical questions is that I, like most readers, wish to identify you with Nora in *Tirra Lirra*. Is there much of your life in Nora, or in Nora's life?

JA: No. But it's a subtle thing. I feel that my life might have touched hers. I've said again and again that I was trying to write about a woman who was born at the turn of the century and who went through three great things: the First World War, the Depression, and the Second World War. The three great destructive events. Nora's was a difficult generation. It must have been a hard time to be born, and especially if you were born in a colonial place. When I was a child I could see pretty women around me, and they aroused my curiosity, and I suppose they made an impression on me with their marvelous dresses and their restlessness, which I came to understand so well as I grew up myself. So there our lives would have touched slightly. It's hard to explain. She isn't me and I'm not her, but I understood her. She is an invented character, but she is my invention so she must have some slight element of me in her. But I do have an imagination and I do have empathy with people which enables me to create characters who are not really strongly like me at all. It's the first person narrative that misleads people.

RW: Does it bother you that people assume you to be Nora?

JA: Yes. Not so much as it did, perhaps. But I long for more subtle readers.

RW: I think the reader admires Nora so much that we want her to be you. We want to meet Nora.

JA: Thank you. I can't arrange it. When I opened the door once to a woman who had read the book, she stepped back, looked at me, and said, "I expected an older woman."

RW: You've told a story about a woman at a party who was following you around scrutinizing your face, searching for Nora's ruined facelift.

JA: I pulled up my hair and said, "Look, look—No scars."

RW: How did you come to write *Tirra Lirra*?

JA: It began as a story, twenty thousand words. It was too long for a story and too short for a novel. I put it away and ultimately I dramatized it for radio. During that process I enlarged it and saw how I could make it into a novel. Later, I worked on it and made a novel.

RW: What changes or additions did you make?

JA: It was a matter of finding the themes and defining each character more precisely. As a story it was like a first draft. The same thing happened with "Outdoor Friends." That was a long story. The action was there but it was empty. I returned to it and defined the characters and left them a bit clearer. It then worked as a longer story. It's a method that isn't quite deliberate. It's largely intuitive, accidental.

RW: But it's a method that worked for you in *Tirra Lirra.*

JA: Yes, though you can see the parts that I wasn't sure of because I hurried over them and didn't return to them.

RW: Which parts?

JA: The suicide attempt, for example. It was only mentioned, then abandoned.

RW: You might have written much more about the relationship of the friends at Number Six. I was interested in them.

JA: I was tempted to, but it would have run away with the book. I think it was long enough.

RW: I don't think the reader pauses to consider a lack of development or wonders if the writer might have done it better. He is too compelled by Nora's story.

JA: I suppose so. But I thought at times here and there that it was a little bit fudged, not quite developed enough.

RW: Did you ever think of writing a sequel to *Tirra Lirra*?

JA: You couldn't do that twice. Actually, in a way, I did try. I've said that I lived in the house next door to Nora at Potts Point. Well, I wrote a story of my own experiences there. It was a personal story—myself in my youth—though I wrote it in third person. It was so bad that I withdrew it from publication.

RW: At what point in your life did you go to England?

JA: Nineteen thirty-six, thirty-seven. I came back to Australia in 1940, during the war.

RW: This is another reason why biographically one would think there was a connection between you and Nora.

JA: Yes. But Nora was there for a long time. Was it thirteen years? I was only there for two and a half years.

RW: How did you support yourself in England?

JA: I worked doing research for a man who had a magazine called *Townsman.* It was donkey work. I did other things—I typed a novel for a woman who couldn't type. I can't type either, but I managed.

RW: Was your husband painting at that time?

JA: In his spare time. He was also working as a layout artist for Lever Brothers Agency in London.

RW: What was it like moving from Sydney to London?

JA: It was a marvelous experience but I didn't feel myself in London. I hated the English climate. There is one way in which I was like Nora—I did get bronchitis every year.

RW: Do you get homesick easily?

JA: Yes, I do. Isn't it horrible? It's a great drawback in one's life.

RW: At what age did you publish *An Ordinary Lunacy,* your first novel?

JA: I was forty-four. I started writing it as I approached forty. I thought it was time to write something that I could own up to. It took me ages to write it. It was awfully long at the start; it branched off in all directions. Then I cut it ruthlessly.

RW: It's been republished recently. Have you read it again?

JA: No. I've been afraid to. I opened it up here and there.

RW: In *An Ordinary Lunacy* one sees the first of your female leads who stands apart, who is an outsider.

JA: Yes.

RW: Is this a consistent theme of yours?

JA: I suppose it has been a theme of mine. Alec is an outsider in *The Last Man's Head* and Logan in *The Commandant,* especially. It isn't always a female character, but yes, there usually is one who remains aloof. Another theme that I have noticed in my work is the theme of authority, how different people have it and how other people resent it.

RW: I can think of a number of your characters who react that way.

JA: It's a strong theme that I've only noticed recently. I think it's probably a personal theme, too. Probably the most personal of all my themes is a resistance to authority.

RW: Again, to your use of the outsider—is this a personal theme as well? Have you felt like an outsider?

JA: At times.

RW: Isobel in *An Ordinary Lunacy* weakens under the pressure of ostracism and loneliness and commits suicide. But she is the only heroine who falters for the lack of a man. I see in the girl in *The Commandant* the prototype of all your heroines to come. Would you talk about Frances O'Beirne as a heroine and the writing of this historical novel?

JA: I made Frances up. Most of the characters in the novel are real people out of colonial history. I introduced Frances in order to observe and comment. None of the historical characters were similar enough to me to allow me to comment through them. I had to have one character to carry my own feelings. So I made her a radical young Irish girl, new to the scene.

RW: You've said that you feel *The Commandant* is your best novel.

JA: Probably because I enjoyed writing it so much.

RW: How long did it take you to research it?

JA: Quite a long time, two years. But I am a bad researcher. I go off course and read round everything and then center again. I had a lovely time. I enjoyed it enormously.

RW: Frances is advised, "You must acquire a manner and refer your intelligence to it, and most of your instincts. That's the way it's done. It does not do to be opinionated." You are writing here of manners in colonial Australia, but the notion of an acquired self and a submerged real self is the subject of your other novels as well, isn't it?

JA: That is an acute observation. That is true. It is one of my subjects.

RW: Want to talk about it?

JA: I can't talk about it. But it is true.

RW: I'm thinking of Sylvia, Greta, and Molly in *The Only Daughter*. Each has a self in abeyance. In Molly's case she also has a secret—her illiteracy.

JA: Yes. I actually met someone who had kept this secret all her life. Even her husband didn't know, and it was easy for her to keep that secret from her husband. She was of so little account to him. He simply didn't notice.

RW: You create in *Tirra Lirra by the River* a very independent woman who must overcome oppression of family, husband, and nationality. Would you comment on the refrain you set up in the novel, "Who does she think she is?"

JA: I think that is a question very commonly asked any clever girl as she grows up. Not today perhaps, but in the past it was a refrain.

RW: Her mother, her sister, her mother-in-law—at every point in the novel just as she begins to move into a new sense of selfhood, she is asked this question.

JA: That was her generation, again.

RW: A larger question, then, does Australia as a country tend to level everyone?

JA: Not now. It did, but that's over, I hope.

RW: In the end of *Tirra Lirra,* in the garden of her sister Grace, you seem to imply that Nora comes to an integration with the Whole, with at least a provisional awareness of Self. Would you comment on this interpretation?

JA: That novel was a story of a girl who had been partly ruined and partly made by romantic notions. The whole idea of the romantic movement worked on her mind in a society that isolated her. In order to make the romantic comprehensible, I had to make it attractive—because of course it did have its charms—but it was a force that almost destroyed Nora.

RW: So when she sees herself as a part of everything and not separate . . .

JA: She finds herself. She is interested even in a stone that she picks up off the ground.

RW: It's a very Eastern notion, isn't it?

JA: I suppose it is. I was just working through her life.

RW: It's interesting that her sister Grace worked for grace all her life while Nora . . .

JA: Grace might have achieved it. In her garden. "In compost?" someone said to me disbelievingly. But there she was, working on the earth, and caring for the earth. She was before her time, perhaps. She tried to found a compost society and everyone laughed at her, remember. So, don't underestimate Grace.

RW: *The Only Daughter* is another novel of manners, of conventions and quest. Is Sylvia another version of Nora?

JA: No. She's more realistic. She's less complicated. She is also much younger. Please take that into account.

RW: I'm thinking of the pattern of exile and return that both women experience.

JA: Yes, that's true.

RW: She seems to grow up in struggling through the reunions with her family.

JA: That is true. Sylvia's father, Jack Cornock, was an interesting character to me. I have seen that kind of semi-criminal career so often in Sydney. It was truly a Sydney novel.

RW: What about his wife Greta's compliance in crime in the novel?

JA: It's interesting, isn't it? She had a dreadful experience with her husband, who was a religious fanatic who had taken her beyond the bounds of ordinary acceptable experience. She was trying to care for all of her children, but having gone through that experience she couldn't marry a man who hadn't been through its equivalent. Jack, too, had been through great hardships in his life. Jack had also been an outcast.

RW: What about Greta at the end of the novel?

JA: I thought she was moving toward spirituality.

RW: You have a good bit to say about real estate development and physical changes in Sydney in this novel. Have you, like Patrick White, given up on Sydney?

JA: No. I fell in love with Sydney when I was a girl, and I still love it. That's partly because it's my home, and because I know it so well. As a city, it's only two hundred years old, and you can still see its history as you travel about it. You can read it as you walk. Then there's its earlier history, when it was lived on so gently by the Aborigines. You can't read that, but you can feel it.

RW: Would you say a few words about your new novel, *Taking Shelter*?

JA: It's about love in the early stages of AIDS. It's set in 1986. It's a novel of manners with a good bit of comedy in it. It isn't told in a conventional form.

RW: Do you follow any of the themes in *Taking Shelter* that we've talked about in the earlier novels?

JA: Perhaps if any one of the characters is an outsider, it's a man. But I don't really think there's an outsider in the novel.

RW: What do you feel about *Taking Shelter*? Is it the best thing you've done?

JA: I don't know. I would need more time to stand off and look at it. There are parts of it I would like to revise, but that applies to all my novels. There's a part from *The Commandant* I would like to do again, but you can't keep revising.

RW: Do you revise a great deal?

JA: I rewrite a lot. I don't actually revise; I'll start again and write it again and again until the tone is right. When the tone is right the characters seem to be right too.

RW: Even as we talk, I keep being distracted by the ships and boats in the harbor and the bridge in the distance. Looking out from your eighth-floor window over Rushcutter's Bay, I wonder if you are able to write here at home, or if the water view is too much of a seduction?

JA: It is lovely, isn't it? But I work happily at home. I just look up now and again, say to myself, "Oh, there's the *Auckland Star* coming in," or some such thing.

RW: Do you write in longhand?

JA: I always begin in longhand. And I return to it if I'm stuck.

RW: What's the most difficult aspect of writing for you?

JA: Anxiety.

RW: What kind of anxiety?

JA: I feel until a book is done and over that I don't quite know what's going to happen to my people. I don't work to a written plan. I plan as I go. I do have a plan in my head, but it's never firm. When I've completed the book I know it has gone according to that plan, but if I made that plan firm and visible at the start, I would not be able to write, so it is like writing into the unknown, and that creates anxiety.

RW: The American writer Ellen Gilcrist once described the writing process as waiting for the mystery to rise.

JA: That is an excellent description of it. That is one of the best I've heard.

RW: You are a very visual writer. Do you see what you are going to write?

JA: Yes, I do indeed. If I can't see it, I can't write it.

RW: What about dialogue? Does that come easily for you?

JA: Yes, it does. It comes easier than anything.

RW: Your daughter, Laura Jones, is a screenwriter. Do you have a close relationship with her?

JA: Yes. Very. She is my only daughter.

RW: Is there a similarity in your work and hers?

JA: I don't think so. She is adapting *Tirra Lirra* for the screen. She is also adapting Elizabeth Jolley's *The Well.* Movies can fall down, but those are the plans at present.

RW: Are you collaborating with her on *Tirra Lirra?*

JA: No. I couldn't return to work that is in the past.

RW: Have you collaborated with her on anything else?

JA: No. I would never collaborate with anyone.

RW: Would you ever consider writing a screenplay?

JA: No. I haven't the skill. I would prefer to trust my work to someone who has.

RW: You've said that you don't feel that you have much in common with other Australian writers. Why is this?

JA: I said once that my work is mainly dramatic and that most Australian writing is of a documentary character. I don't know if that applies today, but it did at the start of my writing career. My work was out of keeping with the Australian tradition.

RW: You've said your work is more in the English tradition; what about American writers? Have any been important to you?

JA: So many American writers have been important to me. I read Henry James in my twenties, and later I adapted some of his work for radio, and he is so good, he is so sound, that nobody could adapt his work without learning something about construction. I've read all your other major novelists as well, right up to the present. So many, I can't name them. You've a wonderful tradition. That is to say nothing of your poets. I've read them all my life. Beginning with Edgar Lee Masters in childhood. If Americans have influenced me less than English, it must be because blood and culture made the English more personally compatible. I don't quite know if this is true, though, not so true as it was.

RW: Which of your own books has been the most successful commercially in the States?

JA: *Tirra Lirra.* There, as well as elsewhere.

RW: Like Nora, you've been an artist, you've created things, you've been independent, your own person. Has your life as a writer been a good one?

JA: Yes. I've talked of trials and anxiety, but there are times when I've had great joy from writing, great pleasure indeed. I would not have chosen anything else.

THEA ASTLEY

Girl with a Monkey, 1958
A Descant for Gossips, 1960
The Well Dressed Explorer, 1962
The Slow Natives, 1965
A Boat Load of Home Folk, 1968
The Acolyte, 1972
A Kindness Cup, 1974
Hunting the Wild Pineapple (stories), 1979
An Item from the Late News, 1982
Beachmasters, 1985
It's Raining in Mango, 1987
Two by Astley (*The Acolyte* and *A Kindness Cup*), 1988
Reaching Tin River, 1990

was born in Brisbane in 1925. After graduating from the University of Queensland and Teachers' Training College, she spent five years teaching in country towns, an experience she draws heavily from in her fiction. In 1968 she moved to Sydney and for a number of years taught in high schools before becoming a Senior Tutor at Macquarie University. Since retirement in 1980, she and her husband, Jack Gregson, have lived in the countryside near Kuranda, Queensland, and more recently near Nowra, one hundred miles down the coast from Sydney. Thea Astley has won the Miles Franklin Award three times: for *The Well Dressed Explorer, The Slow Natives*, and *The Acolyte*. In 1989 she won the Patrick White Prize. Astley's work is characterized by acute observation of character, with compassionate concern for the misfit, the outcast, and scarcely concealed loathing for the institution or the ego which promotes itself at the expense of the other. Particularly Australian in its use of small town settings and verbal slang, Astley's fiction often surprises and delights the reader with its humor, sharp wit, irony, and linguistic complexity. The following interview occurred in Thea Astley's kitchen in her home near Nowra and in an earlier conversation in my kitchen in Memphis, Tennessee.

INTERVIEW

RW: You grew up in Brisbane and have written about it, as have Jessica Anderson and David Malouf. Would you talk about the effect of Brisbane on you?

TA: Altogether, our experience of Brisbane would be about thirty years apart. The essential ugliness of Brisbane had a sort of lacerating effect the way ivy on cottages in the Cotswolds would have a soothing effect. Instead of molding you into a relaxed, dreamlike state that would probably inhibit writing, I think the sheer marvelous discomfort of a timber town in the tropics filled with cockroaches, blowflies, and terrible rains woke one up. I remember my father, who was a journalist working on *The Queenslander,* taking me to see a flood when I was about seven. We went to see houses half underwater. This sort of thing was a stimulant rather than a soporific. When I say an ugly timber town full of cockroaches and blowflies, that is not to say I didn't like an ugly timber town full of cockroaches and blowflies. Some cockroaches are my best friends. I think that's why I responded to *archy and mehitabel* so early. We had all grown up with cockroaches. It was a meaningful poem.

RW: How does Brisbane figure into your novels?

TA: It's in many of them—*The Slow Natives, A Descant for Gossips.* It authorizes my reactions for Townsville, which is the setting of my first novel, *Girl with A Monkey.* It's hard remembering exactly because writers are sort of fictional liars. I'm frightened of people saying, "That's me. How dare you?" You tend to rename places and shift them even if you are using scenes from Brisbane or Sydney. You locate them someplace else. I suppose that's why I've always called Cairns, "Reeftown" and Townsville, "Sugarville," or Mackay, "Sugarville." I used a school to which I was evacuated during the war years called Warwick which I called "Condamine." There is a town called Condamine in Queensland quite near there, but I wasn't writing about it.

RW: Where is Tin River?

TA: Tin River, as I say in the book, is a state of mind. It's somewhere around Mackay or Sarina, a sugar town; it's somewhere up north of the Tropic of Capricorn.

RW: You have lived in Brisbane and in Sydney, but you have also lived a good portion of your life in rural Australia, from the hills above Cairns in north Queensland to the hills south of Sydney near Nowra. You have had a broad experience of ways of living in Australia, urban, regional, rural. Would you talk about your use of the small town and the rural in your fiction?

TA: I think my use of the rural and small town has been based on my experience teaching in very small towns when I was in the public education system in Queensland before I married and came to Sydney. Even then, my experience was limited to the coastal region. I've only been west as far inland as Mt. Isa, eight hundred miles inland from Townsville. I've been in the Far West on lecture tours, but that's not like living there. I've visited properties owned by friends out in the Western Plains, and I have enormous admiration for people who can handle that sort of existence. Unfortunately, for my purposes, these people were all well-to-do and privileged. They were what you would call ranchers, and they owned vast properties with their own airplane and airstrip. The sort of backbreaking rurality I'm thinking of I observed in the hill country behind Cairns, up in the Tablelands. We'd drive out to places like Irvinebank, where there was a small artificially made dam which was the size of a small lake that I used for the setting of *An Item from the Late News.* I used the School of Arts Hall in that town in Irvinebank, but I actually wanted to go to a place called Lake Galilee. It was almost impossible to fly there; the configurations of travel with trains and planes was brutally impossible, so I used this place for the setting. But the North and the Coastal North I found rich was filled with oddballs. I said in an article "On Being a Queenslander" that Queensland isn't the place where the tall yarn begins; it is the place where the tall yarn happens, where it is lived out by people who actually are the *dramatis personae* of the tall yarns.

RW: What sort of people?

TA: Funny people, hard-working people, laconic people, people who put up with a great deal of discomfort. Look, the flies are bad here this afternoon, but in Queensland you can go out West and whole tables appear to move upwards if there are no screens. I don't think anyone had invented the flyscreen for the Far West until well after World War II. They put up with flies and heat and lack of rain. I remember when I was out near Mt. Isa some old-timer was telling me one of those Queensland legends. He said one day his eight-year-old kid ran in screaming. It was raining and they were saying, "Dad, what's happening? What's happening?" It was the first time they had seen rain in their whole lives.

RW: I was thinking, too, of the hippies that you use in *Hunting the Wild Pineapple.*

TA: They were largely Southerners. They weren't Queenslanders.

RW: You have a preference for the drama of the small town over the city, don't you?

TA: It's easier to see conflict taking place within a small group of people. It's easier to understand the reasons for conflict if the group is accessible. Sydney has turned into a brutal, ugly town, where there seems to be a major crime every day. You can't understand the reasons behind it. It would be impossible to analyze crime after crime, but in a small town where the population is a few hundred and everybody knows everybody (I'm taking the easy way out for the writer) people can be assembled like characters on a stage. There are some very small towns. When I was up looking at Irvinebank for writing *Item from the Late News,* we called at the pub. The woman driving me ordered a beer. The guy had his whole range of hard liquor behind him; it was four bottles: a bottle of scotch, a bottle of sweet sherry, a bottle of port, and something else. This was the pub's range. "What do you want, lady?"

RW: Where did you discover the man who was actually a woman that you use in *Item?*

TA: There probably is in Australia a history of women who in order to escape the terrible male dominance have disguised themselves as men. Joseph Furphy in *Such Is Life* has a character who had dressed as a man for years after an accident had scarred her face. Everyone thought it was a chap. My character I read about in a small local paper or in the *Cairns Post.* There was a funeral held in a town up on the Tablelands of this local identity who for years used to ride as a jockey in the local picnic races and win things. Everyone thought he was a nice little bloke. When it came time to do the autopsy, they discovered he was a she. She'd pulled the wool over their eyes for years. This happened in the twenties or thirties.

RW: You said once that you were particularly drawn to the sort of character or situation that Flannery O'Connor uses . . .

TA: The oddball. Very much. But I hadn't read any Flannery O'Connor until long after I began to use this sort of character. I read her very late on. I like the story about the woman with the artificial leg. She might have been a Queenslander. I did read Carson McCullers from an early age. I like her better than Flannery O'Connor. She writes with more tenderness and sympathy for the oddball. I have sympathy for the oddball.

RW: Do you personally prefer the rural or the small town to the city?

TA: When I was twenty-two or twenty-three and transferred to these one-horse towns as a teacher, I can't say I enjoyed them. They were small, nosy; you didn't dare put a foot out of line. They knew everything you did. For me, there was no social life. I was either boarding with a local family or living in the local hotel, which we call a pub. The only social life seemed to be in the pub, which would throb until ten at night, when they would lock the policeman inside because that was the official closing time. He would go on drinking with them until everybody fell outward. I found it ugly because I was young and intolerant. I was discovering books and poetry and good music, and nothing cultural like that was happening in the small towns. I think there is a lot more to be said for the larger place like Townsville, where I was transferred when I was twenty-one. I suppose it must have had a population then of about forty thousand. The Queensland State Quartet would come up occasionally. You felt you were still in touch with some kind of mental life. There was a library. I'm comparing this to a place in the Mary Valley where I had to live once that had a population of three hundred.

RW: What about now? You live down a dirt road on a hilltop near Nowra, a small town a hundred miles south of Sydney.

TA: A hundred miles isn't far from Sydney. A lot of Sydney slickers are moving away, at least for the weekend, trying to get tank water, a breath of fresh air. They are coming this far out. They don't have to breathe polluted air or look at a harbor that's full of sewage.

RW: So the small town is preferable to you now?

TA: Yes. People-sized towns.

RW: You write about your grandfather in your recent novel *It's Raining in Mango.* Have you often drawn on biographical or autobiographical material?

TA: Look, all writers use things that happen to them or that they've heard. I can't write about people I know well at all. I'd rather write about people I hear of or glimpse in the street, because then I can let my mind wander free. Wafer in *Item* I based almost entirely on a character that I'd heard was about in the reaches of the Far North. He was a very good pianist; he had tried to establish a commune which was burned down; I went out to the commune. It was about ten miles up the track from our place. There is nothing sadder than a burned-out typewriter and melted records. I never met the man, but I knew someone who had taken singing lessons from him. I'd rather hear these things, and then I'm not in danger of libeling anyone. It's purely my vision.

RW: Is any one of your books more autobiographical than another?

TA: Yes. I think my first one—*Girl with a Monkey.* It deals more or less with the last day I spent in Townsville when I was on transfer from Townsville to a school in the Mary Valley. I think everyone's first novel is probably more autobiographical than anything else. But my others are just collage—things you see, things you hear, things that have happened to you.

RW: Do you draw heavily on observed people?

TA: Yes. And sometimes you are so wrong. There used to be a character around Cairns who wore a tartan skirt pinned at one side with a safety pin, a green tank top trimmed in yellow, and sand shoes. He was totally bald and used to walk with the utmost dignity down the main drag. He had thick beefy legs coming out from under the tartan skirt and a cheap plastic black eye patch. One day I was in a supermarket with a woman friend and I saw this guy and I was saying to my friend in a patronizing way, "God, isn't he marvelous?" She was wandering off looking for something and she came back and said, "Do you know what he said to me? He said, 'Where's the caviar?'" You can be totally wrong.

RW: Did you ever use him as a character?

TA: I thought of him when I was writing about Reever in *It's Raining in Mango.* Skirts are cooler in the tropics. I had Reever dressing in a skirt.

RW: What about eavesdropping?

TA: Yes, I've been unashamed about eavesdropping ever since I read a marvelous Cheever story, "The Country Husband," where this guy is sitting in a coffee booth listening flat out to people in the little coffee booth behind him. Yes, I do tend to tilt my head backwards when I'm in coffee booths.

RW: Do you have a good ear and a good memory for dialogue?

TA: No, I don't, but I do try. When I was in Port Vila after researching *Beachmasters,* I had to spend three days waiting for a plane. The natives get terribly agitated when they see middle-aged women stalking around on their own, and I really got tired of answering this question, "Where is your husband?" You know, as if I was some sort of aged Old Pro or something. It worried them. I was having dinner in the restaurant that was attached to my hotel one night, and it was full of "beautiful people" who had just stepped off a tour boat. They were having their fish and I was sitting at a table on my own having my whatever. I had a notebook and pencil with me. I was listening unashamedly to their conversation. They were having a wonderful time talking and I was writing down every word, and in the middle of all this the waiter came up and said, "Where is your husband?" I was so angry at his interrupting that I said, "Where is your wife?" He burst into a wild giggle. He'd never had anyone answer him back.

RW: Did that dialogue appear in Beachmasters?

TA: No. I didn't use it, actually. I got masses of stuff up there that I didn't use.

RW: Do you begin writing with a character always, or with an idea?
TA: It's often an idea. I had always wanted to write about the brothel floating out to sea that I wrote about in *It's Raining in Mango.* It's an idea or something or someone I read about in history. I find the history of the early places great source material. It is stimulating.
RW: I'm surprised. I thought you would say character.
TA: Sometimes it would be an idea about a character, I guess. I wrote *The Slow Natives* because someone came into the common room at the school where I was teaching and said, talking about a friend of theirs whose son was fourteen and going through a difficult adolescent stage, they said, "You know, this kid wanted a duffel coat and he said 'duffel coat' nonstop for a whole weekend, so they gave him one; they couldn't bear it. He just kept saying, 'duffel coat, duffel coat.'" I thought, "God. What a kid." And I wrote *The Slow Natives* out of that.
RW: So the character and the idea came together. You'd never begin with a philosophical idea?
TA: I suppose I ought to be pretentious and say, "yes." But, no, I suppose at the back of everything like that kid saying "duffel coat" there is an idea like selfishness or self-absorption, some big abstraction, but I don't start that way.
RW: You are a great gossip, aren't you?
TA: Oh, God. Is that unkind? I love it actually, because I don't go anywhere. I wonder if Jane Austen was a great gossip, or if she flattened herself against coffee booths in her period. She wouldn't have been allowed out on her own, would she? I'm sure she would have if she could have.
RW: What's the value of gossip?
TA: First of all, I don't think I believe half of it, but I find it very stimulating. It's almost as if people are making up novellas as they go along, about characters you know or you know of. Gossip is the creative process in action. It's like making up jazz on the piano; it's improvisation. It's creative. Just as long as it's not too malicious or as long as you don't believe it.
RW: What about your use of gossip, say in *The Slow Natives* or *A Descant for Gossips?*
TA: In *Descant* I was inveighing against the idea of malicious gossip that can destroy people in small country towns. The book was a protest against that sort of thing. The sort of gossip you asked me if I enjoyed and which I love is the sort of flummery gossip you get around the writing traps, which I no longer seem to visit. I don't get to open the cages any more.

RW: Traps?

TA: Writers' conferences.

RW: Some critical gossip about your own work—in your novel *The Acolyte* did you use as your model a great Australian novelist who was once your friend and neighbor, that is, Patrick White?

TA: No. Definitely not. I've said this often and it really is true; I got the idea for the book from watching a documentary by Ken Russell on Delius, the composer, who was blind with tertiary syphilis in the last years of his life and who invited an amanuensis to write down his work. I thought, God, how can that man put up with being booted around? Delius's wife always called him Delius, "Delius will see you now," you know, not Fred, which was his name. I really wanted to write a book about it, about being a subservient character to a great man. I was getting sick of great men. I wanted to see them from the other side of the doormat, you know? I saw the documentary a couple of times and I started the novel with words I pinched from the back of a record, a work of Dag Wiren, a Scandinavian composer: "This is an utterly credible little work." After that, the book practically wrote itself. The main character, the musician Holberg, is based on a young man my husband, Jack, used to bring home from the conservatorium where he was working. The young man used to come out and stay weekends. He was very gifted musically. He had perfect pitch. He had been born with sight, but his eyes had been destroyed by fly-strike. His parents were itinerant farmworkers. The physical description of Holberg was based on this young man. I believe he was a bit annoyed when the book came out, but it wasn't his personality. He was a rather nice guy. With relevance to the question you asked about Patrick White, I do admit that I read just about this time or the year before *The Vivisector,* Patrick's book about the great artist. I thought out of sheer amusement, this is my reply—the vivisected. But as for Holberg being White, no, no, no. Not a bit.

RW: You and Patrick White were good friends for a number of years, weren't you? You were neighbors?

TA: He lived at Castle Hill while we were living at Epping, about ten miles away.

RW: I've heard that you two liked to gossip on the telephone.

TA: We were good on the telephone. We didn't see each other all that often. He'd come down to tea, dinner as you'd say, three times a year or we'd go up there, and that was it. Patrick gave my son, Edmond, his first paint box. I will always remember walking up to the front gate and Edmond, who was about two, picking his nose. Patrick's friend Manoly said, "You mustn't let him do that," and I said, "I just think it's wonderful how God has made the diameter of the finger exactly to fit that of the nostril." But truly, I was overawed by Patrick. He was a mixture of kindness and humor. He made me laugh. He was difficult, too. But then I suppose that anybody of that caliber has got to be difficult. They have more going for them, for one thing. I was telling someone recently this story. Patrick and Manoly used to have someone come to do their ironing. One year just before Christmas I went over and Patrick asked me if Edmond liked jelly. I said, "Yes, he does." He brought out a plastic lunch box with a fold-over lid that kids take their lunch to school in and it was packed with packets of jelly crystals. You call it "Jello." There was a sort of glitter Christmas card in it, and it was a present from their ironing lady to Patrick and Manoly. I thought then that the simplicity of that present given in good heart from someone who was not aware of how Patrick ranked as an intellectual, as a writer, showed just what a really nice chap he must have been to someone who was helping with household work, someone that he must never have allowed his genius to dominate or overawe. I still find this terribly hard to talk about; I couldn't write about this incident. She just saw him as a nice employer and in her humble way she gave him a present he might appreciate; I remember being very moved by it. It said a lot about Patrick.

RW: Do you feel a stylistic kinship in your writing to Patrick White?

TA: Probably we were all affected by Patrick White in the metaphysical sense. He taught us to look at the essence of things. I mean, God, he's had a tremendous impact on any one of us who ever picked up a ballpoint pen. But I don't want to write like Patrick. One doesn't want to be just a pallid imitator of the real thing. But I think he clued us all in to attitudes we should take toward people and even to inanimate objects. Like that remark I told you he made to me one time, "Sit at home and shell the peas and think what it is to be a pea." I think, too, the outrageously ornamented sickly imagistic style of Hal Porter affected us as well. It makes White look spare. Well, White does write spare prose; it's the soul that's dense. He uses ordinary words in strange metaphysical juxtapositions.

RW: Is there one novel of yours that you feel was more influenced by White than any other?

TA: I don't know. I'd written my first book, *Girl with a Monkey*, before I had read any of his books.

RW: We were talking about *The Acolyte*. The word "acolyte" often appears in your fiction, as does the egotistical character who brings the acolyte into his orbit. Would you talk about your recurring use of this theme?

TA: I grew up in the Catholic church, which used serving boys on the altar. They are called acolytes, and they serve at mass. An acolyte is a common enough term in religious ritual. The idea of the server has never worried me particularly, but when I was writing this novel I have to admit I was using the term with a certain amount of irony or cynicism. It was a loaded term. He was more than an acolyte. He had been turned into a doormat.

RW: I'm thinking of other characters in other works.

TA: I think the whole world is divided into feet and boots and mats, isn't it?

RW: You often deal with power struggles on personal levels, with your male characters shown to be egoists, pompous clods. I'm thinking of men in *A Boat Load of Home Folk, The Slow Natives, Reaching Tin River,* "Ladies Need Only Apply." Would you comment about this recurring egotistical and insufferable male?

TA: I suppose I've taught in so many schools where there were insufferable and incompetent males all earning far more than I, achieving promotion and higher salaries purely for their maleness rather than by efficiency. I guess growing up in a time before equal pay for equal work was implemented, I wrote it out of my system. But you do see it all around you all the time. It's not just males, but sometimes I feel really resentful looking at the power brokers who control the whole world, people like Dan Quayle, for example. Looking at him on telly, he strikes me as an absolute bubble brain. I feel this resentment. Just on the grounds of maleness, he's made vice president of the most powerful country in the world. I'd rather see George Bush's wife as vice president.

RW: In your work it's not just the man of ego, but it is usually a conflict between the powerful and the powerless, isn't it?

TA: As a taxpayer and voter I belong to the powerless, the doormat group. I always have. At least I can get some little satisfaction in writing about the boots. It's one's only little comeback.

RW: A specific kind of character that you debunk so well is the priest or evangelist, for example in "The Curate Breaker," and in *It's Raining in Mango.* Do you think there is something fundamentally wrong with organized religion?

TA: I think the Western Christian church is on the skids, but this doesn't affect my belief in God. Remember, I grew up in a church which was totally controlled by sociological attitudes as well—the bog Irish priest, not a well-educated lot. We've got a number of them out here. I don't think the church now of any denomination can cope with the fact that it has a far better educated laity than it was dealing with fifty years ago. I think it has to sharpen up its act.

RW: You are a very moral writer. Do you have any particular religious beliefs?

TA: I believe in God. I hope so much there is a God. Otherwise, I feel the whole operation is pointless. But I think the Christian churches as established promulgators of religion have moved so far away from the concepts that Christ is identified with that He wouldn't recognize them if He came back. He'd go in the wrong door; in fact He probably wouldn't go in any door at all. I feel the Christian churches have become big p.r. organizations. I suppose in every church there are good people struggling to maintain the ideas of the early Christian beliefs, but I don't know if they are very successful. Mother Teresa seems to be; some of the priests in South America seem to be living out religious lives. I do think religion is more than ritual.

RW: How do you express your religious beliefs?

TA: I still pray. I don't think I'm fundamentally a Christian. I would like to be.

RW: What about nature?

TA: The only sort of regrets I have about getting old is that there are fewer days to watch leaves turn over. That really upsets me, that we have such limited time. I think this notion of the whole world as a Garden of Eden is as good a way to approach the Creator as any way is. But man has messed up the Garden. I find myself lately even feeling little spasms of guilt as I pick caterpillars off the acacias and crush them.

RW: In much of your fiction your characters live on the edge of disasters—a cyclone, a political coup, a nuclear holocaust. More often a personal disaster awaits them, an emotional collapse, perhaps. In your own words from *The Acolyte,* you say your characters are "always touching on the edges of cyclones." Would you comment?

TA: Did I write that? Gee, that's nice. Well, of course they are. Just being alive is like living on the edge; well, to me it is. This is what Patrick White is all about. In *The Eye of the Storm* he came right out and said it, but he's been saying it in all his books. Everybody's living on a cyclonic edge.

RW: In your fiction you seem to focus on bringing a character closer and closer to that edge.

TA: To the edge, or to the eye?

RW: Often he is in the eye and he is moving toward the edge again.

TA: I think Patrick's been taking his characters into the eye and I think mine have been misguidedly trying to get right away, out of the entire ambient of the cyclone and, of course, that is not possible, not for any human. The minute you are born you are put into this situation. I get the terrible feeling these days that there is a whole new generation being brought up without any spiritual conscience. I think the philosophy promulgated in the late sixties, "If it feels good, do it," is so improper, so selfish. Kids used to sit in a tute group and I'd ask what they were going to do next year and they'd say, "I'm going away to find myself." I'd say, "Where will that be, dear, Borneo, Pakistan?" In the late sixties and seventies they were looking for themselves all over southern Asia.

RW: And yet your characters are often looking for themselves.

TA: Yes, but I used to say to the kids, "I don't want to hear this selfish garbage. If you start looking for other people, discovering how they feel, you'll find out so much about yourself in the process that you won't believe it."

RW: Do you think it always takes another, or a series of others, for one to define oneself? Does it take relationships for this to happen?

TA: Yes. The umbilical cord isn't just the thing between mother and child; there is an unseeable umbilical cord linking all humans, six hundred billion umbilical cords, which we ignore. Just to sit there thinking about my own problems is so boring and so useless. You get seventy years here biblically to communicate with other people and find out about yourself, and you find out about yourself by talking to others. As we are not God, we can hardly ever encounter our own problems by ourself. It usually takes another person who can stand off from you to peel the plastic covering off a bit. It's much easier to get good advice from a friend over a cup of tea than it is to sit and drink innumerable cups of tea by yourself and try to think it out. I think in that way madness does lie.

RW: In fiction do you use reflector characters to bounce ideas back and forth?

TA: I haven't consciously done this, but I suppose I have done it. I find dialogue difficult, actually. I find it the hardest part of writing to have characters talking and not sounding totally trivial. That's why I have such admiration for playwrights.

RW: You often have as a main character a misfit. You've said, "My novels have always been a plea for charity . . . for the misfit, for the seedy little non-grandiose non-fitter who lives in his own mini-hell." Would you comment?

TA: What more can I say?

RW: What about the misfit interests you?

TA: I've always thought myself to be a bit of a misfit. It was a selfish way of writing out things that worried me. I remember when I was teaching at a high school in Sydney before I started to write *A Descant for Gossips.* I based my central character on a little redheaded girl who was in one of my classes. She didn't have any friends; no one liked her. I didn't even like her myself. I tried hard, but this worried me. She was so obviously used to being unliked it had almost become a shield around her, a force field. She'd come up to me at the lunch break and ask me spurious questions just to be seen talking to me because she didn't have anyone to talk to. Halfway through that year another kid joined the class. You get terrific antennae as a teacher. I thought, "She's another one." I sat these two together and they never looked back. On the playground they had their heads together talking, eating lunch. God, it was marvelous, probably my greatest triumph as a teacher.

RW: That manipulation of a misfit was the starting place for your novel?

TA: That, and a story about another misfit that a friend of mine who was teaching up country told me. The day my friend arrived at the school at which she was to teach, an inquest was being held for a girl who had killed herself. She'd been a fat girl, the daughter of the town rat catcher, and the kids had given her hell. They'd yelled, "You're pregnant, you're pregnant" because she was fat and large, and she went home and took her father's rat poison. My teacher friend, Mary, said that all the kids turned up at the funeral. I thought, my God, what a terrible story; I must use it sometime. The whole time I was writing *A Descant* I thought about the redhead whom I'd taught, who didn't have a friend for six months, and the fat girl. I couldn't give the story a happy ending as in my school, because I was juggling the two events.

RW: How do you feel about the film that was done of *Descant?*

TA: It was terrible. I think the script had ten words of mine. The script was totally rewritten; the actors were wrong.

RW: You've said in terms of your characters' interaction, "Disaster comes out of the most sheltered places." What do you mean by this?

TA: Well, I knew when I wrote it. I guess I was talking about the sudden disruption in people's lives, the shock one gets when a relationship or a situation he's taken for granted does a somersault and he is confronting the other side of it. I think this happens a lot.

RW: I thought you meant that it often comes from what one trusts the most, the knife that turns against you.

TA: Yes, that's true. The awful thing is that the sufferer is just as capable of doing that to another person. The victim can become the aggressor. But I think there are fewer of these than there are total misfits, the one who doesn't learn. If you keep turning the other cheek, that can be a kind of aggression too—"Ah, hit me here, dear."

RW: You've written touchingly about injustice to Aborigines, in *A*

Kindness Cup, An Item from the Late News, It's Raining in Mango, and elsewhere. Have you been more interested in the national problem or in individual characterization?

TA: Both. But the scales weigh more heavily on the side of the individual treatment, because, after all, the British poisoned, shot, or gave disease to most of the aboriginal population in this country. My feelings are based a lot on people, like those in the little settlement of blacks who lived opposite us in the North. We got to know a few of the Murris, which is their tribal name, and found them very gentle and charming and non-aggressive. They were happy and laughing and simple, in the best sense. They just wanted to be left alone.

RW: You learned a pidgin dialect to write *Beachmasters.* Language is a particular interest of yours, isn't it?

TA: I think it's man's greatest invention, without which, nothing, nothing. I was listening to a commentator on the telly recently who said that the beginning of Australian language was the "grunt." He went through the process of how language grew sophisticated. Then he said that with the teenagers now, we've returned to the "grunt."

RW: In some of your writing you use a great deal of Australian slang, more than any of your successful contemporaries. When I first began to read your work it put me off a bit; now I relish it as a kind of verbal museum. Why do you think Australians in general use so much slang, particularly so many diminutives?

TA: It's part of the Tall Poppy syndrome out here, cutting someone down to size. It's so that people won't think you a wanker, using pretentiously long words. If you use a diminutive of a job, it belittles the job. Instead of dignifying someone by asking if he is a teacher, you say, "You are a chalkie, are you?" "You have a uni degree, do you? Say big words."

RW: What's a wanker?

TA: It once meant a masturbator; now it means someone who indulges his ego. "Wanking" means thinking yourself to be someone.

RW: Let me give you a few words and you tell me what they mean. What is a dunny?

TA: A lav.

RW: A lav?

TA: Out-the-back one. Anything where you go to relieve yourself.

RW: A bikki?

TA: A biscuit. A cookie.

RW: A prezzy, a truckie?

TA: A present, like a Christmas present. A truck driver. It's printed in the paper now as "truckie."

RW: You used earlier a word that means dangling sheep excrement. What was that word?

TA: Dags. Dagging a sheep is a job that has to be done to keep fleece clean. People say, "It's a real daggy looking house," meaning grotty, you know, grotesque.

RW: Turning a car around?

TA: Doing a u-e.

RW: The diminutive is made by using an *o* or an *e*?

TA: It must depend on the consonant formation of the word. A musician is always a "muso," not a "musie"; a journalist is a "journo," a "brickie" is a brick layer. Plumbers aren't shortened at all because people are overawed by plumbers. But we say, "Here comes the 'garbo' or the 'milko.'"

RW: Why do you record so much slang?

TA: My characters use it a lot. I've been exposed to it, particularly in all those bush towns I taught in. I just listen.

RW: Your prose style is unlike that of any other writer that I can think of, brambles of wit, puns, flights of metaphors that often make the reader gasp at the dance you set in motion. At other times I am so slowed by the density of the prose that I am exhausted at the end of a couple of pages. Could you talk about the way your mind works as you write?

TA: I often read a lot of poetry when I'm writing a novel. I like poetry. I feel it stimulates me. The metaphor probably rubs off.

RW: Have any prose writers influenced you?

TA: I don't like to read serious fiction when I am writing. I'm afraid of plagiarism, but along the way almost everyone I've read has influenced me. Patrick White, Cheever, Hemingway, Nabokov, Carver. Every time I read a writer I admire, I think, "God, I wish I'd written that." I wish I'd written *The Heart Is a Lonely Hunter,* I wish I had written at least ten of Cheever's stories.

RW: Some critics consider you the funniest writer in Australia. Do you see the world in terms of comedy?

TA: Black comedy. Even if you are in the midst of a domestic row you think, "God, this is awful, isn't it?" and you start laughing. I have always admired a writer who can have you walking that very narrow edge between weeping at the horror of things and laughing. It's comic, but it's horrendous. I think to do that is dazzling. Olga Masters did this very well, particularly in *The Home Girls.* Ray Carver did it when I heard him read "Cathedral," carrying the audience from laughter to wonder. I had a coffee with him in Canberra. We talked. I think *he* might have been a victim.

RW: Your recent novels *It's Raining in Mango* and *Reaching Tin*

River are in terms of style more easily accessible than the earlier novels. Is your writing changing in this way?

TA: Yes, I think it is. I've had a lot of critical flack over my dense style. I've probably consciously tried to make it simpler. Maybe I'm just getting tired. Maybe I'm not reading as much poetry. When I was writing *Mango,* I was writing about simple working people and I thought that I wanted to tell the story in a way that it would be read. I felt it was no good writing about the problems of Aborigines in prose so imagistic that no one would get the message. I think Ray Carver taught me a lesson in the way that Hemingway never did. I didn't know one could be so moved by such simplicity, such honesty. I think that's genius. I thought, if he can do this with such basic English, what am I messing around for? In reading Carver, I felt like I'd met the Mother Teresa of the written word.

RW: You are a very prolific writer. Are you compulsive?

TA: No. I find writing hard work. I think probably there ought to be longer gaps between my novels. I get the feeling from agents and publishers that if you don't have a book every two years you're dead meat. I feel I was pressured a bit over *Tin River.* Even so, I did five drafts of the darn thing. Writing was once a leisured occupation. At the same time, I've always marveled at how Dickens wrote so dazzlingly to a deadline. He must have been the Mozart of the written word. I don't know how he did it.

RW: By *compulsive* I mean, do you need to have work going all the time?

TA: No. I can go months without writing anything, but once I start I feel that I have to write some every day or I'll lose it.

RW: How do you work?

TA: I find the morning the freshest time. I do longhand before I type it. Sometimes I write five hundred words in bed at night.

RW: Once I asked what it's like to be inside your head, and you answered, "A can of worms . . ."

TA: It's awful. Compulsions, obsessions, guilts. It's like badly cooked spaghetti. I think anyone's head is like that, don't you?

RW: Do you have one novel that stands above the others?

TA: I still like *The Acolyte* the best. I did a lot of work on *Beachmasters,* but it seems to have dropped down a black hole.

RW: You live on a hillside overlooking bright green pastures and distant valleys, and in the far distance the Pacific is a shining blue line. Kookaburras fly through the eucalyptus trees; I've seen kangaroos appear and disappear in the bush that encroaches on your land . . .

TA: Maybe we could publish this description . . .

RW: This is a beautiful, natural spot, but it is isolated. Your husband, Jack, is seventy-five; do you worry about growing old and about being so far from neighbors and services?

TA: Of course, I worry. And I am the worst driver in the Southern Hemisphere. Yes, I would be the worst driver. There's a certain cachet in that. I think eventually we'll have to think of moving, but we'll hang in here as long as we can. Eventually we would need a gardener, and that is very expensive. Housework is very exhausting—no wonder men have made sure that women did it. I mean, vacuum cleaners have gotten heavier. Excuse me, I am about to kill another fly.

RW: What do you think matters most?

TA: Being kind. I'm not saying I am. I'm not. I wish I were. I think being kind is probably what matters more than anything in the world.

PETER CAREY

was born in 1943 in the small town of Bacchus Marsh in the state of Victoria. After dropping out of Monash University, he worked in advertising, living first in Melbourne, then in a commune near Brisbane, then in Sydney. Carey's work, varyingly described as it has changed over the years as having elements of science fiction, metafiction, and magic realism, has been very popular in Australia and from the beginning has suggested a new kind of writing in Australia. His novels, lengthy studies of Australia and the Australian character, have all garnered critical praise. *Bliss* was given the Miles Franklin Award and was made into a motion picture. His most recent novel, *Oscar and Lucinda,* was awarded the Booker Prize. In the spring of 1990 Peter Carey was writer in residence at New York University. The following interview occurred in Carey's waterfront house in Balmain (Sydney).

The Fat Man in History (stories), 1974
War Crimes (stories), 1979
Bliss, 1981
Illywhacker, 1985
Oscar and Lucinda, 1988
The Tax Inspector, 1991

INTERVIEW

RW: With *Oscar and Lucinda,* you've recently won England's Booker Prize. How have you been affected by winning the Booker?
PC: I've sold a lot more books. I've gotten known in a lot more places that I wasn't known and I've been translated more easily. I was in London when I won the prize and in the beginning I did so many interviews it was like being run over by a truck, and I became very good at hiding.
RW: Tom Keneally has said to me that winning the Booker came at a useful time in his life. It validated his work and stimulated him to continue. Did you feel any of this?

PC: Tom and I are different personalities, I guess. I mostly live in a state of anxiety, expecting failure. Every book I've ever written since the first published one I've expected to be liked less than the previous one. I've always expected to disappoint people. When I'm writing, I look back into the previous book and think I could never do anything this good again. Each time, though, I've been fortunate to have the new book liked even more.

RW: You must be really nervous now.

PC: Yes. I think what the Booker Prize does for me is just increase that state of anxiety. I don't like what I'm doing now as much as I like *Oscar and Lucinda.* One day I'm going to be right.

RW: I am fascinated by a bit of comparative biography. You've indicated the influence of Faulkner, particularly *As I Lay Dying* on your early work. I've read that you failed your first-year exams at Monash University. Faulkner failed freshman English at the University of Mississippi. Does this say anything about budding genius?

PC: I don't think so. The crude and easy response would be to say that there is something so stuffy and wrong with academic life that it fails people who are creatively gifted. I don't believe that for a second.

RW: What happened that you did fail?

PC: Predominately because I'd spent seven years cooped up in an all-male boarding school. Then there were women and alcohol, and I fell in love. I did well for about half a year; then tragedy of all sorts descended upon me and suddenly academic life seemed less important.

RW: Do you remember what reasons you were attracted to Faulkner?

PC: I'm used to saying something which is not quite true. I love saying to people that I'd never read a good book until I was eighteen. That's upset many people including my old English teacher who taught me Shakespeare and Milton and many books that I've forgotten. But basically I read crap. It wasn't really until after I failed university that I started to read. I read in a big rush, and I read because I was working with people who were writers or who wanted to be writers and who introduced me to books. Faulkner was among those things given to me. I remember it as being the first week of my life. All those books arrived. It couldn't have been that way, but I remember Joyce and Faulkner and Kerouac all coming at once. I haven't looked at *As I Lay Dying* since I read it in 1962, but I remember being struck by the beauty of the language, the rich, unimaginable poetry of these people whom you would look at from the outside and think were nothing. I loved the way they contradicted each other in their versions of reality.

RW: I can see in your stories the way you make use of alternative realities.

PC: Yes. My early stories in particular have lost, apparently loveless people who lead extraordinary interior lives.

RW: There are parts of *Illywhacker* and *Oscar and Lucinda* which remind me a bit of Melville—*The Confidence Man, Moby Dick,* the whiteness of the whale, the whiteness of the glass, the liar. Have you read Melville?

PC: No. I am an extraordinarily self-centered and intolerant reader. One day when I'm adult enough to discover a great work of literature I must read *Moby Dick*. I did start it years ago, and I became impatient with the beginning of it, so I've never read it.

RW: Your short stories and early novels illustrate modern narrative strategies; what contemporary writers have been important to you?

PC: Borges. García Márquez. After I had been writing stories I read *One Hundred Years of Solitude* and it had for me a hugely liberating effect. Donald Barthelme. In retrospect I can see how I was particularly affected in terms of ways of talking about things by his story "The Balloon."

RW: You've said that if you could write a novel like *One Hundred Years of Solitude* you'd be proud and happy. Is *Oscar and Lucinda* that book?

PC: It would be presumptuous of me to even consider it. Quite seriously, there is a part of me that is competitive. I basically disapprove of it because I think writers should help each other. I would like to think that this is my practice in life. But there is this other mean part of me which I have to acknowledge because it affects how I read. But when I think of García Márquez I can only applaud. It's like a knife going through butter. *Love in the Time of Cholera* is such a beautiful book, so imbued with a love of people. If someone thought *Oscar and Lucinda* was in any way like that I'd be very flattered.

RW: When you left the university you began work in Melbourne at an advertising agency. You've said, "Most of my education took place in advertising agencies through people I knew." Would you talk about that education?

PC: The first advertising agency I worked for was quite extraordinary. Like many of the agencies I've worked with, it was run by a member of the Communist Party of Australia, which is one of those lovely contradictions: communism, capitalism, and advertising. During that time particularly, advertising agencies were havens for all sorts of artists and writers. We had no magazine industry or film industry or anything, so advertising had a lot of those people. In the first agency I worked for there was Barry Oakley, who is now the literary editor of *The Australian,* as well as a novelist and playwright; Morris Lurie, whose works I can always find in bookshops in New York on those irritating days when I can never find my own; in the next room there was Bruce Petty, one of Australia's most distinguished political cartoonists. There were other people who were doing similar odd and interesting things. It was through Barry Oakley, who had been a schoolteacher and who at thirty-two was just beginning in advertising, that I began to read books. He encouraged me to read.

RW: It doesn't sound like Madison Avenue.

PC: No. It was quite literary. There was even a copy chief in another agency who had read *Finnegans Wake.* Morris Lurie used to write short stories in the office. None of our work ever went through. We were the most uncommercial sort of people you could possibly imagine. My advertising history has been much like my first job. There has always been room for eccentrics.

RW: In your first novel, *Bliss,* Harry Joy saw his own life in advertising as hell. I gather that Harry's experiences were not your own.

PC: No. I chose some things from my life, so that I wouldn't have to make them up, really, and the fact that Harry ends up in the rain forest is because that was where I was living when I was writing the novel. My reason for doing certain things was not so much to express myself but because I was inventing and taking from things which were around me to use. My big difficulty was with the ad agency itself because it is so often caricatured. It is to laugh at and it's hard to imagine a serious work of literature dealing with one. But I knew a lot about it and I wanted to use it. I could have just as well given Harry a job as an architect or an engineer, almost anything in middle-class life.

RW: Were you, like Harry, living in a commune?

PC: Yeah. People there always said it was a community, not a commune, but it was thought by the local people to be a commune.

RW: How long did you live there?

PC: About four years. I used to live in the community which was north of Brisbane, and I would go down to Sydney for about five days a month and do some ads and come back.

RW: And you could support yourself that way?

PC: Yes. But that kind of living was due in a way to a lack of courage. The brave thing would have been to say, "No more advertising for me, thanks," but because it was more comfortable to do it the other way, I could write almost every day and without having to be anxious about whether my book would sell or not sell; I always chose that sort of option.

RW: I'm surprised that you managed to live two lives in a commune, that you weren't swallowed up by whatever was the prevailing mind-set of the place.

PC: Well, we weren't very doctrinaire.

RW: For a number of years now you've made a very good living with your own advertising agency here in Sydney. How compatible has this been with your writing?

PC: I've spent years trying to answer that question, and I think I'm finally close to getting it right. Once I've answered for myself the question of what I do with the answer, "I am a writer of fiction," then everything else falls into place as a way to make that happen. That's the first thing. But having an ambivalence was the best form of private patronage I could ever have had because my partner worked all the time. I didn't. We never took on any business we didn't want. We were often offered tempting things, for example, a cigarette business worth five million dollars. We had no hesitation in saying no to it and lots of other things as well. If you are going to be in commercial life, it is great to be able to control your own destiny. It was a pleasant feeling. We could even fire clients, which we did. We had a small business, necessarily, if you're going to behave like that; but it was for most of its life a pleasant place for people to work. It wasn't sexist; it wasn't particularly hierarchical even though there was leadership, so it was quite a pleasant place, a little walled building in a sort of bleak industrial part of Chippendale, Sydney, but pleasant inside, which was what the business was like.

RW: Did you write fiction in your office?

PC: No. I wrote at home and went into the office two afternoons a week. That's all I would do. Advertising always provided all the money I needed. I never even expected to make money from writing. But we've sold the business and I'm out of that now. And up until now I've never ever thought about financial success from writing and it's just as well because I've been so riddled with anxiety about artistic matters that I would have hated to be worrying about if the writing were going to sell. I was sure when I wrote *Illywhacker* that I was eliminating the American market completely by writing such a deliberately colloquial Australian novel and that *Oscar and Lucinda* being about Anglican and Australian matters would not interest Americans, either. If I had had to think about commercial matters I think I would never have written those books. I am very, very grateful I have not had to worry about money.

RW: In *Bliss* you set up a positive/negative polarity between Australia and America, with America standing for petrol, cancer, bad advertising, spiritual death; and Australia, through Honey Barbara, standing for a kind of natural, romantic self-reliance. Do you see even now such clear distinctions between Australia and the States, or did you then?

PC: I don't think I made such clear distinctions even then; but it's difficult for me to remember because I haven't read the book in such a long time. I did have a thing about Australia being on the edge of the American Empire, which seems essentially true. One can feel a great deal of reservations about American political actions in the world, the actions of American companies. But I really like Americans as individuals. It's a great generalization, I know, but Americans always seem to me to be optimistic, whereas Australians tend to be pessimistic. I like talking to Americans better than to Australians. I think Americans are more comfortable with emotion than we are and I like that.

RW: Were you happy with the film of *Bliss?*

PC: No. And I think about it quite a lot, actually. There are two or three things I really dislike. I shouldn't have written the screenplay. I followed the book too closely. I think the film is frightened of emotion. I think emotion stays out when it should be in there. I think the director had no view. Visually, there should have been a poisoned paradise. There should have been crap pouring into the sky. Visually, the viewer should have seen what Harry Joy didn't see; then he should have seen Harry seeing it. You should have felt you were in a poisoned place. It was my fault. If I had approached the script with that idea it would have ended up looking like that because the director would have followed. I was too close.

RW: Before the novels, *Bliss, Illywhacker,* and *Oscar and Lucinda,* you published a number of short stories that won you a large following in Australia, particularly among the young. Would you talk about two of your popular stories from this early period, "Crabs" and "Peeling"?

PC: They were written so long ago that I am as usual an unreliable witness. In "Crabs" a young man is keen to take his girlfriend to a drive-in movie theater. It is during a time of great lawlessness, when cars are very valuable and car parts are hard to get in Australia. At the drive-in there is a gang that steals car parts and so the couple becomes marooned. The young man spends all his time trying to escape. Two things happen: he figures that the only way to get out of this drive-in is to be a motor vehicle in good health, so he becomes a tow truck. This is the only sensible solution to his problem. When he leaves the drive-in, having successfully become a tow truck, he drives around and finds the streets empty. What he finds that he has escaped from is the world. Everyone is in the drive-in theater.

RW: How did you get the idea for the story?

PC: Driving past a wrecker's yard in Melbourne. I imagined a world in which people were living in motorcars. That's how the story began. I made notes and worked it out; probably before I started writing I would have known that the man was going to change into a tow truck. But "Peeling" is not like that at all. More than anything I've ever written, that story follows my intuition. Nothing was planned. I once went to a house in Carlton where the woman who was living there used to arrange a lot of white painted dolls on the landing. It was an arty sort of house with writers and painters. It was odd, but not that odd. I wrote half the story, put it away and when I picked it up again it worked itself out. The story line is this: there is a woman who has a mystery, and her mystery is that she makes white dolls. A man in stripping away the layers of her clothing, getting closer to her essence as a human being, finds that as she falls to pieces, all there is at the center of her is a white doll. The mystery is still there. What she is externalizing is this thing that is inside her, but there is no psychological explanation why.

RW: Your work has been described as science fiction, fabulism, magic realism—do any of these terms apply?

PC: I don't care what people say as long as they are nice to me. Science fiction as a descriptive comment about my work was in an odd way self-fulfilling. I had scarcely read any science fiction. Then I went out and discovered the early stories of Vonnegut and *The Sirens of Titan,* and then I started to read other science fiction. Science fiction did have an effect, but it came after I had already begun to write.

RW: Do you start in realism and let your imagination take you into another dimension? How do you work?

PC: In *Illywhacker,* for example, I began with the image of my country as a pet shop, people living in cages, being well-fed, thinking they are happy, but denying the nature of their prison. I wanted to have a story in which a family ends up in a pet shop. Then I spent all the rest of my writing time, three or four years, finding out how that might possibly be so, how those people might have got themselves into that situation. My idea was a fanciful one, but I was intent on making it real.

RW: So you started with a situation even before you had a character?

PC: Right. I always have the situation first. The short stories really didn't have characters.

RW: In some of your fiction you create a narrator who has an insight that reminds me of Vonnegut or even Mark Twain, a kind of cosmic observer who is in a sense beyond morality; perhaps he is amoral. He sometimes inserts himself into the story. Would you comment?

PC: You are thinking of Badgery in *Illywhacker* and the narrator in *Oscar and Lucinda*?

RW: Yes.

PC: I suppose this is giving the writer an active role, isn't it? It's making the writer into another character. It just adds another dimension to what you can do. I don't have a theoretical reason for doing it.

RW: You aren't intentionally playing with reality, creating parallel worlds, the sort of things Fowles does?

PC: Well, yes. In *Oscar and Lucinda* I am doing this, not in *Illywhacker.* When I've finished a book I often feel a little deceitful in the sense that I feel like one who has crammed for an examination. When I've finished the book and it's all over, I press the button and it all ejects. The longer the period after the book, the harder it gets to remember. When I was in New York doing National Public Radio someone asked me a question that I liked, one of those very intelligent reader's questions and I knew that in the back of my foggy mind there were very good reasons why I had done the things that he was asking me about and that he was leading me to the answer; it was a friendly question, and I couldn't remember enough about the book to answer. In a sense writing is like a madness or being very drunk. I look back and say, "I did this!" And I'm not that smart. I know that I had all the different ideas and arguments and threads of things and I kept it all in my head, everything, as I was writing. I would know where everything is and why it is there, but when the writing is over, very soon afterwards, or as soon as I begin to think about another book, all that goes away.

RW: It would have to, wouldn't it?

PC: I don't know. But I always feel inadequate in the face of questions from good readers. I start mumbling and fumbling around, often unable to answer.

RW: Let me try some general questions. Back to *Illywhacker.* Could you say something about the structure of that novel, your narrator, the pet shop?

PC: I've said a bit about the idea of the pet shop. Dymocks Book Store had also a gallery and a pet shop upstairs. That gave me an idea, but later I imagined its being a space in what is now the Strand Arcade, a three-storied open courtyard with galleries going around. This is where the families ended up. I wanted the story to be set in a period in Australian life when people had a kind of entrepreneurial optimistic nationalism. I began the story in 1919 because I didn't want to have to worry about World War I. I thought that was too hard to think about. Otherwise, the time seemed to fit historically. I slowly shaped this family which had some things to do with my own family—selling motorcars, a lot of T Model Fords, setting up what seemed to me to be a very Australian thing—being passionately attached to the American product, knowing that the American product would be easier to sell and that the Australian would be more expensive and probably wouldn't work as well, yet at the same time being passionately nationalistic, this duality of expedience and the feelings of emotions about one's country. Ah, I can't remember all this.

RW: How did you come up with the 139-year-old narrator?

PC: Well, he wasn't that in the beginning. I was going to divide the story into three generations, and the first was going to be about the confidence man, liar, trickster; the second was going to be about a kind of degeneration from entrepreneurial capitalism; the third generation was going to be about the pet shop people. But when I was well into the first part, I thought, I can't lose Badgery; he's too good. I had discovered the thing about lies and lying by then, which I hadn't set out to do. I found that the idea of lies becoming truths was an interesting thing to deal with in writing fiction. One can look at the fact of imagination, saying that which is not true, or as Badgery says, "saying that which is not yet true" as a way of actually shaping the future. Once one says something, it does begin to be true. That's one of the things I myself think about fiction. There is a great responsibility in imagining something. To digress, I'm working with Wim Wenders on a film at the moment which when we first talked had a nuclear holocaust in it. I said I thought it was really important not to imagine it. Carolyn See does imagine it in *Golden Days,* a really extraordinary book that stays with me, and I wouldn't criticize her at all for doing it, but I would personally be very nervous with this sort of imagination. But back to *Illywhacker,* when I started to think about the narrator as liar I began to unlock for myself some bigger issues to deal with and some things that deal with fiction itself. I could have the pet shop and the cage as a lie, as an invented thing. I could make Herbert Badgery the author and these people in the cage creatures of his imagination.

RW: It sounds as if you are making a moral statement about the writer—that he should invent what is morally desirable.

PC: I would never put it like that. But I think the writer has a responsibility to tell the truth, not to shy away from the world as it is;

and at the same time the writer has a responsibility to celebrate the potential of the human spirit. What is good about *Illywhacker* and *Oscar and Lucinda* is made in the tension between those two things. *Illywhacker* has an extraordinarily bleak view of Australia on the one hand, and yet it is celebratory. *Oscar and Lucinda* is similar.

RW: Critics of David Williamson's plays often take him to task for combining the bleak and the celebratory. They want him to be one or the other, but not both at the same time.

PC: This combination is what I am interested in. I used to write these miserable, bleak stories. It used to worry me so much that when I finally began to write a story that was not bleak, I called it "Happy Story."

RW: You write about entrapment a great deal, characters getting into traps . . .

PC: I think one would have to separate the short stories from the novels and I think what the short stories are really about is my childhood. The stories never really corresponded with an expression of how I was an adult. As an adult I've always felt a great deal of potential, but as a child in a country town I felt trapped, with denied possibilities. I am writing about my childhood now in the new novel, and the writing has a lot of the emotional resonances that connect with the short stories. When one looks at cages and trapping in *Illywhacker,* I think that's a different sort of thing.

RW: In *Illywhacker* Phoebe tells Badgery, "We invent ourselves." Do you believe that? Do we invent ourselves?

PC: Yes. I think it's true, at least on one level. Human societies absolutely invent themselves. We don't often enough look at ourselves as being creatures of our imagination, but we are. On the other hand, if someone said to me, "You can be anyone you want to be," I would say he was talking absolute bullshit and it would make me very angry. This is sort of post-hippie middle-class crystal gazing. But in the way Phoebe means it, I think it is true.

RW: You come from a line of automobile salesmen, you've been a seller of advertising, a fictional seller of lies. Do you think everyone is in a sense a seller of his invented self?

PC: I'm not sure I understand the question.

RW: Are we constantly inventing and projecting and delivering versions of ourselves?

PC: Yes. It's an interesting thought, but I'm not sure how I can talk about it.

RW: One more question about *Illywhacker.* What is particularly

Australian about this novel? What are the Australian lies that perhaps would not be American lies?

PC: One lie the Australians tell themselves that comes true is that they are a cowardly, unimaginative people. Badgery in one scene has a finger in a bottle, and he puts it on a counter in front of a policeman who asks what it is. Badgery says, "It's anything you have the freedom to imagine it to be." This is all about being an Australian. I can't imagine that scene in that way in an American book because this is not the way Americans see themselves. One could do a reading of *Illywhacker* and read it as being about the failure of the manufacturing industry in Australia, which is what the current economic crisis in Australia has partly to do with. There are people who try to make things and fail, like the man in *Illywhacker* who invents this wonderful plow and the typically Australian banks won't loan him the money to produce it.

RW: Is this a failure of imagination, a failure to say "yes," a failure of enthusiasm? What sort of failures are these?

PC: I think they are all that you list. We are a culture of fixing something up, making do with what's available, rather than creating something new. Ours is a failure of confidence.

RW: Confidence is also a subject in *Oscar and Lucinda.* Do you recall the beginning point in your imagination for this novel?

PC: Yes. I was living in the country. I used to drive through a particularly beautiful valley every day. In the valley was a small simple weatherboard church down by the river. I never thought about it too much except I loved coming through there. Then I heard one day that the church was going to be taken away. I got really mad. I'm not a Christian, though I grew up in the Church of England, but I thought, this is really weird. Why am I so mad? I wondered, am I taking some false and sentimental comfort from the religion of my childhood, that there's some sort of mummy or daddy somewhere that will look after me? I thought about it some more. I thought, "maybe." Then I began to think that it's really interesting that the Christian culture is the only culture we have. We have a great mass of stories which I grew up on. Now people don't even know what they are. If you talk to someone about the parable of the talents, they say, "The what?" So I thought, this church is going to be taken away and all that is going to be left is thistles and I think that's really appropriate. That's what will grow in where the earth's been broken because we have nothing moral to replace Christianity. I thought that it was not so long ago when people came to this valley and killed the Aboriginal people and destroyed their culture. This whole lovely landscape is filled with their ghost stories. Then I imagined the church—this is the lunatic part, I suppose, like a cartoon; I think often like a cartoonist; if you look at the end of *Illywhacker*, it's rather the way the cartoonist thinks. So I imagined a box full of Christian stories on a barge passing along a river through an Aboriginal landscape filled with Aboriginal stories. I liked that idea. I wondered why that church would be on a barge and I thought that maybe somebody has a prefabricated system for building churches and they want to show it off. But I didn't know, and then I remembered that the Victorians used to manufacture things out of cast iron which they could bolt together, library staircases that were shipped out and then bolted together, sort of a prefabricated technology. So then I asked a good friend of mine, an architect named Richard Leplastrier (Lucinda's surname) who had designed the house in which I was living in the country, "Was there this cast iron thing?" He said yes, but it was only for glass houses and glass and steel. He asked why. I said that I wanted this church to go down a river on a barge. I said, "Don't ask me why yet. I'm not sure," and he said, "Why don't you make it a glass church?" That was the moment! The minute he said that, I thought, my God, that's right. I loved the idea of glass. I loved the idea that it was a folly. That immediately suggests an obsessive character somewhere behind it, and I like obsessive characters. I liked the idea of glass because of the associations: clarity, a sense of incorruptibility, a sort of hard, clear, diamond-like substance. Then I thought maybe someone had done it all for a bet. That could be a way to justify the lunacy of the thing. Then I remembered what Pascal had said about belief in God being a gamble. That clicked together. That's really how the book started.

RW: The characters came after the idea, then?

PC: Yes. I knew I was writing a kind of funny love story. I knew there had to be a clergyman involved and somebody who had something to do with glass.

RW: You have a long and complicated story. Did you tell the story in sequence from beginning to end or did you follow an idea or a segment to its completion?

PC: I spent a lot of time mapping it out, working out where it had to go to. I did a lot of work with notes before I could see roughly what the story would be. Then I began. Physically, my method of work is rather like nervous cantilevering. I get out about thirty pages and lose confidence. I have to go back to the beginning. Then I get up to seventy pages and lose confidence and have to go back to the beginning. I keep doing this because I stop believing in it myself and I feel I haven't got a proper grasp of the characters or the situation or the place.

RW: How did you do the research, the religious research, for example?

PC: I read a lot of things, but the big thing was a wonderful book by an English writer named Owen Chadwick, *The Victorian Church.* It was beautifully written, a real pleasure to read. I read a book by Cardinal Newman called *Loss and Gain.* In fact, some of the preoccupations of Mrs. Stratton in *Oscar and Lucinda* are derived from *Loss and Gain.* I read Geoffery Favor's really mean-minded biography of Cardinal Newman. I talked to clergymen. Mostly, I set out to write before I knew anything. I invented the ship, having no idea what a ship was like or how it was put together, and then I began to realize what I needed to know.

RW: Did you from the outset intend to dramatize the four great Victorian interests: science, religion, technology, exploration?

PC: No. Actually until you said that, I didn't know I had done it. I feel flattered by that question.

RW: In terms of the style of *Oscar and Lucinda,* critics point out resemblances to Dickens in one spot, to Conrad in another, to Trollope, to Fielding. Were you intentionally playing with these Victorian models?

PC: I knew I wanted the novel to sound like the nineteenth century. I obviously did a lot of reading around the subject, but I didn't read too much fiction. The voice is something that was produced from what I thought it should be like rather than being modeled on anything.

RW: You weren't doing Dickens, Conrad?

PC: No. I haven't really read Dickens. Conrad, I certainly have, but a long time ago. I did read *Middlemarch,* but I think the language I used comes through the reading I did in a lot of newspapers and odd guides of Sydney from the period.

RW: Back to the boat carrying the church down the river, the Aborigines on the bank—the imposition of the Christian myths on the aboriginal territory. Do you consider *Oscar and Lucinda* a post-Christian novel?

PC: Yes. But I often think in talking about this how wrong it is to see these as post-Christian times. But, yes I would see the novel in that way.

RW: Let me bring up one of the *isms* again. Do you think the term magic realism applies to any of your work?

PC: I liked the term magic realism when I first heard it and I always thought that this was a lovely way to describe the sort of writing one finds in *Illywhacker*, even *Bliss*, but particularly *Illywhacker*. Then later it became a tag that was thrown around so much that it started to get soiled. In my mind it became a sort of cheap cliché. I became wary of being labeled a magic realist. In a funny way I no longer feel that I am writing in this way. Even though you can say that *Oscar and Lucinda* has elements of magic realism, I don't see the novel in this sense as I do *Illywhacker*. It's less magic, more real. The new novel that I am writing at this very moment is even more real.

RW: Let's talk about your use of realism. You live in Balmain, a harbor suburb of Sydney, still much as it was in the mid-nineteenth century. Long Nose Point, the ferry landing at the end of the street on which you live, figures in *Oscar and Lucinda*. Would you talk about your realistic use of Sydney in the novel?

PC: I always feel very nervous about Sydney because I don't come from Sydney, whereas in *Illywhacker* I could write very confidently about the countryside in Victoria and about Melbourne because I came from there and had it in my blood. Even though I've spent a lot of time here, I feel I have no right to Sydney because I don't know it so well, so I chose carefully. I chose for Lucinda to live in this place where I now live because I knew about it, about the wind and the weather, and it was easy to imagine her here. I looked for those corners in Sydney that I thought I could write about, and then I did research. I didn't feel confident, and this was what made me work very hard to try to get it right.

RW: Would one now find Lucinda's house on your own street?

PC: No, not actually. In my imagination I placed it up the street as a cottage that was attached to a grand house, Birchgrove House, which has since been pulled down and replaced by a block of cream brick flats.

RW: One can still walk about the various parts of Sydney—Balmain, Birchgrove, Paddington—and see entire streets much as Oscar and Lucinda might have seen them.

PC: Yes. Sydney is still much a nineteenth-century city. And every passing year that it remains like that it becomes a more and more extraordinary city to visit.

RW: You create so many different characters in all your novels, all social levels, occupations, intellectual levels, out of the past and from the present; where do all these people come from?

PC: I don't know. They just about never begin with observation. I think they are formed by the pressures of the story. Sometimes it is like finding a comfortable place in bed. Sometimes when you are fooling around for a character, something just feels right. Where does that come from? It comes, maybe, from how I am allowing a part of my own character to grow and become a being of its own.

RW: It is interesting, as a writer who starts from situation, that you have created as many different characters as you have.

PC: It's because I need them. They are all produced by the demands of story. If the story demands a certain character, then I have to work on him and he has to be real. I suppose I do have a passion that if I am going to have something extraordinary happen, I want it to be real. I want the reader to believe that the chairs in the room are solid. If a ghost comes into the room, then you believe it because everything else is so real.

RW: Do you ever take a day to ride a bus, walk about, simply observe people?

PC: No. I often think I should. For the new book I've been doing a lot of research, going up and talking to people, but it's not the sort of thing you're talking about.

RW: What is the new book?

PC: The working title is *The Tax Inspector,* though it may not end up this way. It begins with an idea that taxation is all we have in this society to redistribute income reasonably. I have a woman tax inspector who is a decent person. She goes to do an audit on a motorcar business in Campbelltown, a family business, which ultimately will disintegrate under the pressure of the investigation. She knows from the beginning that this will happen and is sad about it. I got the idea when I went to a dinner party in Rose Bay where these revoltingly rich people started to complain about tax. They were so very unsympathetic to people who were less well off than they, complaining about how much tax they paid. I came away so angry that I said, "I'm going to write a novel about tax."

RW: What is a good working day for you?

PC: Three and a half or four pages a day, from half past eight until about one, sometimes two in the afternoon.

RW: Is the setting of the new novel contemporary?

PC: Yes. It was a bleak book for a long time because so many things have happened to this family. They were terribly loveless. This has been one of my major problems, the bleakness. But at the moment it all feels better. Though it is relatively realistic, I do have a major character who has turned himself into an angel.

ROBERT DREWE

The Savage Crows, 1975
A Cry in the Jungle Bar, 1979
The Bodysurfers (stories), 1983
Fortune, 1986
The Bay of Contented Men (stories), 1989

was born in 1943 in Melbourne, but grew up in Western Australia. He has worked as a journalist, an editor, and for a time as a private investigator in San Francisco. *Fortune* won the fiction prize of the National Book Award. *The Bodysurfers,* Drewe's first collection of stories, has been adapted for the stage and was a popular miniseries on Australian television in 1989. His most recent publication is also a collection of stories. Drewe's characters are modern Australians suffering problems of loss and identity brought about by changing relationships, changing values, and by the violence and chaos of the times. Robert Drewe lives in Sydney. The following interview occurred in his office and in a pub in Paddington (Sydney).

INTERVIEW

RW: You grew up in Perth, in Western Australia. How did Perth in the 1950s differ from the rest of Australia?

RD: To my family, who came from Melbourne, it was as remote as it was possible to be and still be in Australia, as remote as going to Africa or South America. It was a twelve-hour plane flight with three stops. My father was a young executive in his twenties with Dunlop Rubber Company. I was six and it was an adventure for me, but my family mourned. Once there, I felt immediately at home. It was a terrific place for a child to grow up. In the fifties Perth was in some ways a branch manager's town. People who ran things in the world my family lived in tended to be from somewhere else. They were executive material from Sydney or Melbourne. But eventually most everyone got sucked into the West Australian way, which was a social, hospitable, laid-back, rather drowsy, heavy-drinking, summery way of life. People entertained in their homes; friends dropped in with armloads of bottles and their own food. They often came around 5 on Sunday afternoons and stayed until 1 A.M. Invitations weren't necessary. It was considered good manners to drop by and stay for twelve hours. It was a kind of random growing up, but at the same time there were a lot of methodical procedures that a child had to go through; the expected behavior was particularly hard on a teenager and impossible for a young adult. So we all left when we grew up, at least people like me did.

RW: What were you like as a teenager?

RD: A bit rebellious for a time. In my last year at school I decided to play the political game. I did all the right things and suddenly it all came together. I was good at sport and was on the debating team and in the dramatic society. I ran the school magazine. I became a kind of junior politician and the channels of doing things suddenly became clear to me, so I ran things for a year and then, having done it, I was sickened by it and never wanted to do it again. In the years since I was seventeen I've never been a joiner; I've never been a member of societies or coteries. It was as if I got it totally out of my system.

RW: You got married young, didn't you?

RD: At eighteen, the year after I left school, when I was a first-year cadet reporter. In a way, I was still following the expected behavior. I had been taught to believe that a boy married his pregnant girlfriend.

RW: This must have been a surprise to your parents, who were used to having an ideal son.

RD: Yes. And she was a Catholic girl, too. Don't think that wasn't a part of it.

RW: Both your parents died when you were young. From your writing I feel that this had a very strong impact on you, on your concept of the world.

RD: I presume it had an effect on my writing. It certainly had an effect on my thinking, my concept of the world. From the moment those two events occurred I looked at things in a sharper, nervier way. It seems to me I would have been a calmer, less aggressive person if the deaths hadn't occurred at the stage in my life that they did. I'm only guessing, but it seems I would have been a more serene, casual person, if my parents were alive now.

RW: You write about mothers and fathers a lot in your fiction. I'm thinking particularly of "Radiant Heat" and "Sweetlip." Are either of these parents based on your own?

RD: No, they're not. I am interested in mothers and fathers generally, in part because I am a father. I see life almost all of the time as a parent rather than as a son.

RW: For many years you were a successful reporter, living all over Australia. What effect did journalism have in shaping you as a fiction writer?

RD: It's hard to guess. The forming of one's style happens pretty unconsciously, but obviously because of the good training I received as a cub reporter on the *West Australian* I learned to write simple declarative sentences and how to be sparing with adverbs and adjectives, how to make every sentence pay.

RW: I'm thinking in terms of the wealth of material you must have come across in observing human nature, politics, that sort of thing . . .

RD: Yes. It was invaluable. It took me out of an ordinary middle-class background and showed me with a brusk shove what went on in the world: incest trials, multiple murder cases, grubby politics, all the things that go over your head when you are a teenager. This had a big impact and I loved it. I would have paid the newspaper for the work when I was a cadet reporter. If you stay in it too long, however, it can make you a cynic. But I stayed slightly detached and I think got out of it just in time. I had an education similar to Hemingway's or García Márquez's, not that I'm comparing myself to them.

RW: As a writer you've moved about a lot: cities, countries, within cities. Has all this movement given you the sense of displacement and alienation you write about in your stories?

RD: I'm not sure. You know the feeling you get when you travel—suddenly you are in a strange place, in the wrong climate, with the wrong clothes on, and you are at the airport and everyone's gone and there are no cabs. You're suddenly thrown back on inner resources; you suddenly have to try to become wily. It seems as though everyone in the universe that you are now in is wily and you are a moron, and the wrong color and everything. But along with that comes a feeling of newness and excitement, a feeling that anything can happen. It's like being in a story or at the beginning of a film. It's like you're in a film and the credits are rolling up over you standing there at the curb waiting for the town's one cab to come back from wherever it is. While that worries me at the time, I also like it a lot. I like that feeling that anything can happen, and I also think that there is a story in this, even before there is one. If you're in this frame of mind that travel and newness and fatigue and all these things coming together give you, then you are receptive and stories do come from it. It's rare when I'm in a peculiar town or foreign place that a story doesn't happen. There are different neurons operating, different hormones operating. All these things at once buzzing around tend to make something artistic occur. Even a change of residence will to some extent bring this about.

RW: Your first novel was widely praised by critics as a startling and remarkable work. Would you explain the title, *The Savage Crows?*

RD: It's an ironic title. It was one of the derogatory terms used by the early white settlers in Tasmania to describe the black inhabitants, the unique aboriginal race quite separate from the Aborigines of mainland Australia. It was a description that enabled the whites to go out on hunting sprees and kill blacks as if they were some sort of vermin.

RW: In the novel you have parallel stories, one in the present involving Stephen Crisp, the young narrator who is doing research on the past, on the minister-reformer George Augustus Robinson. The other story is set in the past itself. Would you discuss your use of these parallel stories?

RD: I wanted a modern character who would stand in this time in the way that Robinson stood in the past, a kind of popular wise person. I decided to make Stephen Crisp a television presenter, or anchorman, a kind of younger Walter Cronkite figure who sent commandments down from on high. Also, I wanted Robinson in a sense to be seen in the same frame as Stephen Crisp's father, Murray Crisp. George Augustus Robinson was always going around saying, "I am the father, I am the Conciliator," while showing behavior that didn't coincide with that. Murray Crisp works for a gelatin company. Gelatin is a product made from the rendering down of bones from dead things. His occupation is deliberate, and no critic has yet picked that up. It matches what Robinson was doing. In a way then, Stephen Crisp and his father both have their modern parallels with Robinson. In the end, I wanted a sense of irony to prevail and for Stephen Crisp to come out with a bit of self-realization.

RW: In the end of the novel, Crisp's research has taken him to an island in the Bass Straight. He learns a lesson about the adaptability and instinct for survival of the Aborigines there. Does Crisp have a personal epiphany?

RD: Yes. Guilt has been his wellspring until now. He learns that maybe, just maybe, there's not so much need for guilt as he thought, maybe he shouldn't feel that guilty.

RW: Your second novel, *A Cry in the Jungle Bar,* is set in the Philippines. Christopher Koch set *The Year of Living Dangerously* in Indonesia. Certain Australian critics have approved of the use of these and other Asian settings as a correct and logical linkage between

Australia and its nearest neighbors. The argument runs that Australia should begin to identify with and be particularly concerned with Asian ties rather than American or European ties because of proximity. Would you discuss your choice of the Asian setting?

RD: None of us knew when we were writing these Asian novels that anyone else was doing a similar thing. I think the critical or political interest in the setting came later. Asia has always interested me. The *Melbourne Age* sent me at twenty-one to the Philippines to cover the 1965 election which Marcos won. Marcos then was the man of the people; he was the good guy. The trip to the Philippines was my first introduction to the outside world. I was green as grass. I was astonished and intrigued by being thrust into a foreign place where people wore guns on the street, where the women were amazingly attractive and amazingly available. This was prefeminism; in the West it was the Beatles era. And here was this buccaneer, naughty society going on just off our shores. There was a saying that the Philippines had been four hundred years in a convent and forty years in Hollywood and this present culture was the result. That was pretty much how it appeared. I also became quite fond of the society; I met some intelligent, thoughtful people during that visit and was impressed with them and with certain aspects of the place. The desire to write about Asia came during that trip, even before I knew how to go about being a novelist. I went back to the Philippines in 1974 as a journalist when Marcos had declared martial law; by then he was well and truly established. At that time I came up with the idea of using an Australian Manila-based agricultural adviser as the pivot for various events that I wanted to deal with in fiction. I also used other assignments and other trips around Asia and incorporated them into *A Cry in the Jungle Bar.*

RW: Would you comment on the black humor in the novel?

RD: Bangladesh had a big impact on me when I went there, which was just after its war with Pakistan. At this time Henry Kissinger was calling Bangladesh the world's basket case. I would meet very harried, stressed bureaucrats and they would quote T. S. Eliot to me—from *The Waste Land.* This was Monty Pythonesque. It impressed me because it had a sort of insouciant madness about it, but it was also a way the Bangladesh middle class had for distancing themselves from the really poor and all the problems by going on with its old English/American culture. It was darkly funny to be sitting in a conference with the head of one of the Prime Minister's departments and someone would clap his hands and a servant would come in with a gigantic platter full of bananas, and while the current life-and-death struggle was canvassed around the cabinet table, people would be sitting around peeling bananas in a way that a very clever monkey peels a banana. They make a very elaborate ceremony. The peeling is more important than the eating. This took my attention from what they were saying, about bodies gathered from a particular suburb that day or about the scarcity of wheat. This stuff struck me as rivetingly funny and immensely worrying. The way *Time* magazine and Helena Rubenstein could get into Bangladesh when rice and wheat couldn't. The way people will pay any amount of money for these unnecessary things, that struck me as blackly comic.

RW: Among your books, you've said you have a real soft spot for this one. Why is this?

RD: For all those reasons. *The Savage Crows,* my first novel, really stretched my abilities and I wanted to write a novel that appeared straightforward and accessible and a good read and a bit suspenseful. In a sense I wanted to go over the same ground as the symbol of the Third World, the water buffalo, which was the area of interest of the central character, Richard Cullen, and the subject of his treatise, "The Poor Man's Tractor," which is a reference to the buffalo. He is himself a big, buffalo-shaped former sportsman. He as a rugby player is a representative of the Australian middle class, and I thought that sort of person would be doubly out of kilter in the environment I placed him in—poverty-stricken Asia. In *A Cry in the Jungle Bar* I also like the male-female relationships. In 1977 when I wrote it I was very keen on making Cullen behave responsibly and honorably, partly out of ethics and partly out of fear, which is how good decisions are often made. I like the way he did the right thing and still suffered.

RW: Which of your novels do you think is your best?

RD: I think *Fortune,* but in Australia it has been the least well received, or the least understood.

RW: Why has it not been understood, because of the form?

RD: Partly.

RW: Would you talk about the form?

RD: The book is three interwoven narratives which look at three aspects of Australia and its neighborhood using a deliberately classic Australian flawed hero type—the explorer. I bring him up to date by making him an underwater explorer rather than a land explorer. I do this in a glancing but direct narrative line which I describe as a ricochet effect. The ricochet effect, in terms of people bouncing off one another, relationships glancing off one another, things happening off other incidents, can happen in their purest form and in an easily traceable form only in a small place like Australia, where everyone knows everyone else. The thought behind the book is the statement that the narrator makes at the beginning of Chapter 3. I made the point that in a small country if you are over thirty-five everyone knows everyone else—you've been to school with them or played sports with them or made love with them—and so that presumed knowledge, those preconceived ideas, then mark everything that people feel about the person in question. What is interesting and a bit weird is that the very ironies I was pointing out in the novel were proven by the reception to it. In the novel, because I made a narrator a semi-successful journalist, people assumed I was writing about myself because I had been a journalist and a successful one. I was amazed at the naïveté of Australian reviewers. I wanted a narrator who was on the spot and knew the dirt on things and who when properly placed could talk about rumor and the way small communities operate. In reviews overseas this device was perfectly understood and no one tried to presume that I was writing about myself, sort of dishonestly typing up my notebooks, as was implied here. Here, they reviewed the author instead of the book. Instead of following the ricochet in the book, they went from A to B to C in a straight line and missed the interesting stuff on either side. The irony escaped them as well. That was a disappointment to me. There's another irony. *Fortune* did better in terms of prizes than my other novels. It won the National Book Award. It is time for reviewers to get over the fact that they think they know the people they are reviewing. I think they should be able to distance the writer from the work, and that doesn't happen sufficiently.

RW: Is there in Australia a critical hostility toward journalists who turn to fiction?

RD: I think that is the case. Traditionally in Australia the writers came from either the realist outback farming setting, the lone schoolteacher in a bush town background, or from the English Department in universities. Writers who were writing for a living were really quite thin on the ground here. It does seem amazing that bigger, more confident cultures, America, England, even South America, have produced writers who made their living working for magazines or newspapers: García Márquez, Camus, Hemingway, Graham Greene. This sounds almost too trite to mention, but until recently this has not been the case in Australia. It has only been recently that people like Peter Carey were able to work in advertising and write fiction. The universities have been a bit slow on the uptake in recognizing this sort of writer.

RW: Were you labeled a "journalist writer" even with your first novel?

RD: *The Savage Crows* was greeted enthusiastically, but occasionally with a kind of astonishment, like here is a dog that can ride a bicycle and play a trumpet at the same time, which was sort of flattering and slightly offensive. I don't know how many books you have to write before you are actually a "writer." I've been writing for a living since I was eighteen. I've written three novels and two books of stories and a film script and a play and all have been in varying degrees successful. I think that means I'm a writer, really.

RW: You're one of a handful of writers who has spent time living in the States. This is reflected in *The Bodysurfers* and in *Fortune* and in *The Bay of Contented Men.* Have you been affected very much by your contact with the States?

RD: I grew up in Perth reading American magazines my father used to bring home. I was saturated with all things American. I used to read interviews, the ads, anything. My style seems more attuned to that of some American writers than those of any other literature. I admire the way Saul Bellow gives a representation of his time and place with wit and clarity and very keen intelligence in the same ways the nineteenth-century European writers did with such success. As I was beginning to write fiction, many of the British writers seemed rather tired and dusty by comparison. At home here the specter of Patrick White hung over creative writing and little else was happening. I looked to America for my models.

RW: Your first trip to the States was as the recipient of a grant, wasn't it?

RD: Yes. I had a Leader Grant given by the American State Department to members of the arts and political community in friendly countries. America, California in particular, seemed to me to be the place where the contemporary Western world's behavior began. In terms of current modes and fashions in the 1970s, America was impacting strongly in Australia and I wanted to go there. I spent time in Los Angeles and San Francisco. As a result of that, I got even yet another mortgage on my house the next year and took my wife and young family over. In San Francisco I interviewed for a piece of journalism an Australian private detective named Sandra Southerland. We became friendly. I took a job with her firm as a private detective. Because of my journalistic skills it was an easy occupation to get into. Journalism slots easily into private detective work. As it exists now in California, the work depends mostly on the ability of a person to present himself in a plausible, nonthreatening, middle-class way. Private eyes, I discovered, don't have blue-gray hair and they don't carry guns. They look like lawyers or journalists. Journalism is a perfect subterfuge, especially if you have a foreign accent and can say, "I come from *The Sydney Morning Herald*," and if checked, you can name the editor. Your m.o. checks out. It's a perfect background if you want to be a private eye. The things I worked on with Sandra were very much in the news and pure Californiana for me. Angela Davis was on trial; the Hell's Angels, Huey Newton, and the San Quentin Six were on trial. I had interesting oblique and sometimes direct insights into all of this. Sandra was involved in doing things against the Mafia. For me it was a bit like being in a film. I worked on mundane domestic matters from such things as one neighbor stealing jewelry from another to important political matters. Much of the work the firm did was political and still is. I got insights into all levels of American life, from small-time murder to the Mafia.

RW: You use the mysterious, you create a sense of the impending in much of your fiction. Obviously, you used your detective work in *Fortune*. As a writer, have you always been interested in mystery?

RD: I think I'm interested in the way that most people who read the newspapers are interested in crime. It's what other people do and how they mess up their lives which interests us. But it's only part of the picture for me. I would never be interested in writing purely detective novels or murder mysteries. I see it like I see politics, as a subject for conflict. All these things are a part of the tapestry. But the useful thing about crime as a device is that if used properly, it presents suspense. Since I am involved in the narrative business I want people to keep reading, and suspense is very useful for this.

RW: How long did you live in California?

RD: We lived there two years. The experiences formed the basis for several stories and for part of *Fortune*.

RW: As with certain American writers, I see in your work a strong sense of place. In particular, you seem to have made the coast, or the beach, your own fictional territory.

RD: That's true. Even though I've lived all over Australia and in various places in the world, my sense of place was firmly fixed as a child on the coast and around the rivers of West Australia. I am reliving and rewriting that coastline and the rather weird windscape of that sandy coast in my mind whether I'm transferring it to the Pacific Coast in the case of Sydney or to the coast of Victoria or to the other Pacific Coast in California.

RW: Is place more important than character to you?

RD: Character is first, but I don't think you can separate the two. Characters out of kilter with their place interest me particularly.

Characters being in the wrong place at the wrong time interest me.

RW: *The Bodysurfers,* your first book of stories, is in its tenth printing. It has been a prize-winning television miniseries and a drama. Is this your most successful book?

RD: Yes. In terms of sales. *The Savage Crows* would be the second, but that's been out longer.

RW: Do you like writing stories better than novels?

RD: I find novels much more difficult for all the obvious reasons, but I still feel they are more of a challenge and I feel a mixed sense of exhaustion and exhilaration when I've finished a novel. I am happy to finish a book of stories, but you always feel you could have added another three. It is the difference between running a sprint and a marathon. It's still extremely hard to run a hundred-meters sprint but you're not as exhausted as if you've run a marathon. The trouble with writing a novel is that I start off with various ambitions, but because of all the intrusions of everyday life, I end up with less of a book than I intended, whereas at least with a story I really can't make an excuse. They are as good as I can do. But I've always been a bit disappointed with the novels in the end.

RW: Would you talk about *The Bodysurfers?* What does the title have to do with the collection of stories?

RD: Literally, it means people who surf the waves without boards, people who throw themselves into the maelstrom of things without anything between them and the nature force. But it is also partly a euphemism for sexual congress. As I've said, I've lived on a number of coasts and the sea is very important to me. It occurred to me that the sea had not been used in Australian fiction or been given its place in the full picture of Australian culture. I was anxious to deal with this in *The Bodysurfers.* I also philosophically feel that we Australians need the coast in our mind's eye before we can function. It follows from this that I think the image of the outback as it functions in Australia in the 1980s is a myth. Ninety-eight percent of Australians live in cities or in suburbs of cities around the coast. They identify with things coastal in spite of the pretense in Australian writing that we are all laconic outback cattle drovers or that we are all working class. This is a sentimental myth that has been perpetuated a long time, particularly by university lecturers.

RW: Although your stories often have an Australian setting, they frequently deal with problems of couples—relationships breaking up, families breaking up. This has become a universal problem in these last decades, hasn't it?

RD: Yes. It's a luxury that we Westerners have, I guess, that we can write about these things instead of life or death. These are the sorts of lives we live, for good or bad. I think it is the correct function of a writer to represent his or her time and place. These nervy coastal high-real-estate-price times, the marriage breakup, the creation of the underclass made up of Aborigines and white people who haven't had a job in several generations—this is our life; it isn't all dreamy days by the billabong. Lawson is dead; Paterson is dead. These are sentimental ideas that don't have any validity.

RW: You have a lot of sex and sweat in your stories, lots of breasts and bottoms. Are you an autobiographical writer?

RD: No. Not always.

RW: I'm thinking about "Baby Oil."

RD: That's sort of a humorous story. In *The Bodysurfers* the only disgusting story with sex in it is "The View from the Sandhills" in which the central character is a pervert. And the pervert shouldn't be seen as the author, or hardly ever.

RW: How do I register this laughter? "Baby Oil" and the companion story "After Noumea" are good examples of your craftsmanship. "Baby Oil" tells the story of a woman who has two lovers, one present with her and an absent lover who is present in the form of his underpants left casually in the bedroom. The second story focuses on the absent lover. Would you talk about the structure of these two stories?

RD: The other man's underpants left on the doorknob were a symbol of menace. The underpants gave the absent owner a power of dominance, perhaps more so than if he had appeared. I then wrote "After Noumea" from his point of view because I wanted to show him as the victim. Most people over a certain age have been at both ends of the spectrum, the winner or the loser, the person who's doing bad things or the person who is having bad things done to him. In "After Noumea" one finds that the man who has been seen in "Baby Oil" as a malignant male force has just had a nervous breakdown over this same episode and is a vulnerable, sympathetic, and screwed-up person. At the end of the story, just when the reader is beginning to think him sympathetic, he is suddenly seen to be more menacing than anyone. He may be an abductor and a murderer. I particularly liked in the story the idea of the man marking the level of oil in the bottle of baby oil to see if the sensual woman, Anthea, had been screwing around with another man. The conjunction of those stories gave me the greatest pleasure of any in *The Bodysurfers*.

RW: You use the character David Lang and the Lang family in both books of stories, *The Bodysurfers* and *The Bay of Contented Men*.

Do you have an idea of ever doing a novel about these characters?

RD: I haven't thought about it, but I don't see any reason why I shouldn't use them again as characters in novels. I have thought of seeing what Stephen Crisp is doing now, the central character in *The Savage Crows.* Showing characters a decade apart is an interesting idea. Updike did it well in the Rabbit books.

RW: In your latest book, *The Bay of Contented Men,* you set stories in Hong Kong, Tokyo, California; they involve multinationals. Do you see yourself becoming more of an international writer and less an Australian writer?

RD: No. I see myself as an Australian writer writing now and living the sort of life that Australians my age and in my circumstances live now. Australians are perhaps the most traveled people in the world, perhaps because we grew up with great distances anyway. It means nothing for an Australian to drive twelve hours to do something, only to turn around and drive back again. This is one reason that wherever you go in the world there are five Germans, two Japanese, and a couple of Australians. Australians are great travelers. I am just putting that down. I see myself very much as an Australian writer, and when I do write things set in other places there is no doubt that the central character is an Australian or that the interest of the narrator is an Australian one. It probably doesn't make great commercial sense to see it like that, but that is my viewpoint.

RW: There are exceptions, but generally the kind of Australian you write about in *The Bay of Contented Men* is educated, traveled, middle class. Is there any significant difference between your modern urban Australian and his American counterpart?

RD: When I think of the American reading I've done it amuses me slightly to find a lot of American middle-class writers trying to write down, writing "dirty realism." A lot of college boys writing about filling stations and pickup trucks. I get a feeling that filling stations and pickups are put into stories a lot more than necessary. This I see in a number of short stories. I'm trying to look at the Australian picture which is also made of those things, but it is also made up of lawyers and architects and people who work in banks. I'm interested in the middle class because it is there and is a large part of Australian culture. But I'm interested in other things as well. In *The Bay of Contented Men* there is a story from the point of view of a woman living in an aboriginal camp; there's a story describing a Chinese woman's life in Australia. I do try to look at the whole picture. But I am conscious that the vast number of the middle class has been overlooked. I'm not ashamed to write about them. I don't think it's particularly yuppie or trendy. It's just that the middle class is there living their lives of quiet desperation just like everyone else and in larger numbers. I want to record some of that.

RW: It seems to me that there is less difference than there has ever been between the Australian and his American counterpart, his cultural or economic counterpart. There is perhaps more universality in the short stories you write than there is topicality. Would you agree?

RD: Yes. I would agree with that.

RW: Do you see any changes in your writing in *The Bodysurfers* and *The Bay of Contented Men*?

RD: Yes. I think the new stories are better crafted than *The Bodysurfers* stories. Together *The Bodysurfers* stories make up a kind of ethos that hadn't been looked at before for the reasons that I've been talking about. But I think individually the stories in *The Bay of Contented Men* are stronger. I tried to make them different from each other and different stylistically. I think they are a progression forward.

RW: If you had to choose one of the new stories for an anthology of short fiction, which would you choose?

RD: "Radiant Heat," the first story. It does what a story should do.

RW: What should a story do?

RD: For me, it should give me a bit of a slap in the face. It should stun a bit. It should make you think, "Yes, that's right, but that's astonishing." There should be identification and the shock of recognition.

RW: How did you come by your title, *The Bay of Contented Men*?

RD: Ray Lawrence, the film director, and I were working on a film together and we were bantering one day, and he mentioned an idea he had for a film to be set in New Guinea. He had in mind a setting which he said was near the Bay of Contented Men. A little explosion went off in my head, and later I asked him if I could use the name as a title. I was halfway through the book and I wanted a title. In a sense I wrote a story to fit the title. When I went looking for the place on a map I couldn't find it. Ray found it under the name the Archipelago of Contented Men. It was briefly a place in the nineteenth century. In the meantime, having not found it on my own research, I had come to like the idea of not being able to find it. I liked the idea that this sort of serenity that seemed to be inherent in a place like that was in fact very hard to come by and impossible to find. All the stories I wrote after choosing the title seemed to fit into this context. It must be seen as an ironic title. I like to go with the idea that it is this place on the map that we are all looking for and that we all want but that it is really hard to find.

RW: Your writing career is at such a wonderful place with your play, your television miniseries, this new book just coming out, your home life so agreeable—have you reached this Bay of Contented Men?

RD: It would be dangerous to think so.

BEVERLEY FARMER

was born in Melbourne in 1941 and educated at Melbourne University. She has supported herself as a teacher, as a writer, and by doing restaurant work. In 1965 she married a Greek migrant and later returned with him to a village in Greece, where they lived in the house with his parents. Beverly Farmer wrote her first book, *Alone,* while in Greece, and her Greek experience both in that country and in Australia forms the subject matter for many of her short stories. Her first book of stories, *Milk,* won the 1984 New South Wales Premier's Prize. Farmer's stories are strong, sensually perceived records of powerful personal experience. The following interview occurred in Melbourne.

Alone, 1980
Milk (stories), 1983
Home Time (stories), 1985
A Body of Water (stories), 1990

INTERVIEW

RW: If one reads either *Milk* or *Home Time,* he's immediately immersed in both Greek and Australian life. Would you talk about your Greek ties?

BF: My Greek involvement began when I was twenty-one and had just finished the University of Melbourne. Not wanting an academic career, I was going to adventure and just pick up jobs waitressing on the way around Australia, which I had never seen; but the first place I went, I met a Greek man that I liked and the friend I was traveling with went on and I stayed at Mount Buffalo Chalet. The man had just arrived in Australia; he spoke about six words of English that included "poached eggs" and "fried eggs." He was cooking at the Chalet. We met through a woman I worked with who was married to a man he worked with; we became a foursome. I was teaching him

English, he was teaching me Greek, and I suppose we went on from there. We spent month after month closed in in the snow and got to know each other well, and so it just happened imperceptibly. We were going to get married without ever having talked about it. We just took it for granted.

RW: Where's Mount Buffalo?

BF: It's in the Great Dividing Range in Victoria. The Mount Buffalo Chalet was an old place run by the railways European style, with a staff of eighty who were almost all migrants. I was one of the very few Australians there.

RW: How long was it before you went to Greece?

BF: A long time. We married in 1965, and one of his brothers came over and lived with us, then a cousin and another brother. We had a Greek household and we lived a Greek life. In Melbourne it was very easy to isolate yourself in the Greek world. It was like a ghetto—we went to Greek houses, Greek weddings, Greek parties. We bought from Greek shops, went to the Greek cinema. Melbourne has a very big Greek community, and in my own defense I had to become fluent in Greek, since I had three Greek men living in the house at one stage and I never got a word in unless it was in Greek. I had been studying hard since Mount Buffalo, buying books, Kazantzakis in English and in Greek, and translating, then seeing if I got it right by checking the English version. I had trained in French and German at the university and I knew how to learn a language. So I picked up Greek pretty well, but my husband never picked up English because I was so good at Greek. I started writing to his family around 1962, sending them postcards and aboriginal myths that I'd translated, and they thought I'd made the stories up. I remember hearing from a visitor from Greece that my mother-in-law had been going around the village with an aboriginal card and the creation myth which I had laboriously translated into Greek, saying, "What an imagination our girl has." They wrote back to me, so I felt like I was one of the family before I ever went physically to join them in Greece. Unlike many foreign brides, I was welcomed with open arms and made much of, loved and tolerated and all that from the very beginning. I'm sure it was because I had some of the language.

RW: You lived a village life in Greece?

BF: Yes. It's not like Greek island life, which is what most tourists are probably more familiar with. The village where I lived is in a comparatively rich farming part of Greece, an alluvial plain in Macedonia where they grow wheat and sesame, barley, cotton, tobacco.

RW: What size is the village?

BF: Nine hundred people. So half the village were relatives of some sort. The sort of all-purpose title was "cousin" and half the village called me "Nyfi," which means daughter-in-law, sister-in-law, cousin-in-law. It really means bride, the woman who married our boy. So everywhere I'd go, I'd hear, "Eh, Nyfi!" and they'd come and ask me to drink coffee or something.

RW: Did you learn Greek stories that you incorporated into your fiction?

BF: Not a lot. The traditional language was a bit of a difficulty in the village because there were two dialects. There was a sort of Slav dialect, which the original people spoke. My husband's family were refugees in 1922 from the massacres in Smyrna and Constantinople. So they had been settled there in an exchange of populations arranged by the Turkish government after the cease-fire. Years later they still regarded themselves as strangers. They spoke a Turkish dialect, so the older people didn't speak the sort of Greek I knew. Especially since I had picked up the Cretan Greek to begin with from Kazantzakis, but that was a small hiccup from the Cretan past. I'd miss about one word in ten. Even so, my father-in-law, now ex-father-in-law, has always told me that I should sit down and write the story of his life, and I might do that next year when I go back.

RW: How long did you live in Greece?

BF: Oh, my husband and I were there three years straight and then went back for some summers after that, after we'd come back to live here. The last summer I went back was 1983.

RW: Being a liberated Australian female, was it difficult to immerse yourself in a patriarchal situation?

BF: Matriarchal—that was the problem. The household was matriarchal. Especially our house. The patriarch kept well away and didn't infringe upon her territory at all. But having spent my whole adolescence in a struggle to liberate myself from my own mother, it was a bit hard to knuckle down ten years later to my husband's mother. But because I loved her so much, I tried to do it. She was a terrific woman to everyone who knew her; she was gallant and beautiful and strong and brave.

RW: And from your fiction, I'd say generous.

BF: Yes, generous. She had a great sense of humor, so we could deflect our quarrels by one of us making a joke as an overture and the other one would respond. So it didn't become the sort of tooth-and-nail stuff that it often does with daughters-in-law in Greek households. I got on better with her than did my Greek sister-in-law, in fact much better.

RW: When you returned to Australia you obviously continued with your Greek ties.

BF: Yes. Our son was born in 1972, and it was partly so he'd be born in Australia that I was thinking of coming back. My parents were alone here, and I knew we wouldn't be able to afford to come back if we waited any longer. I tell this story in "Place of Birth." So we came back. My husband reluctantly, more or less. That's when we set up our restaurant on the coast in Victoria, and we ran that together for four years and raised the baby. It was very difficult; I can joke about it now, but it was hugely difficult. There was so much work to do, and the restaurant was in an old building with a fire stove. We got a forestry license and went out in the afternoons to cut wood to keep the fire going to cook the steaks. I was the only waitress in the restaurant. No one to help me with the baby—I had two miscarriages in that time. We wanted another child. I think that contributed to the breakdown of the marriage; I couldn't get over losing the babies. I felt that everything I'd lived for was thrown away for the sake of making money. I couldn't bear it. I wanted out and I got out. We split up in 1976. It was very difficult to maintain our ties for a long time; there was so much bitterness. But we're very good friends now. He rings me for advice on this or that and, of course, "the child in common" and that's a big bond.

RW: How old is your son now?

BF: He's seventeen. He is in a school nearby. He didn't live with me after the marriage broke up, but I lived nearby so I saw him when I could. I was working in Melbourne for a long time, but I saw him on weekends.

RW: Are you good friends?

BF: Yes. I would say that we're closer now than we've been in some years. He went back to Greece last year for three weeks. Now that's pure madness, a fare to Greece for just three weeks, but he's been back several times. My ex-husband and I feel it is important for him to be with his family there.

RW: Although you're writing about individuals, individual conflicts, there are in your fiction implied comparisons between Greek and Australian consciousness. Would you talk about this?

BF: I think that's too general a question for my mentality. I pick on particular instances and moments, I suppose, and focus on them; it's such a short focus that I can't really generalize. I'm not good at generalizing at all.

RW: The conflict between individuals is more important than the cultural conflict?

BF: Yes.

RW: What I am thinking of is what you just spoke about—the Australian woman moving into the matriarchal situation.

BF: Yes, it wouldn't have been any different, I suppose, what nationality the matriarch was, or I was. In "Place of Birth," I was observing my Greek sister-in-law's awful quarrel with her mother-in-law. I was interested in recording the abrasiveness in someone, people not hitting it off. I wasn't conscious that I was contrasting nationalities in that story. I can see that it's there, but I sort of averted my eyes from it. I think it's like the sleepwalking you need to do when you've found your subject. I wanted the sharp detail to speak for itself.

RW: Could you talk about the web of the Greek family? It's one of the subjects that you deal with often in your stories.

BF: Yes, I do. I suppose in my view of it, it is the women's side that I give, and the male is almost a drone or a parasite. He's uptight, he's at the café, or he might be earning his keep at the coffee shop or he might be out in the fields or doing something with the horse or the donkey. But the nub of my life in Greece was the household, and its head was the matriarch, the mother, the strong woman figure. Sometimes I've been taken on by feminists for having no strong women in my stories, and that always stuns me because the mother figures in my stories are so overwhelmingly strong. Maybe the feminists just mean their particular sort of women. It strikes me that they mean role models of their own age, and I'm not in the business of providing role models. But there is a strong woman in my stories, for what that's worth. But I've gone off the subject again. I feel the Greek family is a web of duties and obligations; it is a hierarchy, and although in practice it never works out the way it's supposed to in theory, the mother is the head of the female side of the house and she can give orders to all the daughters-in-law, the sons' wives who live there or who visit. And the wife of the oldest son, whatever her own age, has precedence over the wives of the younger sons in their order. And if, say, the middle brother's wife steps out of line, then the father-in-law might come along and say, "I want you to have a word with so and so about such and such." And if you are me, you say, "Oh, Baba, I can't do that." And he'll say, "You must do that. It's your obligation. If you don't, she'll despise you because you have not exerted your proper authority." So, of course, then I wouldn't say anything, or because it would strike me as ridiculous, I would tell the sister-in-law, "I've been told to tick you off about such and such"; then I would be seen as subversive because I'd colluded with her instead of cursing her, so there would be a lot of difficulty about that.

RW: I've made a list of things you deal with in your Greek stories: jealousy, honor, loyalty, piety, cruelty, anger. All of these explode within your family situations.

BF: Yes, they do. I was brought up in a cold and repressed family in which we didn't say what we felt. If it was anything negative, it was to be suppressed or denied. And we weren't allowed to disagree; we were supposed to be nice and polite. If I was angry, even in my teenage years, I was sent to my room and told not to come out until I could behave myself.

RW: You picture this sort of repressive family in "Caffe Veneto" and "Matrimonial Home."

BF: The model I was thinking of for the man in "Matrimonial Home" is the man in Irwin Shaw's "Girls in Their Summer Dresses."

RW: So that's not your real father in the story?

BF: No.

RW: Let's talk about your Greek stories. To illustrate the variety, let me mention titles and you give me the thematic concern.

BF: I wrote some of these eight or nine years ago, don't forget.

RW: I know you remember the title story, "Milk."

BF: "Milk" is about a nine-year-old boy who goes to Greece with his widowed father, who is Greek. They live with the grandparents on the family farm, which, of course, is the village house where I lived. It's the same house, the details of place are very accurate. It's necessary for me to get the place right before I can fit a fiction in a place. The boy is taking milk to a donkey whose mother has died. The milk comes from a cow his father has bought for the grandparents. The same milk is being used to sustain an old woman in the house opposite who is being starved to death by her daughter-in-law. At the end of the story the donkey dies, the old woman dies, and the child is faced for the first time with the reality of death. His mother had died earlier and he didn't know what it meant, but he knows what these two deaths mean.

RW: The donkey is deliberately caused to die, isn't it?

BF: The boy knows they have only been humoring him and letting him feed it and as soon as his bus goes, the donkey will go too.

RW: "Milk" is a very strong story. It suggests more to me of the beauty and the horror of Greece than anything you've written.

BF: I wrote it when my son was nine and went back to Greece with his father. I was often dwelling on what his experiences in Greece might be and how he was coping with it all. And I remembered these two incidents from my own time in the village. In fact, they didn't happen to him and he doesn't like this story. He said once, "You know, you didn't have to make the donkey die in the end. It was your story; you could make anything happen, if you wanted it to."

RW: Would you talk about "Marina"?

BF: That's the one about the young Greek woman who's suffering postpartum depression. The story has been anthologized in a medical journal as a classic example of postpartum depression. The woman has just given birth. She is homicidally depressed. She keeps saying to her husband that she needs a doctor and he keeps shrugging it off and saying, "Well, you know some people have hoards of kids; why can't you handle just one? What's the matter with you?" This echoes a situation I was familiar with. It didn't happen to me, but I knew about it. In the end the woman, who is close to schizophrenic breakdown, in fact, breaks down. At the end of the story, she grabs the baby and bashes it against the wall. And then she tries to suckle the baby, which is a way of saying she doesn't know what she's done. And in fact, the woman the story is based on kept asking her sister, when her sister visited her in jail, "Why doesn't my husband come and see me?" and "Who's looking after the baby?"

RW: The woman's plight is not quite so serious in "Saint Kay's Day." Would you talk about this story?

BF: I wrote it when I was living in the flat with no electricity described in the story. But I wasn't that woman. I was married safely back then, and not hankering after any young Aleko. But I'd seen a particular woman giving English lessons, going from lesson to lesson. I was giving them, too. We didn't have work permits and you always had to scurry around and be a bit furtive in case someone turned you in and you were deported. It was very hand-to-mouth, anyway. So I suppose I put into the story a lot of my experience of living in that flat and my love of Thessaloniki; the rest of it is imagined.

RW: You weren't suffering the unrequited love that Kay suffers in the story?

BF: No, no.

RW: I'm trying to separate autobiography from fiction. What about the story "At the Airport?"

BF: "At the Airport," I wrote it at the same time as the story "Milk," actually, in the same month. That was because my son was in Greece, and the scene at the airport when we farewelled each other, I saw him off with his father, is in that story and how we had a trifle and shared it. And the funny thing about the self-reflectiveness of life and fiction—my son read that story, and years later when he was again leaving for Greece with his father, he took me alone to the cafeteria in the airport and took a trifle and put it on the tray. He looked at me significantly, and I said, "What are you staring at?" and he said, "Oh, don't you remember?" So, that's obviously a story he does like. But that is probably the most autobiographical thing in the book. And even the flashbacks are autobiographical. The long swim we did to the yacht and the visit to the zoo that ended so badly—all that happened.

RW: One of the qualities of your writing that pleases me so much is your use of visual imagery. Let me quote a few examples. In "A Girl in the Sand," you write, "Thunderstorms along this coast have all the savagery of the ones I remember, when lightning bolts struck farmers down in fields and fireballs burst in at windows and burned children in their beds." In "Fire and Flood," about the radiant heat of bush fires you write, "On the day of the fires, birds flying high above were overcome by the heat, fell and were burnt. The wings of others caught alight in midair. Falling, they set more bush on fire." In "Marina" you write, "When he laughed, pink seeds oozed from his mouth. The whitewashed house was hot and sour, full of grapes in baskets." Would you comment on your use of imagery?

BF: When they're pulled out of context like that, they read to me like those things in the *Reader's Digest* called "Toward More Picturesque Speech." I wince and think, "Oh, God." But, actually, those bush fire details are just pure fact. On Ash Wednesday, we call it, in 1983 there was a firestorm, and that story is set during and after that firestorm. As for imagery in general, I suppose I wanted to be a poet first. I think William Faulkner said that everyone starts out wanting to write poetry, and I think it was always the imagist poetry that attracted me most. I'm very visual. I wanted to be a film director for a long time; I always loved photography and I think that probably my sense of sight is overdeveloped, although that could be overcompensation, because I'm very shortsighted. But it's not just the visual; I think I've become conscious about an attempt to integrate all the senses in things I've been writing. Sometimes in a story I've been conscious of the need to emphasize a particular sense. In "Market Day," the blind woman and her niece and her sister-in-law go to visit a relative who is dying in the hospital and there is the smell of phenol and the smell of peaches in the room, and then they go down the hill and are released from the oppressive hospital and they eat salty food like anchovies and they relish fiercely the taste of things because they're alive. I had a conscious need to emphasize other imagery in that story because the main character is blind. The main character in that story is based on someone I knew in the village.

RW: The story reminded me of Joyce's "Clay." The woman is given a joyous reason to live because she's being used.

BF: That's a wonderful story. I wasn't conscious of basing it on "Clay." I thought of it as a Katherine Mansfield story because I was reading a lot of Katherine Mansfield at that stage. Someone had given me her collected stories; a lot of them I had never read and I was overcome. They're so good. "Saint Kay's Day" and "Market Day" were written about the same time and I think they have a strong Mansfield influence, and in fact, you might even notice that Nitsa and Aleko in "Saint Kay's Day" are the same Nitsa who loves the same Aleko in "Market Day," but you get a more sympathetic picture of Nitsa in "Market Day."

RW: In "Place of Birth" your protagonist takes photographs. I see a constant use of light and shade in your work. Is this photographic reference a key to your own way of working?

BF: It has been, but that's another thing I'm militating against in myself because it seems to me that it's static and glassy, and I want things to move and be more fluid now, not ice, but water these days. I tend to shy away from the photographic image, and that was sort of my swan song, I suppose, as far as photographs go. It was also a deliberate attempt. "Place of Birth" was the last story written in the collection. Its white moonlight, the cold, the frost, and the snow balance "Our Lady of the Beehive," which is full of sunlight, the sea, and the summer. In "Place of Birth" you have the dark side of a family which is aglow with love in the last story. It's the two sides of the one family. And I also had in the back of my mind the idea of the white goddess in both of the stories and the white goddess being the moon and the snow woman.

RW: You're not a casual writer, are you?

BF: No, I'm not. But whether people notice it or not doesn't matter, but if they do, it's there. It seemed to me that the snow woman was the white goddess and that there was a spirit of misrule over that house and over the matriarch of the house. Whereas in "Our Lady of the Beehive," she's a benevolent despot and she makes everything happen according to her rules and she even had the mother of God eating out of her hand.

RW: The images in your Greek stories—flowers, fruit, eggs, wine—suggest a stronger sensual life than the images which dominate your stories set in Australia. Is this an intentional contrast in place, or state of mind?

BF: Yes, I think I was more aware in Greece of the austerity and poverty, where the only extravagance is in the light. Dimitris Tsaloumas says something like this. An orange is something you save for, and a banana is something you fight over, as in "Place of Birth." I actually saw the wine being grown and pressed and strained. I went myself to the hay and picked the eggs out. It was more personal and closer. It wasn't like going to the market and picking a kilo of that or a kilo of this. It was something that was hard won. There could be hail or frost and you would have nothing. What you had was what you'd managed to store up and save and it seemed to me much more precious and sacred. I saw it as sacred. It seemed to me that eating to a family in Greece was a sacrament. I'd never felt anything like that in a family in Australia.

RW: Life itself became more . . .

BF: Yes . . . Whereas the image of the bread and wine in Christianity had seemed to me a literary one and had no purchase on my mind at all, when I went to Greece, the physicality of it was perfect, it made sense. I was in a world where that image was created.

RW: Physicality is very important in your writing. Let me give you an example from "Place of Birth" and have you comment. ". . . she hugs herself close to the *somba*, holding the iron door open while she crams pine cones in. She sits with her clothes open. Perhaps the baby can see and hear the fire, she thinks; did he see my hands in there, by the light of the candle? They must have made shadows on his red wall."

BF: I remember thinking these things when I was pregnant in the village in the winter. It was a very hard house to keep warm and you really cherished warmth. There is a retreat into physicality in pregnancy anyway. This state of mind and body continued when I came back to Australia, the sense that you are somehow a nest and that this egg is making itself in you. And the feeling of repleteness and fulfillment that I felt then, was beginning to feel in the village, I think was a matter of being pregnant. I think one reason that physicality is important to me, especially in this relationship of mother and child, is because we were not a touching family, but with my child there was all this physical contact and that was very important. It was wonderful. Having a child was the single most important thing that ever happened to me.

RW: You sound like Helen Garner.

BF: Yes, I can imagine that she would say something like that. Some feminists we are!

RW: You sometimes startle the reader with particularly brutal descriptions, the murder of an infant by banging its head against the wall, the spilled fecal contents of a colostomy bag. Are you calculating in your use of ugly reality?

BF: No, that's not calculation. I try not to flinch from it when it seems necessary. I felt that the story of the woman killing her baby should be told, and I feel one has to tell the truth and face it steadily. I realize that readers would probably wince at that, as they would in real life. It seems to me that these are commonplace examples of real life; this is what happens. I mean, I seem to remember someone reproaching Joyce Carol Oates once about the violence that happens in her stories and her saying, "Well, what world do you live in?" And that's true, the world is full of violence and pain and ugliness and we're not doing our job as artists if we don't show everything. What did T. S. Eliot say? "The boredom, the horror and the glory." You're just a romantic escapist if you don't face those facts.

RW: So, you couldn't put those things in the *Reader's Digest* quotable quotes could you?

RF: No, you couldn't.

RW: In your Greek stories you remind me of Kazantzakis; in the contests between your males and females, you remind me of Lawrence; and in your detachment, of Joyce. Were any of these writers an influence?

BF: I think I'm a pygmy compared to all of them, but they have all influenced me very strongly, very strongly. Joyce first; I discovered him when I was at the university. I picked up *Ulysses* at a friend's house and couldn't put it down; it was banned then. I had read *Portrait of the Artist* and hadn't been greatly moved, but *Ulysses* was a different matter. Lawrence, I love with all my heart. And Kazantzakis, too—it was through him that I first was able to understand the man I was going to marry.

RW: Has any Australian writer been an influence on you?

BF: Patrick White has. It's so long ago now, in the sixties, I tend to forget it. But yes, a great influence in the fact that he had a love for Greece, too, and a knowledge of Greece which also helped me. There is a very authentic Greek male character in *The Tree of Man,* a rather beautiful, simple, physical, natural being, an object of desire. I have a similar Greek man in a lot of my stories. The metaphysical dimension of White, too. I was fascinated that this could be done, that our sober suburban life could be transfigured.

RW: Both *Milk* and *Home Time* contain a number of stories of a woman alone. Would you discuss this recurring figure in your fiction?

BF: I suppose it's so. My very first book is called *Alone,* and it is about a woman alone who has decided to kill herself on her eighteenth birthday because of the failure of her love affair and because she could see no reason to go on living. I suppose that coming to terms with aloneness has been one of the major traits of my life in the last several years in which those stories were being written, after the divorce, and realizing I suppose that it's a part of the human condition and not just a particular personal affliction. Seeing it everywhere. I read in Bertrand Russell's autobiography that he once came upon a woman he knew suffering and in great pain, and he had this illumination of the loneliness of the human soul. I suppose what I'm doing with these characters is in a sense creating that illumination for the reader. Not of my personal aloneness and whatever pain that might cause, but of the existential aloneness of the human soul.

RW: You give the reader such an insight.

BF: That's what I hope to do now that I realize that it's not a personal matter at all, but universal, so that everyone who reads, if it's written right, will know what I mean.

RW: Your work gives the appearance of being very autobiographical, yet there's clarity and precision of detail. I feel the autobiographical elements have gone through a process of distancing and distillation. Would you comment?

BF: I suppose the process of fiction to me is distilling and re-creating in another voice, in another person, things that I have experienced myself. I'm reading a wonderful book at the moment, Ursula Le Guin's *Dancing on the Edge of the World.* She quotes a woman whose name I cannot remember as having said to a group of women arguing about writing theory, "Offer your experience as your truth," and it seems to me that sums it all up and I suppose that's what I've been doing, but not my raw experience, rather my ripened and distilled experience, such as it is.

RW: What about the autobiographical detail in *Alone?*

BF: I think the novel is misunderstood to some degree. Because the love affair that fails for Shirley, the main character, is a lesbian love affair, the novel has been more or less regarded as a lesbian book, a novel about lesbianism like Elizabeth Jolley's *Palomino,* which came out in the same year. But for me, at least, *Alone* is about suicide. I see it as a dramatic monologue. It's told in the first person and present, which can be very irritating I realize now, but didn't then. It's very heightened and intense and adolescent, in a sense, with a sort of heightened emotionality that one has in great moments of one's life. Shirley has resolved to kill herself; she's going through rituals that she has planned for this day and she wants to see the woman again who dropped her. She wants to re-create, she wants to be that woman. She deliberately allows herself to be assaulted on the waterfront, for example, and virtually raped, although there's a degree of consent in it, so that she can be one with this woman who became her lover after she confessed to Shirley that she had been raped. It was this avowal, this intimacy that made them become lovers. So to me the lesbian issue is a side issue, but it has become the central one to most readers of the book, which I think is a pity.

RW: The question I asked was about the autobiographical nature of the book.

BF: Yes, you think I'm deflecting that. . . . It is autobiographical in the sense that my own first love affair was a lesbian one, so I felt that I could not honestly change it to a man because I did not know what first love was like with a man and I would never know in this lifetime. There has to be a grain of truth in the fiction for me to feel it's worth creating, and the grain of truth had to be that it had been a woman in real life so it must be a woman in the story.

RW: But you wrote it how many years after the experience?

BF: Oh, ten years. I wrote the book in Greece and it was about Melbourne, so it was colored with this enormous nostalgia for my lost country, since I had gone to Greece and had intended to stay forever and thought I'd never see Melbourne again. I don't have a sister, for example; my father was not like the man in the book. There are a lot of things that are different, but that one thing had to be true, I thought, or nothing would be authentic about it. Even though I wrote it ten years later, it was supposed to seem like the present. Like I said, it was a dramatic monologue. You're supposed to be inside Shirley's head experiencing what she's experiencing at that moment. In fact, the poems in the book really were written at that time in Shirley's life. So they are genuine documentary.

RW: I find a number of your stories painful. I don't think a reader can sit down and comfortably read right through either of your collections. I think they're so strong, some of them, that the reader has to stop and let time pass before he reads another one.

BF: Yes. But that's great. Flannery O'Connor said that a short story should not contain less life than a novel, if it's properly written. It should have a feeling of the fullness of life you get from a novel.

RW: You have a very chilling story from the point of view of a male rapist. Do you write from a man's perspective as easily as from a woman's?

BF: I don't write easily at all. It's always a great struggle, but I have written other stories from a male point of view. Some of the Greek stories are from the point of view of a male who is a sort of an amalgam of Greeks I've known and of myself. It's as Flaubert says, when you're writing as somebody else, you tend to make that somebody else more and more like you. The rapist in "A Woman with Black Hair" is a male who is boasting of his exploits. He is a curious mixture: romantic, lyrical, dreamy, cruel, and sadistic. He sees himself as romantic until the moment of orgasm. Then he becomes bitter and cruel. I suppose I've known men like that. Fear made me develop it to a logical conclusion in this character.

RW: He rapes the woman and then changes into casual clothing and blends into the crowd.

BF: Yes, he's a jogger and the murder is a quick deed easily done. When I drafted the story I was sleeping in the house I used in the story. I am very shortsighted. I thought I saw somebody sitting in a chair in the room and I didn't move and I must have stared at the chair for about an hour and it didn't move. There was no one there, in fact. My terror is also connected with my revulsion for a man who I felt had these two aspects to his character, although not developed to the degree this man had. And so, my terror as I lay there thinking that there was someone in the chair and my memories of this man and my fascination with him and my submission to him all blended. And when it became light enough for me to see, there was no one in the chair. So I picked up my pen and decided to draft this story.

RW: Several of your stories are set in the States; have you visited or lived there?

BF: I briefly visited in 1980, only for a few weeks.

RW: Would you talk about where you're living now and how you're living financially?

BF: How first. I got a Literature Board grant last year, so I still haven't spent all that yet, and I pick up a bit of work at the local hotel in reception. There are anthology fees and reviews and things, so I scrape a living. But where—it's down on the Victorian Coast in a duney sort of place with salt pans and swamps behind it. Mosquitoes. A lot of wild bird life and mangrove. It's a very strange place and it's misty and ill defined. It's hard to see distances; it's not clear-cut like Greece. I have a feeling, somehow, that this climate is going to or has been influencing my writing. The things that I write about are becoming ill-defined and more fluid and less sharp-edged than they were. It's a sea place, a water place. My next book is called *A Body of Water.*

RW: How would you describe *A Body of Water?*

BF: It's a new departure for me. There are five stories backed up with the journal that went with the writing of these stories. I keep a writing journal as well as diaries of personal events, and it struck me that these were like the nest and the egg or like the embryo and the womb, that they went together so much that they threw light on each other. They formed a whole. So they're being published as a whole, the diary entries and the quotations and the readings that led to a particular story's germination and development. Then you get the story. All the threads are there linking it to the other stories and to other experiences. So it doesn't have a narrative line. It's all in the shape of a web. There are poems in it and recurring symbols. People who are interested in the process of stories coming into being might be interested in seeing how these stories came into being for me.

RW: Is living alone good for you, or should we identify you with your lonely female figures?
BF: Oh, living alone has its good and its bad aspects. I don't know if I really want to identify with any of my female figures. I hope they're separate from me just as one's child is. They have a separate life which is much more limited and defined and small than real life is. Necessarily, so that we can grasp it in the few minutes it takes to read a story. They're on a different scale than real people and contact with them is quite different from contact with a real person. They are encapsulated in story.
RW: Would you comment on the quotation which begins *Home Time:* "Let the soil at your feet be thin, so that you'll have nowhere to spread roots and have to delve in the depths continually."
BF: The lines are from the creation scene in the beginning of the poem "Genesis," where Greece is created from the sea and God is imposing the conditions under which Greeks will live. He gives them little water so they'll understand the value of water, and not many trees, so that they'll know the value of shade, and meager soil so that they'll have to delve deep. This is God's blessing. I suppose I feel it's an injunction against shallowness and a way of embracing, as I did embrace, the austerity, the poverty, and the hardship of living in Greece. I still feel a need for austerity. I live quite frugally. It's almost like a spiritual exercise, to live on as little as possible and to make the most of it, to find everything that there is in it.
RW: I see in the quotation the essence of your questing female character. The woman in your fiction often has this integrity.
BF: I think there's a desire to be tested and to come through.
RW: Do you think aloneness is the proper testing ground?
BF: No, not necessarily, but I'm no longer afraid to be alone. It's no longer an issue for me. I think I've come through that. The pain has somehow gone; it has healed. If I write of people who are solitary now, it's just the bare fact of that. I'd hate to think that there was ever even a grain of self-pity in the way it was portrayed in the past, but certainly there is nowhere for even a grain of self-pity to come from now, because I don't have any.

HELEN GARNER

was born in 1942 in Geelong, Victoria, and was educated at Melbourne University. She taught school until she was fired for using "gutter language" in the classroom. Since then she has supported herself as a fiction writer, as a journalist, and as a screenwriter. Her somewhat shocking first novel, *Monkey Grip,* won the National Book Council Award in 1978 and was made into a motion picture in 1982. Helen Garner has been writer in residence at several Australian universities as well as in Tokyo. The following interview occurred in Sydney.

Monkey Grip, 1977
Honour and Other People's Children, 1980
The Children's Bach, 1984
Postcards from Surfers (stories), 1985

INTERVIEW

RW: Where in Australia did you grow up?

HG: I was born in 1942 in a town called Geelong, about forty-five miles from Melbourne. I grew up there and in a tiny place on the sea called Ocean Grove.

RW: What was your home life like?

HG: There were six kids, five girls and one boy, and I was the oldest. It was a middle-class family. My father came from the country; my mother came from the city. They compromised in the small town. My father was in the wool trade. It was all quite proper. We had on the face of it quite a privileged, cheerful childhood. Not very intellectual, but we were all looked after and there were no material hardships.

RW: *Monkey Grip*, your first novel, is set in Carlton, a suburb of Melbourne. When did you move to Melbourne?

HG: I went to the University in Melbourne when I was nineteen in 1961. The University is in Carlton. I actually haven't lived in Carlton all that much. I've lived in the nearby suburb of Fitzroy.

RW: Would you describe Carlton in the 1970s and your way of living there?

HG: For me it mostly had to do with households which worked as strong families. That was the most interesting part of this period. My first marriage broke down and I had a kid to bring up. So as not to go crazy, it was necessary to find people and to share the job of bringing up a kid. That is the nub of it. There was a lot of music, a lot of drugs, a lot of theater. We had fun. People didn't seem to have jobs in those days. I hate to use the word "bohemian," but everyone was trying to be an artist of one sort of another. Everyone I knew back then was either a musician or an actor.

RW: How did you live?

HG: If you were a musician or an actor you could scrape up a bit of money from being in a band or in a show. I was a teacher for quite a while. In the middle seventies for a couple of years I lived on a small pension called a supporting mother's benefit, which you were entitled to if you were bringing up a kid on you own. Actually, I suppose that was my first grant. I read a lot. It meant that while my daughter was in school I could spend my day in the library or lying on my bed reading.

RW: Would you imagine that the bohemian life was as vibrant in Melbourne as it might have been in Sydney in the same period?

HG: That I can't say. We never had a very high consciousness of what was going on in Sydney. We were much too broke to go anywhere. Our lives were very narrowly centered around a small part of the country. To get anywhere we had to hitch.

RW: Were you conscious of being a part of a counterculture in the same way that the hippie movement in the States was?

HG: Yes. I think so. I worked for a countercultural newspaper for awhile called *The Digger.* We had theoretical positions on most things, feminist Libertarian positions.

RW: Would you describe the public reception of the publication of *Monkey Grip?*

HG: It came out in November of 1977 and I don't even remember the reception of it very much. I went away to Europe about six months after it came out and I didn't come back for about eighteen months. When I came back, I found that it had been noticed and, to my amazement, that people wanted to interview me.

RW: I know there were problems with censorship in Australia into the seventies. I would assume you would have had a lot of notoriety over the book, because of its language—the use of the work "fuck" over and over, because of the drugs and the lack of any conventional morality on the part of the narrator.

HG: I can hardly remember. I think I blot out a lot of this stuff, perhaps because it is too ghastly to remember. I don't remember encountering a great deal of hostility or criticism. Clearly, there were reviewers who were disgusted by the stuff. I think what reaction there was on this score was probably over by the time I got back from France. I certainly didn't set out to shock or be appalling, but it might have been a ground-breaking book for women. Later, even seven or eight years later, I would be invited to middle-class ladies' reading groups and what people wanted to talk about, and what I think the book presented to them, was less the sex and drugs than it was the rather unorthodox arrangements of households. Women particularly were struck by it. They would question me over and over, "But who did the housework? Who minded the children? Did everyone have their own separate room?" They were obsessed with the organization. I don't think it was because they were embarrassed to talk about the sex and drugs. I think the sex and drugs were so far from their own experience or from their own fantasies of experience that they passed them by.

RW: How would you describe the story line of *Monkey Grip* to someone who hasn't read it?

HG: A woman in her thirties with a small daughter falls in love with a guy who is a heroin addict. The book follows a year in their lives, of his comings and goings in sickness and in health and her attempts to balance herself against his wild fluctuations.

RW: The novel is taken in part from your own diary entries. Is that correct?

HG: Yes.

RW: Would you say that the novel is marginally autobiographical or heavily autobiographical?

HG: Heavily autobiographical.

RW: What gave you the idea to turn the diaries into a novel?

HG: I didn't ever have anything that might be described as an ambition to be a writer. I've always kept a diary, since I was a girl; I don't know why, I just have, so I've always been in the habit of recording things as they've happened. I guess after about a year of a relationship with a bloke like the one in the book I thought I could see a story in it and I thought I'd just get out the stuff and see. A lot of work has been done on it. The book isn't just diary whacked down on the page. But I don't think at any state I told myself, "I am working on a novel." I just started working on this material to see what I could shape it into.

RW: And did you have a place where you went every day to work on it?

HG: I went to the reading room of the state library every morning while my daughter was at school.

RW: How long did the writing take?

HG: About a year.

RW: How do you explain the almost hypnotic effect that reading the short chapters have on the reader? Do you have any notion what produces this effect?

HG: No, I don't. No one's ever told me that it has an hypnotic effect. I don't know what to say about that.

RW: The domestic routine, the absence of the man in Nora's life, his presence, his absence, falls on the reader like ocean waves, always a little different, always the same. Would you agree that this rhythm is there?

HG: Oh, sure. Yeah. I think that rhythm is there. The rhythm is dictated by the events. There was a movie made of *Monkey Grip*. The guy who wrote the screenplay had a lot of trouble adapting the structure of what you've just described to what is required in the movie, which is a much more classic kind of structure with a peak and a resolution and so forth. He remarked at the time that it had more the structure of a long-running serial than that of a novel, which is true.

RW: There is a sexual rhythm to it as well.

HG: Umm. That's interesting. I'd never thought about that sort of thing very much until recently when I read a book by Mary Fallon, who is a lesbian writer. She's written a book which I've noticed has a wavelike, sexy quality. It's filled with sexual imagery of a quite vivid and unusual kind. The book struck me as being extremely feminine in that sense. The rhythm of it was orgasmic; it had a kind of wave pattern which is distinct from what I suppose is the classic idea of a male pattern which peaks and resolves.

RW: I think *Monkey Grip* has the male pattern.

HG: I hadn't thought of it like that.

RW: You weren't conscious, then, that you were making such rhythm in the writing?

HG: Absolutely not. I hadn't a clue. Things unconsciously happen in books. This is something that has really surprised me a lot. A critic who was very keen on *Monkey Grip*—he's written a novel himself—asked, "Why has Nora consulted the *I Ching* twelve times?" I had no idea. I didn't know she had. She consulted it and I never thought to count. He was amazed by this. Someone who was reviewing my book *Postcards from Surfers* counted the postcards in the title story and there were twelve postcards. This was totally accidental.

RW: A metaphysical number. Twelve Apostles, twelve signs in the zodiac . . .

HG: Twelve months. I don't know. An enormous amount of *Monkey Grip* was accidental, completely unconscious on my part. I had no idea what I was doing. I didn't know how to make a novel. I still don't.

RW: When Nora consulted the *I Ching* it gave good advice, but it was often the wrong advice for her. Were you doing anything with this?

HG: No. The first review that the book got was one of the worst ones it has ever had. This woman, who later went into state politics, by the way, said, "The quotes from the *I Ching* are set in the text like lumps of lard."

RW: Not true, I think. On one hand *Monkey Grip* reminds me of Wordsworth's celebration of the commonplace, but Wordsworth would never have had his characters shooting smack, nor would the heroine have been obsessed with sex and talking about it. Is the power of the novel due in part to these sharp contrasts, the commonplace juxtaposed with the shocking?

HG: It may work that way. The reader could say better than I could. When I look at it, all I see is a web that is a changed and reorganized version of actual experience, so all these things that people see in it often go right past me. They do. I open the book and look at any page and off the page comes flooding a whole mass of associations and memories which are quite specific in time, whereas a reader who isn't me can open the book and get a whole different flood.

RW: Nora reads a lot in the novel—Jean Rhys in particular. Do you see any similarity between Nora and the passive female protagonist that Rhys uses over and over?

HG: I liked Jean Rhys' books, although I don't think I would like them so much now, though I think *Wide Sargasso Sea* is a wonderful novel. But there's something about Jean Rhys' women—they are ultimately seduced by failure and wretchedness; they are never going to get out of their mess, whereas it seems to me that Nora is struggling all along to go through the experience and emerge on the other side. She hasn't actually dropped her bundle. Some people who don't like *Monkey Grip* say that it is a downer and that there is a sort of dying fall in it, but I don't see that myself. I don't feel it.

RW: Maybe the Jean Rhys heroine was a positive influence in Nora's reading. Not to go down, down.

HG: Maybe. Jean Rhys is a fabulous writer.

RW: Some critics see *Monkey Grip* as an early feminist marker—the first Australian novel in which a woman fucks a man, or like a man, or with choice like a man, or talks about it like a man. Were you aware of a feminist stance when you wrote the novel, or did the term apply after the fact?

HG: That was a period of my life in which we were all feminists. Right from the early seventies that was the weapon we had, the lens we had through which to examine our experience and try to make sense of it, but a really doctrinaire feminist, I suppose, wouldn't have gotten mixed up with such a bloke and wouldn't have plunged into it. I didn't set out to write a feminist book, but I think I was very much both bound by and enlightened by feminist thinking. Now I think I am less bound by it, but still enlightened by it.

RW: I can't imagine changing *Monkey Grip* fourteen years later. Could you?

HG: I wouldn't try. It was translated into French about two years ago and that was a strange experience, because some of it I found quite mortifying. I sat with the translator occasionally to make sure he hadn't misunderstood the English idiom. I feel that now I have a much greater psychological insight into what that character is doing, some of the dreams she has for example, which at the time I was just pulling out because the imagery was striking, or whatever. I can now make a stab at understanding certain things that were mysterious to me then. Sometimes, as I read for the translator, I was appalled. One thing that struck me was how much the man's addiction was a kind of turn-on to Nora. You don't notice that running through the book as a strong theme, but occasionally there are hints of it. I think the theme of the book is that Nora loves Javo psychologically because he is not able to love and that provides her with a battle to get him to love her. It's not something that is won or lost; it just waxes and wanes.

RW: I've been in a situation like that myself.

HG: A lot of people have, I think. Especially if there's been some difficulty with one of your parents. If you have an unresolved relationship with that person, you can drag it into your own emotional life and try to act it out in different forms.

RW: What does the title *Monkey Grip* mean?

HG: When we were young girls we played games where we gripped hands and turned round and round. We said, "Monkey grip, monkey grip!" and the harder you pulled apart, the tighter the grip became.

RW: Love was Nora's habit as smack was Javo's?

HG: Yes.

RW: Is the Javo character still alive?

HG: Yes. He's off junk as far as I know. He lives in another state now. I saw him last year.

RW: Were you involved in the filming of *Monkey Grip*?

HG: I didn't write the screenplay. I didn't know how to write a screenplay then, but I was there for the filming because my daughter played the part of the little girl. She was about ten. She was young and had to be tended to so I was hanging around, but I didn't have very much to do with the filming.

RW: What was it like seeing Nora on the screen?

HG: Awful, actually. I liked the actress, but I didn't enjoy it. It was embarrassing to me. I only saw the film once. I took my mother to see it and I was worried about how she would react. While I sat there grinding, projecting all my anxiety onto her, she just sat there simply enjoying it and being touched by it. She loved it. I think she was a bit shocked by the sex, but not all that shocked. I was so mortified that I could hardly even look at the screen.

RW: Is the film on video release now?

HG: Yes, I think so. People tell me that when there are sexy scenes on videos people run them back and forth.

RW: That's an awful thing to think of—your life being run back and forth in someone's bedroom.

HG: Horrible. It's gruesome.

RW: Let's talk about the books that follow *Monkey Grip. Honour and Other People's Children* and *The Children's Bach* are astonishingly different in style from *Monkey Grip.* What happened?

HG: I got older and I didn't want to write about myself anymore, at least not in the unmodulated way of *Monkey Grip.* There's a bit of myself in everything, I guess. I like *Honour,* but I don't like *Other People's Children* very much. The characters are all right, but its narrative is all out of whack and it's clumsy somehow.

RW: Take *The Children's Bach,* then—if *Monkey Grip* flows and is wavelike, the latter novel is tightly structured, chiseled. What I am asking is what happened to your concept of writing? Did you deliberately begin to study other people's writing at the point between these books?

HG: Well, you write your first book unconsciously, and if it is well received you have to begin thinking of yourself as a writer. It's impossible not to. I don't know how it happened. I just changed.

RW: Why the title *The Children's Bach*?

HG: It's the name of a piano book that I was trying to study from. It has a rather pompous little introduction which says, "Bach is never easy but that is why we should all try to master him." I wanted music to be a linking theme. The moral element in it has very much to do with music. Anyone who has ever tried to play Bach knows that what seems simple and clear is actually the product of a great deal of manipulation of thought and sound. We discover this about Athena's life. Vicki says about Athena's house that it is sunny and charming and full of joy and pleasure, but really underneath it there is a hell of a lot of psychological and emotional labor being done to sustain its simple surface.

RW: The critical response to your recent collection of stories *Postcards from Surfers* was very positive. You've taken a direction opposite the route followed by most writers, from the long form of the novel to the short form of the story. Do you like working with the short story?

HG: Yes, I love writing short stories; you can learn a lot from trying to write a short story, but at the moment I am trying to get another novel going. I've had a hard time starting it. I've gone into it at various points over the last year. I know who the characters are and I know roughly what I want to happen, the area in which I want to find out what the truth is, but I've come up against a brick wall every time I've tried to start it. I am a slow worker. I don't plan much. I work by feel and sometimes I get into blind alleys. It's as if I'm not ready to do the novel yet. That is something I've tried to learn from David Malouf. He says over and over that the thing a writer needs most is patience. I always try to rush things. I dive in head first and then hit the bottom because the water is not in the pool yet. I have a puritanical drive which is counterproductive. Some days I think I haven't done anything when actually I've done quite a lot. Even when I think I'm not working, I am. I always have my notebook. I never go anywhere without it. Once I have the right viewfinder that fits the material, then out comes pouring all the stuff that's been in my mind and my notebook for the last year and it comes in and slot, slot, slot—it falls into place. Even walking around I'm actually working, so it's pointless lashing myself the way I do, feeling guilty. There is only so much in writing that you can do with your rational mind. Once you're on the track, things appear on the paper you didn't know you knew. That's the best thing.

RW: In *Postcards* as well as earlier works, I am constantly made aware of the physical, particularly as it pertains to the body. Physicality is very important to you, isn't it?

HG: Yes. Everything starts in the physical as far as I'm concerned. I think the physical part of it is absolutely crucial. At a reading once with Gerald Murnane I read from a story in which I describe a cut on someone's hand, what it looked like when it had partly healed. Gerald came up to me afterward and said, "When you described the cut on that person's hand, I realized how much your work is physical and how much mine isn't." I was quite struck by that because I suppose it had never occurred to me that that's the way I come at things.

RW: Do you have a story in *Postcards* that you like more than others?

HG: I like "Little Helen's Sunday Afternoon." The one I like the best is "The Dark, the Light," the one about the wedding. It's a very short one. Only two pages.

RW: I like the story about the gay man, Philip. You have a lot of Philips in your work. You must like the name.

HG: Philip has turned into an archetype in my work now. He's the sort of man who is very attractive to women for the very reason that he is unreliable. Philip in *The Children's Bach* is one of them. He's charming, talented, kind of seductively independent, a sort that women find irresistible. In recent stories I've developed him even further. I've written a story called "What the Soul Wants" where the Philip stuff is taken into a dream archetype. I'm interested in him. You'll be seeing more of him.

RW: Do you feel a kinship with any other Australian writer?

HG: I admire Elizabeth Jolley enormously, but I couldn't really say I felt a kinship because we talk about different things. We belong to different generations. With your own contemporaries in your own country often it's too close. I feel sometimes perhaps I shouldn't even be reading them. Other writers—I admire Raymond Carver. I think the sun shines out of him. I also like Jamaica Kincaid, particularly *At the Bottom of the River.* I think Alice Munro is fabulous; a story of hers sometimes has as much meat in it as a novel does.

RW: You've been doing screenwriting. Is that satisfying to you?

HG: Yes, it is, in a completely different way. I've written two screenplays, one called *Two Friends,* directed by Jane Campion, and *The Last Days of Chez Nous* for the ABC that hasn't been made yet. I like writing screenplays; it is much faster work, less obsessively perfectionist, and you get paid for it. That's the wonderful thing.

RW: Is there another work in Helen Garner that can knock 'em dead the way *Monkey Grip* did?

HG: Who knows? There is not a work in me that resembles *Monkey*

Grip. I'm not interested in that anymore. Maybe not. I haven't got much ambition of the external kind. I'm trying to get rid of ambition, to tell the truth.

RW: Why?

HG: Because it takes my focus away from what's real in me, and then I lose myself. Because it doesn't get me anywhere.

KATE GRENVILLE

was born in 1950 in Sydney, where she now lives with her husband, cartoonist Bruce Petty. She has lived in London, Paris, and Colorado, and in addition to writing fiction has worked as a film editor, journalist, and teacher. Her novel *Lilian's Story* won the *Australian*/Vogel Award in 1984. The following interview occurred in her home in Balmain (Sydney).

Bearded Ladies (stories), 1984
Lilian's Story, 1985
Dreamhouse, 1986
(written before *Lilian's Story*)
Joan Makes History, 1988

INTERVIEW

RW: On finishing a degree at Sydney University, you lived five years in London and Paris. Afterwards you did something I find unusual; you went to the University of Colorado to study fiction writing. How did this come about?

KG: Like everything I do, it happened by accident. When I lived in Paris I met a lot of sophisticated, intellectual Americans who had a quality I liked—curiosity, interest about the world. They kept lending me books which I responded to very badly. They were innovative modern American novels by people like John Hawkes and Robert Coover, people I'd never heard of. And I thought, I want to go to the place where these extremely interesting people are coming from and where this extraordinarily challenging writing is coming from, where people are writing the way people speak without worrying too much about grammar. Because I had no money, one of the few ways I could go was as a student. So I applied for and got financial assistance from the University of Colorado. Then I found myself in the middle of the Rockies with the raccoons coming in my window, wondering what a nice girl from Sydney was doing there.

RW: How did taking the fiction-writing courses affect your work?

KG: I learned more in those two years than I probably would ever have learned on my own. It accelerated the process a hundredfold. I had no idea that you could approach the great classics in any other than the way that I had been taught to approach them, that is, as a critic. To approach Wordsworth and Shakespeare as a writer, rather than as a critic, was for me an amazing, liberating process. Writing is by nature linear. How do you get around that? To see Wordsworth trying a dozen ways to get around the problem of everything happening simultaneously was fantastic. Not only did I see that I could ransack the whole of English literature for things that I might be able to use, but that I could also enjoy the process as a reader. The other thing of value was being a graduate student with twenty other serious and knowledgeable graduate students who had all done a bit of writing but not a great deal. I had had no experience of that kind of group of peers unselfconsciously criticizing each other's works without it being personal, and within that very healthy context of a classroom. The only experience of feedback I'd had before was showing my work to friends or agents. If they said it was terrific, I didn't believe them; if they said it was terrible, I didn't believe them. Another thing was that the writing program at Colorado had several innovative writers in it and I was exposed to ideas that in my Australian Anglo-Saxon education I had never been exposed to. The idea of going to a poetry workshop the first week and, instead of being told about meter and rhyme, being invited to chant in order to free up the mind was a startling idea for someone who had gone through Sydney University. Working through the writing program was the best thing I ever did.

RW: You wrote a collection of stories called *Bearded Ladies.* Were these stories written while you were in class or were they written in Europe?

KG: Most of them had been written in Europe. But what I did, under the impulse of the workshop, was to rewrite a lot of them. By the time I left Colorado the stories had the shape that they now have.

RW: Why the title *Bearded Ladies?*

KG: It cost me such agony, that title. I went through so many disastrous titles. I obviously wanted to get in the paradox of someone who is a woman and yet who doesn't fit the stereotype of a woman. A slightly freaky thing happened. I don't know if we have epiphanies, but I think this was one of those epiphanies that you hope will happen. I had always thought real writers had epiphanies all the time, so it was a great relief to finally have one. I had a deadline. I had been dithering around with the title and the publishers had said firmly, "At five o'clock this afternoon—and that's going to be it, whatever you've said, that's going to be it." I was walking home from work and my finger reached out to press the Walk button on the pedestrian thing and it was as if some electrical contact came to me in that moment through the stalk of the traffic light. I knew the title—*Bearded Ladies*, as if it were written in neon in the sky.

RW: Your form changes quite drastically from *Bearded Ladies* to *Dreamhouse*. What was going on with you? Did you write through something in that first book of stories?

KG: I think I wrote out a lot of great anger. That's not very hard to guess in *Bearded Ladies*. By the time I came to write *Dreamhouse* I could see that pointing the finger at the other, at men, was not quite enough to deal with that anger. I myself was happier when I was writing *Dreamhouse*, slightly happier, so I didn't quite have that fury, that rage that I had to express. The other thing was that I wrote *Dreamhouse* while I was at the University of Colorado. I was heavily under the influence of writers like Hawkes and Flannery O'Connor and I think that there is a lot of those writers in *Dreamhouse*, not that I would put myself in their category at all. I think I was still trying to find the voice that was my own fictional voice. I was still allowing myself to be influenced by others because I thought that was probably one of the things you did when you learned to write.

RW: How about Carson McCullers? *The Ballad of the Sad Café*, had you read that?

KG: I'm not sure, actually; I had certainly read *A Member of the Wedding* and *The Heart Is a Lonely Hunter*.

RW: The sexual ménage in *The Ballad of the Sad Café* is similar to what you create in *Dreamhouse*.

KG: I might easily have read it, though Carson McCullers is not someone that I've been particularly drawn to as a writer. The Hawkes books sort of follow that misalliance, too.

RW: *Dreamhouse* is a very strange novel. What were you doing?

KG: Well, it began with a photograph that I had of a couple who spent all day saying to each other, "I love you, darling"; "Oh, yes, I love you, too, darling." But when they went to bed at night, they dreamed about killing each other, cutting each other in little bits with axes. That seemed to me to be a very fertile starting point with a lot of friction. But as I wrote, I realized I wanted to explore another idea, which was the idea of how we arrive at knowledge. In this situation you have two people who are misreading the signs. Instead of listening when the other person says, "I love you, darling," one ought to be listening to the other kind of information which that person is giving through behavior. I wanted to write a book that didn't explain anything. I wanted to write a book that was more like a film script. In a film script all one has to go on is what people do and say. And from that, one has to try to deduce correctly what is actually going on. And, of course, none of the people in that book did deduce correctly. They all got it wrong. That seemed to me like the human condition and worth exploring, that whole thing of not what we know, but how we know it or how we think we know it. And that's why the novel has that strange distance, a kind of non-analytical quality. It has surprised me that nobody has wanted to make the novel into a film. It was written almost with that in mind.

RW: *Dreamhouse* seems to me a bold novel for a beginning writer in that it has an unsympathetic narrator. In fact all the characters are pretty unsympathetic. Was this hard for you to do? Were you aware that you were setting up such a difficult way of engaging the reader?

KG: I suppose I wasn't experienced enough as a writer to know. No, that's not true because in *Bearded Ladies* I made sympathetic, very awful women. I look back now at the *Bearded Ladies* women; they don't deserve the kind treatment the author gave them, so I think perhaps in *Dreamhouse* I had worked that out in some unconscious way and wanted to come in a different way at those problems, not taking sides. The other thing was that, and I think I'm doing it with the book I'm writing now, I wanted to force myself as the writer and also the reader into the uncomfortable partnership of having to identify with the characters as one does in a novel, especially a first-person character, and yet knowing that the character or characters are not people one likes. That's a really interesting, uncomfortable stance for writing. I think it's interesting reading, although it is a bit of a strain for a reader.

RW: Why do you want to write in this way?

KG: One of the things writing is about is expanding one's own notion of what it is to be human and to explain or explore without judging. Then at some point one has to ask, "What do I do with these reprehensible people? Do I just consign them to the outer darkness, or do I somehow say they, too, are human?" So if I'm going to do anything useful here, I have to understand what it feels like to be their kind of human. If they are human beings, what do they feel like? That seems to be worth doing. With *Dreamhouse* I hadn't worked that out consciously. With the book I'm writing now, which is about a much worse character than any of those, I'm very conscious of wanting to say, "It's too easy to divide the world into the goodies and the baddies." The hard thing is to recognize that there is the "baddie" in all of us. There is also the other thing. There is some deep rapport with those unpleasant characters as well as a deep repugnance.

RW: And that keeps us turning the page?

KG: Well, I hope so, yes.

RW: Would you talk about the black humor in *Dreamhouse*, the bird imagery, the excrement imagery—what were you doing here?

KG: The use of this sort of thing is partly a hangover from *Bearded Ladies*. When I started writing I felt an incredible rage and frustration, not only with the world, but also with the books that had been written about the world, because they seemed to draw a veil over so much human experience, like the pissing and shitting part of human experience, the plumbing, the squalid physicality of it. Books recognized our spirituality but not the fact that we are also bodies and that those two things are connected, especially for women. Women are constantly being told that we are all goddesses. On the other hand, women are told that their bodies are revolting and a lot of things have to be done to them before they are acceptable. So for a woman, having a physical body, especially the unacceptable things that happen about it, is a really important political and philosophical thing, as well as just an accident of physicality. Part of the *Dreamhouse* stuff is a hangover from that. Also, I wanted to write very confronting fiction. I wanted to shock people, I suppose, which I did. I was angry that too much fiction was soothing and just entertaining. I certainly have always wanted to do more than entertain. All the animal imagery—I was terribly conscious of the snake, for example, what a corny Freudian image it was. But Freud wasn't wrong about a lot of things.

RW: What about the bird in the refrigerator?

KG: Again, I suppose it was the idea of what's hidden beneath bland surfaces, which is what the book is about. There is the bland social surface, where people have refrigerators full of bottles of milk, and there is another reality when one opens the refrigerator and confronts dead birds.

RW: What is the significance of the dissertation the husband is writing concerning Malthus and "The Doctrine of Necessary Catastrophe"?

KG: I wanted to make the dissertation sound ludicrously pompous.

I also wanted it to be a clue to what the book might be about, which was in a way tumbling toward catastrophe. I read about Malthus' belief that because of the way we kept populating, we were doomed to a cycle of famine which would reduce our numbers. This seemed to fit with the brutality of my book. And the character who's writing the dissertation can talk about catastrophe in a cool manner like that, as if it's not human beings that it's happening to. This sort of callousness that I always attributed to Malthus I wanted to give to my callous and self-obsessed character, Rennie.

RW: What about Louise, your female lead? Are we supposed to be sympathetic towards Louise when she returns to Viola, or is this just another dead end?

KG: I don't think I was really thinking about sympathy. I did want it to look as if for the first time she makes a choice of her own that has to do with her own destiny. So, I wanted it to be like a door that has opened. I actually wrote a long sequence that comes after that, where Viola and Louise have set up house in London. But it seemed to be much better, later, to leave it there where in fact she might not have ever gone back to Viola. But she had got herself out of that terrible death trap with Rennie and that was all that mattered, and if the mechanism for that was this probably equally doomed relationship with this peculiar woman, at least it was an escape.

RW: Why did Rennie suddenly flee from Daniel?

KG: Daniel makes sure that he and Rennie share a room. I imagined at some point in the night that Daniel makes an overt, physical pass at Rennie. Although Rennie likes to flirt at the idea of being seduced, and although it is wonderfully attractive to have somebody hovering over you in that seductive way, when it actually comes down to it, particularly since men are very ambivalent about their homosexual inclinations, because culturally it has that awful load which women's homosexuality doesn't have, women can be much more exploratory without it threatening our—whatever the equivalent of our manhood is—when it finally comes down to it, Rennie can't do it. So at some point in the night they have that confrontation and Rennie has to see, even with his blindness and self-delusion, that Daniel wants to screw him. Rennie leaves. He is a bit of a prick tease, really.

RW: You moved from a very passive female lead in *Dreamhouse* to a very aggressive female protagonist in *Lilian's Story.* How did this novel come about?

KG: After writing *Dreamhouse* I was sick of those characters. I loathed them so much and I was very sick of writing about people I hated. I had a great repugnance for all those people and for their passivity. I wanted to take them all out of the book one by one, grab them by the shoulders and shake them. So I thought, all right, next time I can allow myself a character that I really like, and I think also in the process of the evolution of my own thought I'd come around to thinking, well, okay, *Bearded Ladies*, that's all that anger; *Dreamhouse* is an exploration of suppressed/repressed passive resistance. So the next logical step is to have somebody who is fully her own person, what Louise might have conceivably become ten years down the track, a woman who is not a victim in any of those ways, although she had all the disadvantages that might make someone a victim. And for some reason, the image of a Sydney eccentric named Bea Miles came to my mind. I was still in America, but was about to come back to Sydney and I was obviously starting to think about Australia. I knew very little about Bea Miles, but I had seen photographs of this enormously fat, ugly woman radiating a sort of satisfaction with her life. She had made a life that she quite liked. And so I named her Lilian and started to write about her. It was time in my own life, as well as fictionally, to write about a woman who had come out from under the shadow of all that oppression and dishonesty.

RW: Would you call Lilian a grotesque in the sense that Flannery O'Connor or Elizabeth Jolley create characters who are grotesques?

KG: I think the characters in *Dreamhouse* are grotesques in that way, but I think Lilian is right on the edge, if I'm right about it, because the reader is forced into a very close rapport with her and he has to submerge into her way of seeing the world. I think it would seem part of the nature of the grotesque that the reader has a bit of distance. Although that's not entirely true, because you think of that wonderful novel of O'Connor's where you actually live with Hazel Moats.

RW: I'm thinking of the word "grotesque" in terms of being oversized, overly emotional, larger than life.

KG: Perhaps Lilian has two identities, in fact. Perhaps she has the identity that she projects, which is deliberately a bit larger than life, especially in her maturity, when she is almost self-consciously parodying herself; she's playing up to the role she has written herself. Then there is the other person within that act, who is just an ordinary size person, who doesn't want to die and who misses out on things.

RW: Did you ever meet Lilian?

KG: I saw her from a distance when I was a student a few times, but I never met her.

RW: The style in *Lilian's Story* is radically different from that in

Dreamhouse. Lilian's Story is a series of snapshots tightly organized and named, or would you describe the style another way?

KG: No, that's a very good image.

RW: I've never read a novel structured in quite the same way. The stories are very tight and they move forward in a smart cadence. How did you arrive at this narrative method?

KG: Partly it was a revulsion against *Dreamhouse* because I had worked from notes. I had a great stack of notes, because I had been told it was good to keep a notebook. So I had a sense of methodically working through. I got very worried in *Dreamhouse* about things like motivation and what the book was about and what was going to happen, the big picture. With *Lilian* I thought, look, let's do it another way. This was one of the many things I learned in the writing program. I wrote *Dreamhouse* while I was studying; *Lilian's Story* is the flowering of everything I learned. One of the things I had learned was not to worry too early about what the book is about, or where it's going, or what it means, or why people are doing things. Just get them to do it and worry about those things later, that was one thing. The other thing which was a result of being a student was that I reread *Moby Dick*. I think that is the model for the structure of *Lilian's Story.* My snapshots are very much shorter than Melville's, but it has that same idea, that a book does not have to progress along a line like a string of beads, because life doesn't actually progress like that. At least our grasping of life works in vignettes, more like a film. I was also allowing myself to use the bit of film background that I had, because film doesn't have to show people coming in the door, opening the door, closing the door, walking through the room, sitting down. You just cut from one thing to the other. And because of film, people are used to that grammar, so you can now use it in books. I don't think it was terribly original. In the beginning I thought all those short bits would be a first draft; then I tried to combine them into a seamless narrative, because I sort of still thought that's really how a novel should look. You had big chunks of narrative. And when I did that, something very peculiar happened; it was the same material but the whole thing went flat like a soufflé you take out of the oven too soon. It just died when I tried to string it all together into a conventional narrative, so I hastily cut it up again and put the title on each section. And that seemed to be the right form for that content. For the first time, I allowed myself to be led by the material rather than the other way around.

RW: One thing that is dazzling to me is the number of facts that Lilian's father, Albion, quotes. How did you collect all those facts?

KG: Actually, I made most of them up. The new novel I'm working on has Albion as the main character, and now that I'm writing his book I'm actually trying to find some real facts. I've gotten some wonderful ones today about how many square yards of skin the human body is covered with. How much the average liver weighs. But I think I made most of the ones up in *Lilian's Story.*

RW: Albion has an incestuous relationship with his daughter, so we think. Are you doing here, as well as elsewhere, an England/Australia parallel?

KG: You bet. I think the British shadow lies over Australia and has since the beginning. It's a powerful thing that an Australian artist has to come to terms with. It's also a very powerful image for other kinds of colonial oppression. Obviously the male/female colonial analogy is another version of the same thing. That's why when it occurred to me to call the father Albion, it seemed like a neat sort of parallel. I suppose most cultures have some version of an Albion figure that they have to come to terms with. I was interested in both of them, the British oppression, and my oppression as an Australian woman writer.

RW: You have Lilian say, "Books should have toilets in them." What does Lilian mean?

KG: It's what I was saying earlier. I think that if you are hiding, if you are drawing a veil over some part of your human experiences then that infects the other part of your human experience. If you are being dishonest about one thing in your life, you can't possibly be honest about everything else. It's very contagious. So if you want to try to be honest or honestly exploratory about what I think of as the big issues, with capital letters, of Good and Evil, what it means to be human, what it ought to mean in moral terms, what we ought to be trying to do, then you have to clear away that undergrowth, those great shreds of concealment that we hang over so much of our existence. It's only when you come to terms with physical grossness that you can move on to the spiritual. I suppose it's a bit like the Catholic paradox, where you mortify the flesh in order to transcend it, so you notice the body a lot more and in some paradoxical way that enables you to transcend and to think about the nonphysical.

RW: Are you as an individual transcending through the writing? Or is the reader to transcend through the reading?

KG: As a writer, I often feel that it's not that different from being a reader. I write the thing with the same sense of discovery as I hope the reader reads it. In a way, I feel we're all in there together, being explorers. And certainly I think there's not much point in writing books that are just entertainment. Not that I want to be some didactic moral preacher because I don't know what I'd preach, but I think the thing about trying to make everybody, including myself, keep on thinking about human dilemmas, insolvable though they are, is one of the things that, if there is any point in writing, seems to be one of the points.

RW: The women in your fiction which you persuade the reader to dislike are passive, are pawns of men, conventional; those you like, such as Lilian; Lilian's friend, Joan; the pipe-smoking Miss Gash; all the Joans in your recent novel, are unconventional. What does this consistency of characterization say about Kate Grenville?

KG: I think it reveals a profound longing to be less conventional than I think I am and a profound longing to be braver and bolder and more independent than I really am. It is an extended wish fulfillment, I think. I have just enough of those qualities in me to wish I had a lot more. It's a very great pleasure to write about those women and to imagine myself for a moment in their enormous skins and walk around with their confidence.

RW: With *Lilian's Story,* you won the ten-thousand-dollar Vogel Award. Did this convince you of your arrival as a writer?

KG: It could not have come at a better time. I had just written a book which was absolutely my own book written without influence. I didn't think anyone would even publish it and here judges were saying, yes, this is the book that has come straight out of your sensibility and we like it enough to give it a big prize. This was fantastic, because if one of the others had won, I would have thought I should have continued doing the same sort of thing. The prize also came at just the right time in my career; I had written two books. I had decided that a writer was what I wanted to be. It was terrific, although a bit of a shock, to be asked in the first interview to explain what I was doing. It was quite a challenge, but a good one.

RW: So you had a new way of looking at yourself?

KG: It made me very self-conscious. I had a hard time getting going writing again after that without sort of imagining the questions I would be asked.

RW: Your most recent novel is *Joan Makes History,* commissioned by the Bicentennial Commission. What was your concern in this novel?

KG: The hidden underbelly of Australian history, that is the underbelly that consists of half of the human race that was here, the women, and their experience which has not made it into any of the Australian history books. That, at least, was the initial impulse. I wanted to put the women in, and I also wanted to explore the whole notion of what history is and what it ought to be and what we ought to do with it. Is it more than facts and dates, and ought historians to take a moral stance, as some of them do? What use is history? Is it just to tell us what happened? Or should it tell us something about what we should be doing today? So the novel expanded from that initial desire to have a bit of a poke at men to trying to engage with fairly serious ideas about history.

RW: Are you playing off all of the various Joans that you set up from chapter to chapter, which are a kind of expanded allegorical type, against the one Joan that we follow through a lifetime? Or are you making some statement against public history and private history, or stereotypical history and individual history?

KG: Yes, all of the above. And the other thing I was trying to say was that history is not something that happens to other people. The Joan that we follow consistently throughout the book is also the same person as all the Joans that were born in 1700. In other words, history is what makes all of us what we are. We can't say that it happened to other people in another place. We have to acknowledge that history is our history, even if it's not our personal history. It's what makes us what we are. I think the novel isn't technically a huge success. But I wanted somehow to say simultaneously that Joan is a woman in the middle twentieth century and she is also simultaneously all these historical women in a sort of Every Woman way.

RW: You bring a character over from one work to another. The central Joan in *Joan Makes History* is the same Joan from *Lilian's Story.* Would you comment on this moving of character from work to work?

KG: Partly it's my self-esteem, the desire to recycle when I've got something good, to recycle it endlessly. But more than that, again when I was in America, I read most of Faulkner's Yoknapatawpha series. Reading him for the first time as one who was trying to write, I was struck with what a terrific freedom it is not to be bound by a novel, but to expand, and if you believe as I do, that there isn't any such thing as objective reality or only one interpretation, then to have a series of novels that circle around the same set of incidents is probably the ideal way to get closest to the actual truth of the matter. It is like one's having to read a dozen newspapers to get any version of the truth. I enjoy doing that leaping from head to head, and I think within the confines of a single novel it's pretty hard to do that. You want the reader to be completely seduced by each version as it happens, then right at the end perhaps to be able to say, well, I was seduced in turn by each of those realities, so what does that mean?

RW: At one point Lilian yells on the street, "Do not worry about getting old gracefully, girlie; be foolish and loud if you feel like it." Joan certainly follows that advice, but by the end of the novel, after changing in appearance into a man and then back to a woman and mother, Joan moves into contentment, being a wiser but ordinary woman. Is this a kind of rite of passage, perhaps a feminist's rite of passage?

KG: You've picked up what a lot of feminists haven't. I've had flack from feminist critics in this country who think I've betrayed the cause by making Joan in the end a mere housewife. But one of the things I wanted to say was that the reason why women have been written out of history is that certain things have been defined as important and worth doing and other things have been defined as being unimportant and not worth doing. It just happens that the things that women usually and have always done, and a lot of us want to keep doing, like having babies and so on, have been relegated to the not important part. What I wanted to say was that too is glory, and that too is achievement, and that too is history. So, you don't have to become the Prime Minister to make history. You can make history just as much by being a good human being, by doing terribly humble things like washing the socks and bringing up the children. You can make history as do a lot of men, by doing meaningless jobs that are never going to make them famous. That's a version of history, too.

RW: That's a very Zen idea, isn't it? Chop wood, carry water?

KG: Well, it's an idea that I suppose is a logical extension of a lot of philosophies. History has changed. Social historians look at what ordinary people were doing as opposed to the sort of "great man" theory of history. So it's a sort of inevitable evolution in thinking, I suppose, and it seems to me much more useful since most of us are going to lead pretty ordinary lives and much more hopeful in a way because it says that the destiny of humanity may not be carried by one or two people, who carry a torch on behalf of all of us. We're all doing it. We all have a tiny input. That's pretty idealistic but it seems to me not a bad image.

RW: You are writing about a gender rite of passage and at the same time it has to be an individual rite of passage, where each person goes through the stages of consciousness. Perhaps one ends up where he started, but at the same time the journey is part of that wholeness that has always been there but has to be returned to. And that's what I see you doing in Joan's history.

KG: Yes. You do have to acknowledge all of the alternatives. I think you're right; you do have to take that big trip through all the things you could have done, all the paths not taken, before you realize that actually the path that you are on is okay. But it is only okay if you acknowledge the other paths.

RW: Exactly, if you have an awareness that the other paths are there. The novel ends with a kind of Eastern mysticism, the many and one, each and all are important, the unimportance of the individual ego. You create a holographic paradigm with Joan's realization, "I'm the entire history of the globe walking down the street." Is this how you see it?

KG: I suppose so; it is deliberately overly grandiose because I want it to be a bit funny and to be slightly self-mocking as well as what I really believe. I suppose it is possible to consider those things at once. But while I came to history rather skeptically when I started writing *Joan Makes History,* the more history I read, the more convinced I was that the one subject that ought to be compulsory at school is history. It does tell us what it has meant to be a human being, and there can't be any thing more important than that, how communities of people have tried living together. We ought to be able to get clues from some of the things that have gone before. The other thing is that awful individual search for fulfillment which is incredibly destructive. Most of the worst things that have happened in our culture have come out of that belief in the individual's right to grab for self-fulfillment at any cost. I would once have defended this. Since becoming a mother I've had no question about feeling myself connected. Suddenly you're connected back with all those people. And forward. And you become very insignificant. That's probably a healthy thing, given the fact that most people have plenty of ego and feel that they are the center of the universe.

RW: It's almost a koan. In fact, I wrote out what I was thinking when I finished reading your book, which was that another way of perceiving this is to say that the ego is a lie, and if the ego is a lie, then history is a lie. The phrase that Joan often repeats, "I am to be a woman of destiny," must be seen as self-delusion.

KG: It's self-delusion in the way she means in the beginning, but by the time she gets to the end of the book, she realizes that it means something different.

RW: It depends on how you look at it, or the position on the path from which you're looking. Implicit in *Lilian's Story* and *Joan Makes History* is the notion of parallel universes. In your interview with Candida Baker you say about your writing, "I'm always conscious that I'm choosing one version from an infinite number and any version can be just as convincing as another." Is this the way you feel about yourself or all "selves"?

KG: Yes, I think we are absolutely contingent; some of us are more chameleon than others. We are only a sum of the information and data that is coming to us. People can be blamed for not searching out better data, better information, and I suppose that is what I'm trying to say in the book: "Look, it isn't just one line of information, there is this whole spray and it's all rough in a way." It's like we're vessels filling up with stuff; it just depends what gets poured in. And one of the things books can do is to pour in another set of stuff and if it's done sneakily enough, it might even be stuff that would be normally rejected by the filter system. But if you can sneak it in past the filter, you can actually get another kind of input in there which will then affect the mixing in the vessel.

RW: The current theory in physics of parallel universes is that all one's choices are happening simultaneously, that one is living them out. Whatever "yes" you've said is going on at the same time with whatever "no" you've said. You are simply in tune with only one choice at a time, but they're all going on. All the choices and all the decisions of everyone are going on on various planes.

KG: Intuitively, I think that's how we feel.

RW: At the end of *Lilian's Story*, Lilian tells her taxi driver, "Drive on, George, I'm ready for whatever comes next." Do you feel this positive?

KG: Tht's a hard question to answer. I do feel fairly confident, except that I am conscious that I'm very weak and easily seduced by the alternative, by laziness and taking the easy way. That makes me feel not positive, but I have a lot to be positive about; I've been extremely fortunate in my life and my work. In a way, I suppose that should make me feel less than optimistic in the sense that it's time for the pendulum to swing the other way. Gee, I hope that doesn't happen.

RW: It won't happen; you won't make that choice in this parallel universe.

KG: Right. I won't.

ELIZABETH JOLLEY

was born in 1923 in the Midlands, near Birmingham, England. She began her fiction career by writing stories for the BBC World Service. In 1959 she immigrated to Western Australia with her husband, Leonard, who became the Librarian at the University of Western Australia, and her three children. Trained in England as a nurse, Elizabeth Jolley has also worked as a "flying domestic," a real estate agent, and a teacher. Jolley's fiction, laced with wit, quirky characters, and black humor, is very popular both in Australia and in the United States. The following combined conversations occurred in Sydney in 1988 and in the Jolley living room in Perth in 1989.

Five Acre Virgin and Other Stories, 1976
The Traveling Entertainer and Other Stories, 1979
Palomino, 1980
The Newspaper of Claremont Street, 1981
Mr. Scobie's Riddle, 1982
Miss Peabody's Inheritance, 1983
Woman in a Lampshade, 1983
Milk and Honey, 1984
Foxybaby, 1985
The Well, 1986
Stories, 1988
The Sugar Mother, 1988
My Father's Moon, 1989
Cabin Fever, 1990

INTERVIEW

RW: As the history of Australian immigration goes, you are a fairly recent Australian. Could you speak a bit about your background?

EJ: I grew up in the industrial Midlands in England. My father was a teacher and my mother came from Vienna. My father was in Vienna at the end of the 1914–1918 war, with the Quakers, doing Quaker relief work. He was in prison during the war for refusing to fight, and he brought my mother back as a bride from Vienna just after the war and his father turned him out of the house. He wouldn't take him back, so my mother didn't have a very good beginning. But things sorted out. I grew up in the Midlands. I went to a Quaker boarding school near Oxford, and then I was trained as a nurse. I had one sister and both of us wrote stories. We played with dollhouses, and dollhouse characters still exist in our letters. We still talk about them.

RW: Do you conceive of your characters as kind of dollhouse figures?

EJ: Some of them have come from the dollhouse game. We used to have dialogue for them, little dolls in dollhouses and bigger dolls talking to each other. We used to continue the game in buses and trains, still talking as if from the characters. It became one long novel, but of course I didn't know then it was some kind of novel.

RW: Is your sister still living?

EJ: Yes. She's in England, in the Midlands. We write regularly.

RW: Were you nursing when you met your husband?

EJ: Yes. He was a patient of mine. When he recovered he was better for a long time, not because of me exactly. As he has got older, his illness has caught up again with him. He's an invalid now.

RW: Were you married before you came to Australia?

EJ: Oh, yes, yes. When we came to Australia we already had one daughter of thirteen. Our little boy was six and the younger girl was four. We came in 1959.

RW: Your novels depend a good bit upon your memories of the Midlands and of England. Was leaving England and coming to Australia a good catalyst for your writing?

EJ: Yes. The new country makes an enormous impact on you. Because of this impact, something fresh, you attempt to make a bridge between the past and the present, something which you might not do if you stayed in the same place. I think when you do move, such a big move as this is, I mean coming to Australia, though the language is the same, it is a foreign country compared with the Midlands of England. People often ask me what would my writing have been like if I had stayed in England; well, I don't know, but I think it would have been very different because of the experiences that I've had over here. I've been teaching out in the remote parts of the wheat belt and going to very faraway places, the kind of thing that would never have come my way, you know, so that I've had lots of experiences here that I would never have had in England.

RW: Do you identify anything particularly Australian about your writing?

EJ: Well, I think perhaps the isolation of the wheat belt, the drought conditions. The wishing for land was already with me. My father had a great wish for land. He came from a farming family in Salisbury, and I think I always had a wish for land. But it was an idyllic wish. Knowing more about it now, I know the land can turn really bad on people, with the drought and all the difficulties, and that kind of thing.

RW: You live in a brick, tin-roofed cottage on a quiet street in Perth. Roses and climbing vines are blooming in your garden; the Swan River and the Indian Ocean are a few blocks away. The setting is gorgeous—yet Sydney and Melbourne, the literary centers of Australia, are some 2,500 miles across the desert. Has this geographical isolation been of any effect on your writing?

EJ: As I said, the wheat belt has been an influence. It is quite spectacular and different from anything I've ever known in my life. You can travel for miles on the road and never see anybody. You can get lost and not know where you are. There is a certain wind that rushes through, and sunrise is pink, and the sunset is pink, and it is cold at night, even in the summer. I've used this setting for some of my fiction. As for the isolation of the desert—if you wanted to get published and you sent off a manuscript from here some years ago and you weren't known, the stuff just came back unopened. That was a real disaster. It's not like that now. Things have changed a great deal.

RW: In terms of your writing, does it bother you being so far away from another center of population?

EJ: No. I've lived in Edinburgh, Glasgow, Birmingham, London, and I spent time in big European cities with my father and mother. I think I have always been creative. I was writing before I came to Australia. You have to work very hard wherever you are living. You have to persist and write. It's not any easier to produce it here; you can be just as busy here as you are in a big city. It depends on what your life is.

RW: Tell me about your boarding-school experience. That has certainly influenced your writing.

EJ: Yes. I think boarding school would make an impact on anyone. I, you see, was kept at home for some years before I went to boarding school, so that my first year in boarding school was really a hard thing to manage because I hadn't been in a classroom with children, except when I was very small. When I was about six, I had a year in school; then my father took us away and we had a series of German and French and Swiss governesses and my father taught us. When I first went away to boarding school I was very homesick and I really couldn't stand being with the other children in a classroom, let alone a dormitory, but I got to like it very much. It was a Quaker boarding school, and I feel it was a great privilege to be there.

RW: You write about characters who have lesbian experiences. Did you own time in the boarding school give you insight into this sort of relationship?

EJ: I'll put it this way. I expect that I was a very late developer. And I think I've noticed this in some of the students I teach. Some may not be sexually active, but they are sexually perceptive, you know what I mean? And I think I must have perceived things in other people, not knowing what they were. I didn't even know the word "lesbian" then. Not for many years. You see, in boarding school and then in the nurses' home— when I was training as a nurse you had to live in, you weren't allowed to live out—I think I was very aware of people's relationships in those circumstances, not necessarily having such relationships myself. I suppose a writer is like that. A writer notices or is aware of something, perceives something, then builds on it in imagination, but doesn't necessarily have the experience. Sounds rather dull for the writer, doesn't it? When I was a child, and this was before your time of childhood, many women did live together, but there was no suggestion of lesbian relationships. Schoolmistresses or unmarried women for economic reasons would share a house, share a small car, and it was never suggested, but obviously there must have been relationships because people need them. People take what they need from each other and if they don't have a relationship in one direction they will have it in another direction.

RW: Would you say in your fiction that you are most interested in character?

EJ: Yes. I start with character. I don't write anything until I've got my people. I get my people into a confrontation, or a situation, a dialogue of some sort, and then I start going ahead from that. I start with a little picture of one character, or two characters, and then perhaps a third character that has an impact on one of them, an intruder perhaps.

RW: The conflict comes from the third character coming in?

EJ: Very often, yes. Very often the conflict is either in something that is in one of the characters when one of the characters is demanding too much, or not giving enough, or a relationship that can't take anything from the outside. I'm very interested to observe that there are many relationships that really cannot stand the intruder. And this could be on any level, just the ordinary superficial social level, or the family level, or a close relationship. A relationship between two people that cannot take any kind of other person coming in is a distorted one, really, and many people live in a sort of distortion, but they don't know it. I mean, a writer knows. Do you know what I mean?

RW: I'm thinking of two women I know who live together. They haven't had a sexual relationship in ten years, but one woman cannot bear to have the other woman out of her sight.

EJ: Well, that's what I'm talking about. This happens between husbands and wives. They keep up the social conventions; they have dinner parties and barbecues and they go to bridge parties with groups of people, but in actual fact one is being so possessive of the other that it's like a kind of curse. I'm interested to explore that. And when you explore it, it becomes heightened, and for fiction you exaggerate, but you don't heighten it beyond reason.

RW: Have you had much lesbian response to your books?

EJ: Yes, I have. I've had very touching letters from people who are obviously very lonely. I think possibly they would be very disappointed. On the whole, I don't discuss my married life. I met my husband, Leonard, when I was seventeen and I'm still with him, you know. I was a nurse in hospital and he was a patient. I was in that hospital for two and a half years. We weren't allowed to socialize with patients. Of course, I liked him very much. He was very poetic and very fond of music. It was the kind of hospital where you got to know the patients because they were there for a very long time. But you were not allowed to be overly friendly. But then I kept up a friendship with him and then we married later on. I get letters from people who have never had anything like that. They've not had anyone that they can completely trust or who sustains them. And that's very hard, really. I think they are disappointed that I cannot make either in correspondence or in reality a relationship with them. I can't always write, you know; I have an awful lot of correspondence.

RW: Do you get any militant lesbian correspondence? You haven't done us right, that sort of thing?

EJ: Oh, yes. And the feminists don't care for me. Because in that little film that was made of me I do say, which is a perfectly true thing, that I can't do any writing until I've got my house things in order and I know what I'm going to cook for dinner. You see, I cannot work unless I've got a superficial order. I can't bear to come out from working, if I've been working in the daytime, to find the breakfast things there, no shopping done, no idea what I'm going to cook for dinner. See, the feminists would say, "Why should you do the dinner in the household?" But I've always taken it as my responsibility. A woman once said to me, "Why ever are you making Horlicks for your son?" She was visiting in the evening and I had said, "Excuse me, I must go and make my son Ovaltine," that's what it was, not Horlicks, and she said, "Couldn't he make it himself?" He was fifteen. I said, "Yes, he can, but I like to take it in to him." That was my feeling for my boy.

RW: If you do the cooking and the housework, when do you write?

EJ: I get up about four-thirty in the morning. I used to work right into the night but I found I wasn't working very well. I was too tired. I've tried this four-thirty thing now for about a year. I do find it hard, but I find I get more done before I need to take Leonard his tea. That's around six-thirty or seven. I get more done in that time than I was getting done staying up till twelve or one o'clock. I'm really working better.

RW: When you finish, is that your writing day?

EJ: No, no. I work all the time while I'm doing other things. I use a notebook. But this is the sustained time when I need to sit down and read back a bit and work on a bit. But I often nowadays work in the afternoon, since Leonard has an afternoon sleep. And I am at Curtin University, and I have a room there and I often take my own work there as well as student work.

RW: I like the humor in your writing.

EJ: I can't help seeing the ridiculous side of everything.

RW: For example, the letters at the beginning of *Foxybaby.*

EJ: Yes. The letters are really what triggers off the nightmare, the writer's nightmare which is sort of hinted at in the letters. But luckily, I do have a sense of the ridiculous. I can be very anxious and very frightened as a person, but at the same time I can see the ridiculous.

RW: Have you ever thought of writing a novel of sustained comedy?

EJ: Well, it might fall flat on the page. Someone once asked me to write a funny piece for a journal and my husband explained to me—he's a very clever man—that what makes things funny in my work is where they are placed, what things they are placed next to. That makes the funny situation, or the thing they are leading to. You can't just write a funny thing on its own. It's really a great skill which I don't think I've got.

RW: I think you do have it.

EJ: What I manage to do is to place something so that it will make a funny situation.

RW: An Australian critic recently remarked that in Australia humor is regarded as a lesser form than the tragic. Do you have any feelings about this?

EJ: I didn't know anyone said that. I suppose it depends on what the humor is. I think black comedy, which I've tried to achieve without knowing the name of black comedy—it was only labeled as such by a reviewer of *Mr. Scobie's Riddle*—is the only way in which I could handle that material and of course the only way in which a reader could handle the reading of a book that is on such a sad subject. I can't agree that people think that in Australia. I think Australians have a very laconic and dry sense of humor that comes out and they can make these little side remarks which have you in fits of laughter. Even in writing they feel it.

RW: Sometimes critics refer to your novels as gothic. Do you think of them in that way?

EJ: I heard the word "gothic" attached to *Milk and Honey.* I think sometimes, and this mustn't sound rude, people lose sight of what gothic means. Doesn't gothic mean going into the supernatural?

RW: It can mean that, or just exaggerated.

EJ: I don't think I ever go into the supernatural, but it's clear there's heightened claustrophobia in the relationship in *Milk and Honey.* In the relationship of Hester and Kathy in *The Well* I've heightened the claustrophobia and I suppose the word "gothic" could be applied to that, but nowhere do I strike out from realism, apart from hysteria and fantasy in *The Well,* when the man is having the conversation allegedly with Katherine, but again, I don't regard that as gothic in the true sense.

RW: Then you don't think gothic is a fair label?

EJ: I don't mind, if people feel they need to label. I'd rather have "gothic" than "lavender and lace," which was applied to me, because I'm not a bit that sort of person. I'm not a bit dainty.

RW: Do any contemporary American writers interest you?

EJ: Oh, yes. I like *Paradise* by Donald Barthelme, Thomas Disch, *Poems.* I recently read Carolyn See's marvelous book, *Rhine Maidens.* I like Raymond Carver's short stories. Also, I like John Updike. I suppose I feel that Australia and America have a lot in common and I feel that Australians and Americans don't mind how each other succeed. Britain is not so keen on the success of Australians or Americans. This is a terrible thing to say, but I am British, even though I'm an Australian citizen now. In England there still is a hangover of not wanting to accept something good from somewhere else.

RW: How are your novels selling in England?

EJ: They've sold well to the publisher. The public have been slow in buying. You see, Australian fiction in general doesn't do well. There's a slowness about being enthusiastic about it. There is a tendency in England for people to remain conventional. The Australian bush ballad and the bush yarn will be very acceptable because the British will say that is Australia, ha, ha, ha. But serious fiction may worry them, I think. But America's not like that, do you think?

RW: No, I think we welcome new insights.

EJ: So does Australia. I mean, if you're in Western Australia you've got to welcome and welcome and *find out,* because we've got sea on one side and desert on the other. In order to manage we've got to get across to the Eastern Seaboard; people don't worry here about what's going on in Western Australia, and we've got to get to Europe and to America.

RW: Speaking of getting across to America, millions of Americans saw you on the NBC *Today Show* when it was broadcasting from Australia. How did that come about?

EJ: I don't know really, I guess through my agents in Melbourne and New York. But it was extraordinary to be on that show. It was quite an ordeal, really. Mr. Gumbel didn't ask me what they said he was going to ask me. They told me the subject so that I could be a bit prepared, and then he started with something entirely different. My jaw almost dropped down. I was quite unprepared for what he said.

RW: You've had very good reviews in America.

EJ: Yes. I'm very fond of America.

RW: Let's talk about your recent novel, *My Father's Moon.* I have a feeling this book is autobiographical. Is your protagonist, Vera, a version of you?

EJ: *My Father's Moon* is probably the most autobiographical book that I've written, though there's lots of me in lots of the stories; but Vera as a character is not really me. Her background is my background. The background of hospital and the school and of wartime is very real. The things that the father says to Vera, my own father said to me. But I am not Vera. She outwits people. I don't think I've ever had that quality, although I might have been crushed by people the way Vera was. I've made things into fiction, but it is very hard for me to know where truth ends and fiction begins; do you know what I mean? Certainly the thing the father says about the moon, my father used to say to me. That was a real thing. Does it spoil the structure of the book for you that it was a real thing?

RW: No. I like that it's a real thing.

EJ: Do you? Good. I sometimes get a bit irritated when someone who has written something says, "This has really happened, you see." I don't want to be the kind of person who sticks by the truth, because I am essentially a fiction writer, but I think you need bits of truth to write from. I am doing a lot more with my father in the novel I'm writing now, *Cabin Fever.* It knits together with *My Father's Moon.* I'm filling in with things I left out. For example, my father started school dinners in the school where he worked, because the children were very poor. He bought them meat and paid two women to cook the meat and vegetables, and he served dinner to a whole lot of children who didn't have enough to eat. He did that before there was the policy of school dinners in England.

RW: Your father remained important to you all his life, didn't he?

EJ: Yes. We had a tremendous communication with letters. When he was run over, the curious bereavement was the bereavement of not writing letters. I hadn't seen him for eleven years when he died, but he was always in my mind. I was composing letters in reply to his letters. The minute I got a letter I wrote one back to him. I would just make time that day to send him a letter back. On the day he was run over, on his way to the dentist, he had started writing a letter to me. He never finished it. My mother sent the half-letter on to me. It was a big shock, a big bereavement. On the whole, I suppose I go on talking to him in my head, now, even when I'm grown up and old. It was in 1977 that he got run over.

RW: Would you talk about the structure of your novels? I'm particularly interested in the discontinuous scenes in *My Father's Moon.*

EJ: I wrote some parts of those scenes, some episodes, as long ago as 1953 or 1954. Then I couldn't face writing them anymore. I have a whole terrible novel in a whole lot of notebooks where some of that material occurs. What I then did was to pick out and make little episodes. It was the only way in which I could handle the material. Really, what the reader does is to weld the pieces together by the spaces. The reader reads very creatively for a book like this. It might be a book that's difficult for some people to read. I don't know.

RW: It keeps the reader turning back and forth to see if he's missed something, to see what's been left out, but I didn't mind doing the work as I was reading. I was curious as to whether you were trying to pull together a lot of different pieces, or whether you were intentionally putting the gaps in.

EJ: I think I left the gaps because I just wanted to pick out the essence of the girl's experience and her rite of passage, her personal journey. Instead of putting in every cup of tea and every bit of the journey, I just put in bits that were vivid for me to write.

RW: I've heard you say that sometimes you write your ideas or bits of a scene on scraps of paper . . .

EJ: I do that. I have lots of little pieces of paper that I will clip together and then I can spread them out. I also have another method. I have a manila folder that I open out, and I might make little squares and write little bits in there so that the pages are actually resting on what is like a map of the structure of the book. Very often some of the things I write on that folder are the very last things of the book. They will be the actual end of the book. One of the troubles with *Cabin Fever,* the book I'm writing now, is that I haven't actually written the end and I'm putting it off all the time. I keep going back and reworking the pieces I've done. For some reason, I can't seem to face the end.

RW: Are you saying that you often begin with the ending?

EJ: Yes. In *Sugar Mother* the thing that I wrote first is the scene in which Daphne and Edwin are changing a baby. At that state I didn't know whose baby it was, but they are changing a baby and they are not very competent and its legs are stuck up in the air. Daphne is giving a violin lesson to someone. I wrote this scene first in the novel and then I worked toward that. It's an odd way to write, isn't it?

RW: Yes. It's interesting that you can write a novel in all directions, crablike and in reverse.

EJ: It's the way my brain works, or doesn't work. Many people write a novel beginning with the beginning and work right through to the end. I don't do that. With *The Well* I wrote some bits with two women brushing each other's hair and then I wrote the piece again and discovered that one woman was older than the other and that there were silver stalks of corn in the moonlight that they could see through a high-up window. Then I wrote a passage where both these two were trying on clothes and they were trying to make a parcel for an orphanage, so then I realized that the younger one had come from an orphanage. You see, bit by bit, it sort of grows and you can piece it together. By this time I'd given Hester her name and gotten her age more or less in mind, and I then wrote the part in the shop where Hester sees the thin white face of the orphan in the shop and decides to take her home. I had already written those other bits and I had to have something that would lead up to that. I didn't discover that Hester was lame until Kathy was having the imaginary conversation with the thing that is in the well and she actually tells him that Miss Hester wears a leg iron. So then I had to go back and have a rewrite because you can't just have something in one place that doesn't occur all along. To start with, I made a great mistake in *The*

Well in trying to make the conversation between Kathy and the person in the well a confrontation conversation, when really the way to do it was to have Kathy report it in hysteria to Miss Harper. Then it was all right. Otherwise, it was hopeless.

RW: As a report, it didn't have to be realistic.

EJ: No. Also Hester has a migraine, so we are not quite sure if she is hearing properly what she is listening to. It took me a long time to discover how to write this scene. I had this dreadful, wooden dialogue between Kathy and the man in the well. It was so wooden; I thought, I just can't do this book at all.

RW: Are you revising all the time as you write?

EJ: All the time.

RW: You use the open ending often. Why does this form appeal to you so much?

EJ: People say I do this, but in *The Well,* for example, everybody is pointing in the direction that they are going. Kathy is going to meet Joanna at the station. She is obviously going to go off with her on the religious kick. Miss Hester is having a lift with Mrs. Borden and going back in the other direction. She is going to pick up Kathy. The Borden children have asked her to tell the story of how the lamp got smashed on the front of the Toyota, and Hester will tell them but nobody will believe her. It is all pointing toward the fact that Hester has been through an internal drama where she confronts herself over her attitude toward Mr. Burns. She's met the woman in the shop who is going to be a writer and has given her the outline of the novel she is going to write like *The Well.* She will probably make friends with her. She won't be on her own; she'll manage. Both Kathy and Hester have got something from each other. It's true that Hester created a distorted relationship, but Kathy has gained a great deal about living that she wouldn't have known. Hester has lived out a teenage childhood that she never had, so that they have both gained. I see it as an optimistic ending with them pointing toward going on living. Hester will probably be revisited by Joanna and Kathy and it won't be such a terrible experience after all. I didn't write that in so many clear words; I just feel that. When I've listened to people at book clubs talking about *The Well,* I have noticed that they've made their own book. I've been amazed, but I guess it's good if people create.

RW: What about the open ending of *My Father's Moon?* Your protagonist Vera thinks she sees her friend Ramsden on the train. Out of confusion she doesn't speak but thinks she might take the same train the next week, might see the woman again and might speak.

EJ: You have to go back to the beginning of the book, where Vera is leaving Fairfields. She can't expect to find Ramsden in London. It's been too many years; Ramsden may be anywhere. I know some reviewers feel the ending is a flop because Vera doesn't speak to the woman on the train and find out whether it is Ramsden. But if she finds that it is not Ramsden on the train, it will be an awful pity. It's better to hope that it might be Ramsden, and the only way to have hope is by not speaking. Also, if she really met Ramsden at the end of this book, it would be rather like rounding off a romantic Victorian novel.

RW: So you do like the open ending? You like forcing the reader to participate.

EJ: Yes. A reader can make up his own version. I always feel if a person has something to hope for then he has something.

RW: Why is Ramsden a woman? Why not a man?

EJ: That's an interesting question. You mean, why didn't Vera adore some man? She did adore Dr. Metcalf and was seduced by him. She thinks him marvelous, while in fact he's part of an older couple seducing a young girl, isn't he? They are a *bon vivant* pair who get their excitement by initiating someone.

RW: There are suggested lesbian characters in the novel whom Vera is not attracted to; why is she attracted to Ramsden?

EJ: She admires her so tremendously. I feel humans need someone, or something to look forward to doing. I have a short story called "The Shed" in which the woman never puts the shed up. A woman once rang me up and said, if it had been her, that shed would have been up years ago. My woman is dreaming about where she will put her shed. You've got to have something to look forward to. In the case of Ramsden, Vera needs someone she can admire. In *Cabin Fever* a character points out that Vera has been lucky in that she has loved someone that she didn't know all about. Perhaps that is a great joy in loving; you love someone when you don't really know the whole person. I think there is something in that too. I hope that doesn't just sound like a sour old woman talking. But you keep the dream of the person. It's like seeing a piece of land for the first time. You buy the land and you get to know it quite well and get to know its difficulties. You never really see that land again as you saw it the first time. It's a bit the same with people, getting to know someone, developing a loving friendship. After that the friendship is marred by all sorts of things, relatives, mortgages, all the things that come in and crowd a relationship. Does this make sense?

RW: Yes. And particularly in regard to what Ramsden stands for.

EJ: A good deal of the things Vera thinks about Ramsden have never taken place between herself and Ramsden. They are purely in her mind. In *Cabin Fever,* she says this. Ramsden is something unattainable that she keeps at a distance. Therefore, she never really speaks to Ramsden, or to the woman she sees on the train and thinks might be Ramsden.

RW: You frequently use a protagonist whose morality is questionable, or at least against what is seen to be the norm. Choosing such a protagonist is a risk for a writer. Why do you use this kind of character so often?

EJ: Do you mean like Daphne in *Sugar Mother,* or Miss Snowden in *Miss Peabody's Inheritance,* people like lettering sticks so you can have the bizarre or eccentric next to them? I do do that. Mr. Bird in *The Well* is a good person without being boring. Is that what you mean?

RW: No, I mean characters as protagonists who are flawed, who are a bit immoral. The protagonist in *Foxybaby* or Vera in *My Father's Moon.*

EJ: Vera is cunning; she will do somebody down partly because she has been done down. She is a survivor and that is her way of survival. I am really interested in survival, people who survive by fastening on to someone or by some resource within themselves. I divide people a bit like that. I think Vera is resilient; she will survive, even though she is naïve.

RW: Do you ever use an unreliable narrator in your fiction?

EJ: I don't know. What about Miss Thorn in *Peabody?* Matron Parks in *Mr. Scobie's Riddle?* I saw her as a person who is really evil but not able to help being evil because of the circumstances she is in. I wouldn't want to put her forward to the reader and say. "This is a bad person"; I would rather show the character in such a way that the reader can look right around the character and decide what is good about her and why she is bad. The same thing with Vera.

RW: Vera is really amoral, isn't she?

EJ: When you say amoral you mean "without morals," that she hops right into bed with Dr. Metcalf . . .

RW: Yes, and she does dirty tricks.

EJ: She does small hurtful things; it's a bit pathetic. But I think the things Vera does are for her survival. She feels that there are things in the world that she could manage and do, but to get to them and to those people seems out of the question. I'm still not answering your question, am I?

RW: Perhaps your characters are complicated in the complex way that modern characters are presented. Maybe you don't see things in terms of moral or immoral.

EJ: I don't see anything as being that easy. To come up against some sort of conflict and resolve it and then another conflict and another resolution. There is always something that will turn back on the person, or the person will let himself down. With *The Well,* I wanted the characters to be really flat on the page and easy, just to make a mystery story, but I couldn't do it. It became very complicated.

RW: What stimulated you toward the particular claustrophobic, bizarre fiction that you write? I don't know any other Australian or any contemporary, for that matter, who writes as you do.

EJ: I don't know. Maybe I've got something growing in my brain.

RW: You spoke earlier about your childhood.

EJ: Well, my parents were very didactic people; they told things. I listened in to grownup conversations and then invented things. My parents used to read aloud to us. Mrs. Viggars in *Foxybaby* comes from a grotesque person who used to visit my mother. I was charmed by listening to her; but I enlarged her. Fiction has to be larger than life. At eight, I was kept home from school and given lessons from over the wireless, as well as from a governess. Listening to the radio lessons and to books performed over radio was very good for my imagination. And then, as I've said, there was my sister and the dolls. We invented a whole world of people.

RW: *My Father's Moon* is very beautifully, very poetically written. Were you trying for a different effect than in earlier works?

EJ: No, I just wanted to have the voice of the narrator. She is telling everything, how she sees things, how she feels, how she talks to herself. I've done the same way of writing in *Cabin Fever.* I am very fond of our language; I like to use the language to what I feel will be the best advantage. I was afraid somebody in the editorial side might want to alter the language because I have repetitions when Vera is going over things in her mind. But they didn't want anything altered.

RW: *Sugar Mother* was your first novel about married people. In *My Father's Moon* you are back to single people. Are you more interested in singles and their conflicts?

EJ: There are some married people in *My Father's Moon* and *Cabin Fever.* I am interested in both. But it's true, I do have a lot of unmarried people, don't I? I don't quite know why, but I am not interested in writing about the ordinary suburban marriage. It tends to bore me. I would have to put something a bit bizarre or odd in it if I did write about it.

RW: There is sometimes a similarity among your characters. Are certain of your characters versions of your former ones?

EJ: Oh, yes. I would think so. I would think that Miss Thorn could end up like Miss Hailey in *Mr. Scobie's Riddle.* When I first wrote *The Newspaper of Claremont Street,* though I altered this, the flashbacks in Weekly's life were the stories about the mother and son and daughter in *Five Acre Virgin.* Weekly, the old cleaning lady who wants a bit of land, could well be the continuation of many of my characters. Vera and her family are used in both *My Father's Moon* and in *Cabin Fever.*

RW: Would you talk about your use of entrapment in fiction?

EJ: I think we are all trapped. Sometimes, by something that we do, or think. Even by our own standards, by what we regard as being necessary to do, say in keeping house, or in our work. We are trapped by routine, by other people's needs. I see marriage as an endless trap. I don't mean to say that you're not happy in your marriage; you can be quite happy, but still be caught in it. I belong to an age in which early on there was very little freedom for women in married life. I've struck out for a kind of freedom. Not that my husband intended to entrap me, but conventionally you are invited out as a couple, not as a single person. That has changed, but even now if I am invited out by myself, I have to make a reason for wanting to go. That's just the way our conventions are. My mother and father had a bit of a separate life. My father was very religious and he had his church life. My mother had no part in that life at all. She didn't want to. She was a lapsed Catholic. They were Quakers together for awhile. My mother went out on her own because she had a lover, a person that she taught German to. I traveled with him and her to Europe. My father was very gentlemanly about the whole thing. My mother's friend would come to Sunday lunch and both the men would talk about their different sermons. They would talk about the sermons during the first course and the weather during the second course. Then my mother would go with her friend to his house and have afternoon tea which was made by the housekeeper. Then my mother would give him a German lesson. My father used to be very restless sometimes on those days.

RW: I can imagine.

EJ: I didn't understand things until I was really grown up. The only thing that made me think many years later, only just a few years ago, that my mother's relationship was a lover relationship was that when all three of them got old my mother used to be very unkind to this friend in a way that if she hadn't been intimate with him, she couldn't have been so unkind. Do you understand what I'm saying? There are certain ways of being unkind that people have between each other that only exist because they have been very close at some time. People who have not been that close could never be unkind in that particular way.

RW: This goes back to the situation we were talking about which you create in your writing. The third person coming into a relationship and everything then becoming shaky.

EJ: I like looking at what distortion occurs and how people react.

RW: This must have been formulated in your own childhood.

EJ: I think so, very much so. Only now at sixty-six does it begin to dawn on me. I don't say when I am writing that I'm writing this because of this and this that happened when I was a child, but when someone like you so intelligently speaks, then I begin to understand something about what I'm looking at. But I think it's fascinating, really. My mother used to teach an evening class and she used to come home very late if the weather was bad, and my father used to pace up and down quite white-faced until she had got in. Then she would pour out the whole thing; she'd tell him everything and I'd be hanging over the banisters to see if they would quarrel. I would run down and placate at the age of seven or nine, or whatever, if they did quarrel. If it was all right, I would go back to bed. On those evenings my mother seemed to need to talk to my father.

RW: I'd like to read a passage from *My Father's Moon* which is quintessential Jolley. "The storm is directly overhead. I am wet through and the mud path is a stream. The trees sway and groan. I slip and catch hold of the undergrowth to stop myself from falling. When I look up I see there is someone standing half-hidden quite near." Will you comment?

EJ: Why is that Jolley?

RW: You have to tell me.

EJ: What am I introducing? Something a bit sinister and a bit odd, and an outsider who comes in.

RW: Even the earth slips away.

EJ: I have that also in a series in *Stories.* Three times a boy calls out. He calls, "Help! I'm stuck! Help! I'm drowning! Help! I'm falling!" I think that's what we do. We're stuck, drowning, and falling.

RW: You seem often interested in creating a sense of impending disaster. Even the elements are contributing.

EJ: That's one of the beauties of using landscape, especially the wheat belt and the landscape in Australia which can be so menacing and frightening, at the same time so beautiful and magical. I've used this landscape in *The Well.* You can parallel the character's thoughts and feelings by the external things and that makes it stronger to me. You can also show something about a character by putting in a piece of music. Landscape, trees, weather, they're all a bit ordinary, but they are important.

RW: After all the novels you've written, is it getting any easier for you to write?
EJ: No. I have to make myself write. When I'm actually composing I get quite worn out. During the day while I'm doing other jobs I'm composing and making notes and I think, "Ah, if only I wasn't doing this. If only I didn't have to go and write this down." And I have to write things down, because I don't remember. When I'm driving the car, I'll say to my husband, Leonard, "Will you remember these three words to recall?" On the whole, he will remember. It's awful to have to keep track of your characters and your ideas. I would like to be quite free and be a vegetable sometimes or just go somewhere and sit and knit.
RW: Why do you keep writing?
EJ: I don't know. If I did, I probably wouldn't do it. I don't feel compelled to write, but when I am writing I've got to write down the things that I think because I'm creating something, but it is an act of the will that makes me go on writing. It isn't something that wants to pour out of me. I have to just get it out of me, or get it from somebody else. I listen to other people and put down things that they say.
RW: In your fiction you are intrigued with the reality a character imagines; do you think that through the imagination we construct the worlds we live in?
EJ: Yes. Things do exist as they are, but how we feel them often determines how they are for us.

THOMAS KENEALLY

The Place at Whitton, 1964
The Fear, 1965
Bring Larks and Heroes, 1967
Three Cheers for the Paraclete, 1968
The Survivor, 1969
A Dutiful Daughter, 1971
The Chant of Jimmie Blacksmith, 1972
Blood Red, Sister Rose, 1974
Gossip from the Forest, 1975
Season in Purgatory, 1976
A Victim of the Aurora, 1977
Confederates, 1979
Passenger, 1979
The Cut-rate Kingdom, 1980
Schindler's Ark, 1982 (published in the United States as *Schindler's List*)

was born in 1935 in Kempsey, New South Wales. He was educated at St. Patrick's College and studied seven years for the priesthood, but was not ordained. After leaving the priesthood, Keneally taught school and began to write fiction. He has twice won the Miles Franklin Award, for *Bring Larks and Heroes* and for *Three Cheers for the Paraclete. The Chant of Jimmie Blacksmith* won the Royal Society of Literature Award and was made into a motion picture. Although he had for a long time looked beyond Australia for his subject matter, Keneally gained his strongest international critical attention with *Schindler's List,* which won the Booker Prize and the *Los Angeles Times* Fiction Prize. In 1983 Thomas Keneally received the Order of Australia for his service to literature. Thomas Keneally lives in Sydney and New York, where he has been writer in residence at New York University. The following interview occurred in Thomas Keneally's New York apartment, with a few statements retained from an earlier interview in Memphis, Tennessee.

A Family Madness, 1986
The Playmaker, 1987
To Asmara, 1989
Flying Hero Class, 1991

INTERVIEW

RW: You've published eighteen novels and several books of nonfiction since you began to write in the sixties. As an Australian, what has it been like earning your living solely by writing?

TK: Writers can go broke in America living off a population of 250 million. The Australian population when I began writing was 10 to 12 million; it is now 16 million. This fact is a powerful determinant of Australian writing and publishing. American culture is self-sustaining. The nature of life in America and the values in America are a source of material which Americans who read can all readily relate to. It is terra cognito to them. There are only 16 million people to whom Australia is a known planet. For this reason Australia is not a self-sustaining culture. It can't afford to ignore larger cultures. You see it in our film directors. Of the six films nominated for the Academy Award for 1989, two of them are by Australians—Peter Weir, *Dead Poet's Society*, and Bruce Beresford, *Driving Miss Daisy*. They can make *Poets* and *Daisy* and all the ichnography, the subtext of those films, doesn't have to be explained back to Americans the way an Australian subtext would have to be explained back. These two sets of circumstance create great strengths in American culture; the self-sustaining thing means that there are many American writers who can earn a living out of the American market. The Australians have been forced from childhood to take an interest in other worlds; this produces a characteristic strength in them and produces a corresponding strength in their imagination about the rest of the world. But it is simply a fact that the size of the country does govern the prosperity of Australian writers. Combined with that, there is less private patronage in Australia and the state has had to be the major patron of the arts. This creates a powerfully different atmosphere in Australia from the atmosphere in America.

RW: You set out to be an international novelist from the beginning, didn't you?

TK: This was partly a commercial consideration. You see how I stumble over that word. Commercial considerations are thought to be the lowest of artistic considerations in Australia; the state is supposed to look after these considerations by giving the writer grants, and I am delighted that the state does do that. But yes, I did start out looking beyond Australia, but even before there was a commercial reason. In Australia we were raised to believe that there was another world out there where Europeans really lived. I was about to begin my first year of primary school when A. D. Hope wrote his famous poem "Australia" in which he said we were "second-hand Europeans pullulating timidly on the edge of alien shores." That was a common perception which pervaded society in Australia when I was a kid. Australians have had a passion for travel, a need to get out and compare, whether it be Memphis or Minsk, to try to understand that new place. Before people know who they are, the passion for self-definition is a driving force. We are desperate to know who we are, to put ourselves in a world context and to understand ourselves in that context. I've always been a traveler. I have also always liked to return home. Travels and returns have been mirrored in my books.

RW: You are Australia's best-selling serious novelist, yet the Australian critics have often been less kind to you than critics in other English-speaking countries. Why has this been?

TK: I don't know. The Australian critics are getting kinder. I think there is a pattern of premature canonization in Australia. Australia wants writers and it makes them bigger than they are at the start and sometimes it turns on them if they don't obey the rules. Then if the writer sticks around a lot he ultimately becomes a protected marsupial. The same pattern occurred in the life of Patrick White; the middle years were bitter for him. He was attacked by great men, like A. D. Hope, let alone philistines. There has been a pattern of not liking expatriates. Australians also tend to feel that anyone with talent shouldn't be writing about anything but Australia, because Australia needs to be labeled and classified. There might have been some of that with me. But in the pattern of departures and returns, I am happy to sense a kind of modest return going on, with some of my works being looked at more sympathetically. I have also had it said to me that no one can write as fast as I do and have quality. There is probably a certain truth in this, but the speed with which I write is a temperamental thing.

RW: If you wrote less, would you write better?

TK: If I wrote less I would probably write technically better, but I do feel a conviction that there would be a driving force missing from the work. I sometimes feel that too much of the driving force of my early work, which was young and mad and chaotic and nihilistic and alienated and had problems in it, may be gone because of the limited degree of technical sophistication which I have acquired. I think writers are driven to write at a particular pace by two major forces: temperament and the meter of their talent, which is different from writer to writer; the other one is economics. The publisher says that if you can finish the revisions by December we can publish the book in time for next year's Christmas market. Then one is severely tempted to fit in with that. Anyone who denies that writers are driven by such considerations is living on some other planet. I find that the pace of writing which I have been sustaining for some years is about the right thing temperamentally for me. The vision of the present book I am working on is always very important for me. That intensity only has a certain life span. I wish the weight of that intensity could last longer, but again that is temperamental. There are writers who keep an intensity ten years over one small novel, and there are others who simply have to write a book about every eighteen months. However, I feel some really long book coming on. I see it spreading over two or three years. I see myself spending a longer time than ever before on a book.

RW: Were you particularly shaped by growing up in Australia as an Irish Catholic?

TK: Yes, it did shape us because in many ways Australia was the most Irish of all the New World countries, so there was a heavy Irish component from convict times forward. With it came an attempt to live a monolithic Catholic life in the midst of a protestant and nonconformist plurality. That attempt ultimately broke down and Australia turned us all into what it would, which generally has been strange subtropic paranoid hedonists. Until after my childhood, Australia was much like Ulster translated to the Western South Pacific. To be a Catholic and to be Irish was a political identity as well as a cultural and religious one.

RW: What led you into the priesthood?

TK: The priesthood was a powerful institution, not only religiously but socially and politically. It was attractive from many points of view, but particularly to somebody who wanted to do good. It was when that kind of priesthood was demonstrated to be impossible in a pluralist society in the late mid-twentieth century that I and many others left the clergy.

RW: What do you mean *that* kind of priesthood?

TK: The kind that was effective. The priest was not only the confessor of sins, the consecrator of the bread and wine, but he was also a social worker in his community in a very real sense. He was the only social worker available in those days before there were courses and degrees in the subject.

RW: Your major interest in going into the priesthood was in this area of social service?

TK: It was a powerful motivation, yes. It seemed to be a worthy way to live a life. Celibacy seemed a small price to pay.

RW: You trained seven years for the priesthood and then took yourself out of seminary. What was it like coming out of the priesthood? What effect did it have on your becoming a writer?

TK: I had always done a bit of writing; therefore, writing became an objective after I got out. The reason for my getting out was that I had something very close to a crack-up. I had the sort of absolutist tendencies which led me to become a writer, I suppose. In the era when rock and roll was being born, I was trying to achieve a kind of mystical perfection. Part of the proposition of having a religious life, as in transcendental meditation the world over, was to get to the divine presence, to touch the face of the Absolute or to experience the Absolute. This was a heady ambition. I was very interested in the mystics, Teresa of Avila, Saint John of the Cross. I suppose that at the same time I was too young and neurotic to make this pursuit in a meaningful and unneurotic sort of way, so there was a great deal of ego bound up in this attempt. I found the solitude of the seminary life, which I tried to keep fairly exactly, increasingly difficult to deal with, to the point that by about a month before I was to be ordained I was emotionally exhausted. It became apparent to me that I was too weird to be ordained. I went away and spent some time in the outside world and was to come back and be ordained; I'd already been ordained a deacon. Among the places I spent time was at Hay as a builder's laborer for an uncle. This introduced me to a broad spectrum of Australian society. I began to realize that there was a robust world out there that couldn't give a damn for my main objects in life.

RW: How old were you?

TK: I went into the seminary at seventeen. I was about twenty-two at this stage. I went back after Hay, and I knew as I prepared for ordination that it felt wrong. I was in a better mental condition, but I knew it wouldn't wash anymore. I had changed. When I left the last time I almost immediately began writing. I worked for the Department of Territories for some months, then taught in a private school. Desmond O'Grady published a couple of crazy stories of mine under an assumed name in the *Bulletin*.

RW: Your novel of the priesthood is *Three Cheers for the Paraclete.* Among the things of concern in the novel is the story of a priest who has a nervous breakdown after he falls in love. Was this based on your personal experience or on observation?

TK: I wish my crisis had demonstrated itself in such a direct and unignorable manner. Seminarians didn't have much chance to fall in love, not even with each other. I didn't have contact with many women at all during those years. I remember that the robust Baroness von Trapp came to the seminary and insisted on eating with us, which was considered an extraordinary event. She brought three of her great strapping Aryan daughters, with whom half the seminary fell in love, even as they ate the mutton and trifle at the top table where women had never eaten before. The crisis of love in the novel wasn't my own, but I was aware of it happening to other people, after ordination in particular. It was looked upon as being one of the classic perils of being a priest. The priest in the novel is based on a New Zealand priest I met when recovering from my seminary experience. He was convinced that the Pope was going to relax the rule of celibacy. He was in love with someone he wanted to marry and his certainty concerning the Pope was unbalancing him with hope.

RW: Your wife, Judy, was once a nun. How long had you been out of the priesthood when you met her?

TK: About three years. She was no longer a nun. She was a very glamorous looking nurse who had hordes of boyfriends and was very worldly. She was more worldly than I was because even though she had been a nun, she had been in a nursing order and she had come up against the range of humanity. She was nursing my mother and we fell in love. Inevitably, if you have a strong personal experience which you share, in our case the church, you don't have to explain the subtext of who you are and what you have been doing with your life. In a way we had both been marked and inhibited by the experience. I felt two things that were powerful in my life and which I had to get over: a profound disappointment in the Australian church's failure to live up to its ideals of good treatment for its own people (seminarians leaving the seminary either very ill physically or mentally and with no involvement on the church's part in their care); the second thing was a growing loss of faith. *Three Cheers for the Paraclete* is part of the writing out of that anger and disappointment. One's individual anger and disappointment is not an excuse for imposing a novel on the world, but the young writer doesn't know that.

RW: Many of your early novels are stories of alienation. Much of contemporary American fiction still deals with this subject. Your characters now seem to act more than to mull. Have you grown tired of personal angst?

TK: I'm glad that you feel that my characters tend to act because the greatest problem of the novelist, and not many writers talk about it, is that novelists are passive people by and large, and if they are going to put themselves in the central character, the problem everyone will tend to have with the book is trying to work out why the central character is such a wimp. It is true that my characters tend to act more, and you probably feel less like shaking them than you did in the early books. The novel of alienation was more popular in the sixties when Vietnam was on and when everyone was so prosperous that they could be alienated. Look at the kid in the movie *The Graduate.* He has graduated and is assured of a job and a future affluence and this prospect fills him with such spiritual despair that he puts on a wet suit and stands at the bottom of a swimming pool. Subtle despair and alienation of the apparently mad but truly gnostic seeing individuals was the stuff of many sixties novels. It was accentuated by the fact that the greatest Australian writer, Patrick White, always seemed to write in those terms. There was always a small body of true seers in the book; the rest were people whose only birthright was their antipodean brutishness. This is certainly a viable view of Australia, and Australians in the fifties and sixties seemed to go to a lot of trouble to prove that they were like that. I was heavily influenced by White and still am, but I began to question some of his artistic and temperamental tendencies when it came to dealing with humanity. I began in the Patrick White vein, but in that vein there is a writing off of many individuals, of the society, even of the species. After awhile with such alienation, you run the risk of painting yourself into a corner. It is a fine corner, but it is still a corner. If you write off the race except for a few people upon whom the spirit breathes, you undermine the necessity for further novels.

RW: You said once, "I went through a long phase when I couldn't understand or deal with the present at all in my writing. I felt the best way to deal with it was through the past. I find history the easiest mode to deal with." Would you talk about this idea and the novels which have resulted?

TK: There are several novels, among them *The Chant of Jimmie Blacksmith, Gossip from the Forest,* and *Confederates.* Let me take *Gossip from the Forest.* There is a direct fuse line, a fuse that is still burning between the past and the present, and the fuse that runs from the railway carriage at Compiègne where the delegates made the armistice at the end of World War I is still burning in Eastern and Central Europe, and it is still burning in Australia. Australia has never been the same since World War I. We were raised to believe that Europe was the center of everything. No one told us in Australia that Europe was finished in 1919. That is what *Gossip* is about—the decline of Europe. By understanding something about that decline we can understand something of the present. There is also a lot of that connecting the downfall of Europe to the present in *A Victim of the Aurora*, a much-neglected book of mine.

RW: One critic has pointed out that you are more interested in the large questions of history rather than in seeing history from an intimate or personal point of view. Is this true?

TK: It's partly true. I've got a theory about history. You don't take the big figures; you take the more peripheral figures like Erzberger in *Gossip*, or in the case of an extremely neglected novel of mine, *The Cut-rate Kingdom*, the press secretary to the Australian Prime Minister. I've tried to look on events in my historical novels from a peculiar slant to see the vision of the time through the consciousness of either an extremely individual or somewhat peripheral character. I am interested in large questions of history and attempt to have them reverberate through the individual. The connection between history and dreams and history and intimate emotion is there in Erzberger's experiences, in dreams and intimate emotions. I feel that it's okay to be involved in the large questions of history, but there should be some added value, some component of value in the novel which is of the kind that only the novel can give.

RW: What particular ingredients do you look for in a historical situation that would make it right for fiction?

TK: I look for some connection to the present, an event in the past which is like a lightning flash that lights up the present. You know figuratively, symbolically, and imaginatively why we have what we have through reading the book. That's the aim.

RW: What was your interest in *Confederates*?

TK: This was a very benighted effort to write a book on the Civil War because the Americans have been no more interested in the realities of the Civil War than the Australians have been interested in confronting the convict system. When Robert Hughes published *The Fatal Shore*, a lot of people in Australia said, "Ah, it's overstated." You have to pretend that the place in which you live wasn't once like Auschwitz or Siberia morally, or in terms of brutality. *Confederates* was an effort to correct certain tableaux of the Civil War which changed America forever and generated modern America. The tableau of the plantation house and the roaring cannon and the bloke with a sword in his hand—all those inappropriate images they used. That war seemed in a way the beginning of World War I or a model for World War I. If it had been studied more, it would have had its appropriate impact on the planning that led to World War I. It would have had an impact on what the generals knew in World War I and might, therefore, have saved lives. That fascinated me, the fact that the war was fought by a Southern proletariat who didn't necessarily have any investment in slavery at all. I thought this was very interesting because of the way the war has been portrayed. Southerners weren't necessarily dying to preserve slavery.

RW: Irony, then, is one of the things which interests you in the historical situation?

TK: Absolutely. In *Confederates,* the contrast between American politeness and the savagery of the events was something that interested me. But it's very hard to get beyond stereotypes. They are even now represented on the cover of *Confederates* in the present American edition. I was also interested in the novel in things like the verbal felicity of the rustic expressions of that period. I am very interested in dialect and am often criticized for my passion for it. In *Confederates,* most of the exotic figures of speech were taken from the journals of the day, the sermons of the day, the political and military speeches of the day. I was criticized for my use of dialect in *The Playmaker,* but some of the early dialect has survived into modern Australia, and that interests me.

RW: Your novels often deal with a character making a moral choice . . .

TK: This probably comes from temperament and conditioning, a tendency to see the world as a battle between the great dinosaurs, good and evil. All lapsed Catholics like me are concerned about morality because they are afraid they'll be struck dead if they're not. There's that concern even in *To Asmara,* so it doesn't look as if I'll outgrow it. Moral choices are something that I find very dramatic in human beings. It puts them on a knife edge; it brings great drama into their lives.

RW: Does doing the right thing replace God these days?

TK: No. The characters in my book don't take any particular moral comfort from trying to do the right thing; they are all mad monks in a funny sort of way. Even Delaney in *A Family Madness* who is a rugby league player is a bit of a mad monk and wants to save this beautiful blonde Belorussian girl. In the case of Darcy in *To Asmara,* he is driven by a sort of moral deception into Africa in a way which he can't escape. It's more like the writing of a novel. The writing of a novel can often seem to have an inescapable destiny. Characters like Darcy and Delaney are driven by moral imperatives which they would often rather not have to deal with, but which seem to them to be inescapable and which have an obsessive impetus to them. The moral dilemma is bearing down on them and driving them along like destiny itself. It's a force, a force like the fates. It's more that idea in my fiction; I haven't sorted out for myself the idea which you propose. The phenomenon of someone being driven is something that is in all the novels.

RW: Robert Stone in his *New York Times* review of *To Asmara* says, "Thomas Keneally has always been a quietly passionate student of the impulse toward love and light in a fallen world." Is this an accurate statement?

TK: I'm not going to look that gift horse in the mouth. But the question with which I was raised, which we were told was the biggest question of our childhood, was not the question of social progress or Utopia on earth; it was the question of the redeemability of humanity. How does humanity redeem itself? Is the race a goer, will it float? This is the question that concerns the great Patrick White in his novels. This has been a general artistic preoccupation for a long time. A lot of people have written as if there is no hope, that there is no use even asking the question. Other writers have written as if they take it for granted that the race is oddly redeemable through the crazy and the benighted grandeur of the way it behaves, Steinbeck, for example. I explicitly address this question in two recent works, *Schindler's List,* where you have a man who is a savior despite himself, almost without knowing it; and it arises in *To Asmara* through the question of whether it is possible that the Eritrean rebel society has made a moral step forward, as I suppose you could say the American revolutionaries made a moral step forward. Some ideas then were released into the atmosphere which would be forever after used by other human beings as a means of defining their own dignity. We see this sort of thing in the rebellions in Beijing and in Eastern Europe. Are the Eritreans on the cutting edge of the moral evolution of human kind? That question is explicitly asked in the book. A number of critics have said, "No," and that it is a sign of the author's partisanship that he thinks it possible. But I've been there and they haven't, and it is possible, so the question of redeemability, social and individual, is something that I seem to write about without being able to help myself. In some books I show my skepticism by writing about it in ironic ways, the nature of Schindler's virtue, for example, but there is not a lot of irony in *To Asmara.*

RW: Do you think the modern novelist hides too much behind irony and alienation? Or, should the novelist take a moral stance as you do in *To Asmara?*

TK: We are a very morally insecure generation because of the decline of the old systems of belief and our uncertainty about new ones. I suppose in these matters it is easier to expect the worst, especially at the end of a century like ours. If you look at what has befallen the people of the Horn of Africa, of the Sudan, or even the Australian Aborigines—we'd like to believe that we have learned something from every disaster of this century, but in fact a lot of things are in a worse state now than they were at the start of the century, particularly in the Third World. Cynicism is a justifiable refuge for writers writing about other human beings, and it is sometimes easier reading cynicism. I suppose some writers hide in irony and alienation; perhaps I do; other writers write that way because it is their greatest strength and they are defining a problem.

RW: Again, quoting the *New York Times* review, Robert Stone says of *To Asmara*, "Not since *For Whom the Bell Tolls* has a book of such sophistication, the work of a major international novelist, spoken out so unambiguously on behalf of armed struggle." In the war, you do clearly believe that there is a right side?

TK: The right side is the side in favor of a settlement. The Eritreans are more in favor of one than the Ethiopian government has been up until this point. To this extent, there is a right side. It doesn't mean that there are glittering spirits on one side and evil spirits on the other. I don't have a naïve addiction to the idea that the Eritreans are all good and the Ethiopians all bad.

RW: Do you feel that novelists should become more engaged with real issues and less concerned in playing a game between the writer and the text?

TK: It is not as critically fashionable to write a novel of real political engagement, though such a book is fashionable with the reader. It is considered by some critics as a sort of bad taste. But if what Robert Stone says is true, then there are a lot of such issues which could benefit from a look by a fiction writer. Books of this nature are relatively rare. I have written in this genre just this one time. It doesn't mean my other books will be like that. But it is curious that this sort of passionate and political tale-telling used to be more critically respectable.

RW: *Schindler's List* and *To Asmara* are differing forms of the non-fictive novel. Is this form more compelling to you now than the more usual novel form?

TK: No. *Schindler* is on its own in that it was a book based on interviews with specific people. Those people are rendered in the book. Their names are given and they are identified, so there is an immediate connection with reality. *To Asmara* isn't meant to be documentary. It is a fictional journey, but it depends heavily on my own record and memories of a journey I made in April and May of 1987.

Nonetheless, it is not a literal rendering of my journal. It's a novel. It is distinct from *Schindler* because it takes liberties with characters and events. There is an entire segment about the traveler's background as a community adviser in Central Australia, and the point of that section is to set up an emotional resonance for him as a character and also a continental resonance between Australia and Africa. This is entirely dreamed up.

RW: Where did you get Lady Julia?

TK: She was based on an English woman who had taught in the Sudan for many years and had been engaged in the question of the mutilation of girl children since she was quite young. I knew about her, and I met a small number of women who had been to Eritrea and were galvanized by this question. I learned more about the issue from women filmmakers and from a doctor I consulted in the Sudan. Ten thousand years of this generation-by-generation mutilation is about to end. It is an extraordinary change in this society.

RW: Did your characters grow from your accumulation of notes and interviews along the way?

TK: Yes. Christine is entirely fictional but is based on the only sort of tourists in the Sudan these days, occasional long-haired youths from the West who want to see the confluence of the Blue and White Nile. Henry is based on various cowboy water-drillers whom I met in the Sudan. Fictionally, I wanted to put together a party of travelers, a sort of *Canterbury Tales* group. There is a bomber pilot whom I know who is a prisoner of the Eritreans and upon whom Fida is based, and there is a French filmmaker upon whom Masihi is based, but neither of my characters is the real person.

RW: Do you write to formula? Conflict, love interest, betrayal?

TK: No. I don't sit down and think this out, though these things do occur in *To Asmara.* There can't be a deliberate acknowledgment of these strategies; you can do them, but they won't resonate if they are not automatic, if they are not what the book demands. I have very little faith in writing to formula because you have to make your plans up front. I've never written a book when the plans were made up front except to an extent in *Schindler's List* because all the research had given me what was going to go into the book.

RW: Would you talk about your problems in re-creating Schindler, a real person? I am interested in the accuracy of the small things in the novel. For example, how were you able to make such a simple statement as this, "Oskar was a slow reader"?

TK: Various former prisoners of his mentioned that. If enough of them mentioned something like that I just put it in. I was careful to put in things that other prisoners could agree with so that there was more than one source. I remember a number of people saying that he wasn't a reader or that he was a slow reader.

RW: It is remarkable to me the work that went into this book, the layering and layering of material and all of it real. Would you talk about the research?

TK: I met Leopold Pfefferberg in late 1980. He had a great deal of documentation, photographs, letters, even SS telegrams, things taken by the Jewish people who ran Schindler's office. He was the Schindler survivor who first mentioned the idea for a book to me. I used his two filing cabinets of documentation as the basis for a treatment for a publisher, trying to get backing for a research journey which we ultimately took the following year. I interviewed Schindler survivors in Australia, New York, Frankfurt, Munich, Warsaw, Krakow. We went to Austria and Israel and with Pfefferberg's help I interviewed many survivors, including Schindler's wife, who was in poor health and living in Argentina. When I got back to Australia and was ready to write the book, I sat down and color-coded the details, different color codes in every document for each period of time and for all the details. I had a lot of photographs, so it wasn't hard to visualize.

RW: Writers often take up a certain place or a certain time, yet your novels jump from century to century and from country to country. Joan of Arc, a polar expedition, the Civil War, World War I, World War II, war in the Sudan, Australia at the time of Federation. How are you able to re-create time and place without long periods of study and immersion in these times and places?

TK: Most of my books have been written about people and periods about whom I've been thinking since my adolescence. I have, therefore, a head start on most of the subject matter. Even a travel book I'm writing at the moment about the American Southwest—that's been an obsession of mine for years. I've been in the Southwest a lot over the years. I didn't choose to write this book; I was asked to do it, but it is typical of a lifelong process of absorbing a large amount of information and then turning the heat up when the time comes to write the book, reading more and absorbing a lot to fill up the flotation cells of the book. You simply let the strange air of other people's memoirs and histories enter the flotation device until there is enough buoyancy there to lift the novel up.

RW: You've written in novels and in nonfictions about the Aborigines in Australia, as recently as in *To Asmara.* Your best-known work on the subject is *The Chant of Jimmie Blacksmith.* Many of your consistent interests as a novelist come together in this novel—

historical setting, political/social/religious oppression, failed love, obsessive characters. Is *The Chant* a particularly Australian novel? Is it important that it be read in terms of Australia?

TK: A bit of yes for both questions. Just a few weeks ago down in Northern Arizona we happened to go to one of the oldest towns in America, Walpi in the Hopi mesas. There was a ceremony going on in which a number of initiates had descended into a ceremonial lodge with a hole in the roof and a ladder down through it. A Hopi priest and his acolyte emerged from another lodge near us. The priest was dressed for the ceremonial initiation, but the acolyte was wearing a Bruce Springsteen American Tour T-shirt. This conflict writ so large on that kid's chest is one that still fascinates me. It is a conflict which occurs in Australia and amongst the Pueblo, the Hopi, the Navaho. The fascination for me is with the fact that one culture is a virus on another, that one culture can be so pernicious to another without any malice, that there are cultures that find it hard to coexist in the same world. There are many Aborigines who believe sadly that our culture is a virus on theirs, and there are many who are caught between the two worlds, the gulf between the two being very difficult to bridge. Those who do bridge the two are the great heroes of this whole berserk process. Jimmie Blacksmith was someone who was trying to bridge the two cultures. Great emphasis is put in *Jimmie Blacksmith* on the malice of others, the malice of whites. If the novel has a fault it is the young man's tendency to make the settlers appear as malicious as I could make them. The question of straddling the gulf recurs in *To Asmara* in the part that deals with Central Australia. It recurs crucially in the book that I'm writing at the moment. There is a character in it who is in a way Jimmie Blacksmith updated. He is an actor, a dancer; he's been on the *Today Show,* yet he has tribal and ritual responsibilities. He is straddling two worlds with some success. The book is partly about the pressures on the people in the dance troupe who live within the two cultures. This is a continuing fascination with me.

RW: What effect did winning the Booker Prize have on you?

TK: The Booker was important at the time I won it because I was in a bit of a mid-life crisis. I had tended to be written off to Australia at that stage as someone who just wrote about non-Australian subjects. The Booker served as a symbol. I've found myself coming back in Australia, being considered a writer worth taking some notice of. I hope my future work will continue this trend because it's nice to be read in a serious way at home. For those reasons the Booker Prize was important to me. I think it is the most significant prize in the

English-speaking world, if the truth be told. Unfortunately, it doesn't impact upon America because America has been a separate publishing world.

RW: Do you feel that there is still out there one large theme, one large unwritten novel which will be *the* Keneally novel?

TK: Yes. I think there is a massive Australian novel, but I'm not sure what its form is. I'm thinking of going back to the town in New South Wales where my grandparents had a general store. I would like to write a novel which is both fantastical and at the same time based on newspaper reports of the incidents which occurred there in the Edwardian era when Australia was still Mars, when it was still the backside, the blind side of the universe. I am interested in the odd forms that human consciousness and human behavior took there, isolated on the North Coast of New South Wales, accessible to Sydney only by coastal steamer, the odd forms that human consciousness took on in that environment at an age when Aborigines were still initiated there, at a time before the great ruination of innocence and the great bloodletting of World War I. But that's only one aspect of what the book would be concerned about. I would like it to be a quintessential Australian novel the way that Günter Grass's *The Tin Drum* is such a quintessential German novel. I see it primarily as being a celebration of ancestors and of weirdness.

RW: Will this be the great Thomas Keneally novel?

TK: I hope so. There's got to be one one of these days.

DAVID MALOUF

Bicycle and Other Poems, 1970 (published in the U.S. as *The Year of the Foxes and Other Poems,* 1979)
Neighbours in a Thicket (poems), 1974
Johnno, 1975
Poems 1974–1976, 1976
An Imaginary Life, 1978
Voss (opera based on Patrick White's novel), 1978
Wild Lemons (poems), 1980
First Things Last (poems), 1980
Selected Poems, 1980
Child's Play, 1981
Fly Away Peter, 1981
The Prowler, 1982
Eustace, 1982
Harland's Half Acre, 1984
Blood Relations (drama), 1987
The Great World, 1990

was born in 1934 in Brisbane into a well-to-do family of Lebanese and English extraction. Educated at the University of Queensland, Malouf has taught at his university, in England, and at Sydney University. As a young man he spent ten years in England and Europe. In 1978 he stopped teaching to write full time and now divides his year by living in Australia and in Italy. David Malouf has received numerous prizes for both his poetry and his fiction, among them the James Cook Award and the Australian Literature Society's Gold Medal for *Neighbours in a Thicket,* and again the Gold Medal for *Child's Play* and *Fly Away Peter.* His novel *The Great World* won the 1991 Miles Franklin Award. Australian critics responding to a recent poll named Malouf's novel *An Imaginary Life* as one of the top three contemporary Australian novels. The following interview occurred at Malouf's house in Sydney.

INTERVIEW

RW: Unlike Stow and others who seem confirmed expatriates, you live a kind of migratory life, dividing your year between Brisbane and Sydney and Italy. How have you evolved your pattern of living and writing?

DM: I didn't necessarily think of myself as becoming an expatriate when I went away. When I decided to leave my job at Sydney University in 1978, I did that because I thought I had things to write and that I might as well write while I had the energy to do it and while they were clear in my mind. I cashed in my superannuation and bought a house in a place where I could afford to do it, and that was Italy. I also had friends there. I wanted to take myself right outside the literary world here and all the pressures that are on you if you are in a literary scene. I wanted to take myself where I wouldn't get reinvolved, so there was no point in going to England. In England I would have been reading the reviews and the magazines, and these were things I didn't want to do. So I took myself to a place where I didn't really have the language for doing that. I've always been pretty certain that you write best in isolation, and the greater the isolation, the more pressure you put on yourself to write. I wanted to go and lock myself away and see what I had in my head. I did that for the first two years. I came back briefly, but mostly I just stayed in a small house in Italy in the village where I was. I didn't think of myself as living in some exotic place or in a place that was romantic to me, because it wasn't romantic to me. I know Italy too well for that. I didn't think of myself as living the literary life of an expatriate. People think you sit around cafés. There was one dreary little bar in the village, and no one would want to sit in it. There was nothing in my mind romantic about it; I was really putting myself in fairly harsh conditions of isolation under which I thought I might find out what I could do.

RW: That began a pattern for you, going and coming . . .

DM: Yes. I actually like Australia very much. I like living here. I came back as often as I could afford in those early years. I didn't have a house in which I could live in Sydney, so I went willy-nilly to Brisbane which is where my sister lives. I stayed in her house as I would my place in Italy. I didn't get myself involved in any way in life in Brisbane again. Brisbane, which is the place I come from, is a place which I really only know as I knew it when I left at twenty-five.

RW: Most of your fiction has been set in or near Brisbane. How important is the sense of place to you?

DM: Where you begin in the world is always a kind of magical and paradisal place and also a hellish place. You get it all at once. No other place you ever go to has the same richness of sensory phenomena as the place where you first experience things as a child and as an adolescent. Often when I find myself moved by something I want to write about, it presents itself to me in a place that has the light and texture and air of that place I grew up in. A large part of my formative life, adolescence, and early manhood was spent there. It was a smallish place with a very different history and a different social structure from the rest of Australia. It also seemed like an interesting place that no one else had got into fiction. Both of those things kept me going for a long time.

RW: You've said that particularities of Brisbane have made you a different Australian writer than writers from elsewhere in the country, the river that divides the town into sections, the hills, the architecture of the houses. What do you mean?

DM: I've always been interested in the mapping of the city you live in, the way you mythologize, make it symbolic. I have written a long piece in *12 Edmonstone Street,* which is about the first house I lived in. The architecture of Brisbane is quite different from that of the rest of Australia and I was interested in discovering how the people who come from southern Queensland see things differently, read the world differently, because the first architectural spaces that they come upon are unique. I wrote a long exploratory piece about that large wooden house with its verandas and its area underneath the house as an attempt to discover what the model is that I used for mapping the world. I assume that once you have discovered that model, you go on using it and applying it elsewhere and it becomes a model for all sorts of things: for your body, for your psychological reading of things, maybe even your moral, your metaphysical reading of things. I wrote sixty or seventy pages about my first experience of that house and how a child gets inducted into the world of space and light and time, how you get inducted into the world of objects which are the bearers of the culture in a society; how a household creates a mythology, a model for how a mythology gets made. I am interested in knowing why I see things the way I do see them and how useful as a continuing thing those early models might be for going on exploring the world.

RW: You've said, "It seems to me that it takes about fifteen years to catch up with my own experience." What do you mean by this?

DM: It's less an interest in the events of the past than the way you deal with them, the pattern of the way a mind deals with reality. I have no particular investment in the past. It seems interesting only in that it is inside the present; it's also going to be inside whatever future there is. I don't have any particular nostalgia for the past. I don't see the past as some people in Australia do as being more admirable because it was simpler. The past is always simpler because we see the pattern of it. It was also a crueler and more conformist and less tolerant Australia. I don't have any particular investment in the country's past or my own past. I am interested in the way I read the past, that more than the events or the objects of the past. I'm interested in an evolving interpretation of the world. A lot of what a writer has to do is to go against the grain, to go against your own nature if you are ever going to shock yourself into discovering new things, so the past is something I can go against and reject in terms of what I want to do now.

RW: What do you mean, "go against"?

DM: People tend to believe that what you do to create things is to go with what you are. Quite often things really happen because you are going against what you are as well. There is a passage in *Harland's Half Acre* about the artist creating himself by going against his nature. To go with your nature sometimes is too easy, too much a passive giving yourself up to what is acceptable, what is already there. You have to go against that to see what else you might be able to do or to see what happens, what comes out of the pressure of pushing hard against what you are. I have a great belief in the energy that comes through opposition.

RW: You have spoken of the notion of time as continuity, a kind of continuous present. In *An Imaginary Life* Ovid says, "It is summer. It is spring. I am immeasurably happy. I am three years old. I am sixty. I am six. I am there." Would you link these ideas together?

DM: I think of time—if you put it in spatial terms, it seems to be less like something strung out in a line than a medium you might be floating in. I've always been interested by the way in which when we dream we are in a kind of no time. It is very difficult to know how old you are in a dream. That may be a deeper version of how we are related to time than the more useful and practical way of dividing it up into days and weeks and moments, maybe a more healing one too.

RW: In your first novel, *Johnno*, the reader finds the first of your co-dependent young men, Johnno and Dante. What are you doing here? Are these two parts of the same nature?

DM: I think so. The book is read a great deal in schools in Australia, and on occasion when I am at a school I am asked if it is an autobiographical novel. I usually like to say, "Well, if you mean am I the Johnno character, yes." That usually stops them because they assume as people always do that a character who says "I" is the writer.

Again, I'm interested in exploring those oppositions. The powerful attraction and rejection between those two characters is a way of working out my own swings between a kind of recklessness and anarchy and a wish to be centered and not to move. I think all the writing I do has to do with this sort of opposition between the two complementary or oppositional types, involvement and withdrawal, action and contemplation. I go back and back to that kind of opposition. In some ways I've always found that the most interesting thing to write about. I realized quite early on that the thing that made something like *Macbeth* work and why it can't quite work when it is played is that Macbeth's argument about the murder is argued out in the play by being dramatized between the two characters. It only really makes sense if Macbeth and Lady Macbeth are two halves of the same total personality. I realized that at about thirteen—I think it became my only notion of how you could do that kind of thing in a work of fiction. I have done it over and over.

RW: Your second novel, *An Imaginary Life,* is considered to be among the finest novels in Australian literature. Would you talk about how you came to write this novel, perhaps say something about the story line, about your intent.

DM: I can't remember when it first occurred to me that I might like to write a book about Ovid. But I know that what I was really interested in first was the problem of the poet who has to begin all over again because language is taken away from him. The idea came out of poems I was writing at the time. The central idea of the book is, I think, an original reading of why Ovid is exiled. In my book he is not exiled because he has seen anything or done anything; he is exiled because of who he is and what he is. The punishment is not that he should be sent to somewhere at the edge of empire, but that he be exiled from the languages he speaks, that he should be put in a place where he loses both Latin and Greek. That seemed to me to be the most extreme thing that could happen to a poet who lives through language. This was where I actually began. I suppose I had written most of the early part of the book before I hit upon a complementary idea which was that of the wild boy, which came out of the notion of having somebody at the other end, somebody who has not yet discovered language and who might be given language and through language might discover that he is not an animal but a human being and after that a god. All this was related to the idea of metamorphosis. But all of that really came as a plot when I was well into what I was writing about Ovid. The preface, which is about the child, got written after that. What I was also working on at the same time was a book about Australian experience. When Europeans say that this is a book that no European would have written, it has something to do with that question about being at the edge of the known world and having to discover how you make that the center. It has something to do with how you make an authentic experience for yourself that may run counter to both history and geography. It is a kind of book about Australia. It has taken us a very long time—only in the last couple of decades have Australians stopped thinking of themselves as being at the edge of everything, feeling that history always happens somewhere else, that experience elsewhere is authentic and that ours is not, that literature could only exist somewhere else and not here. It has taken us a very long time to believe that where you are is the center, and I wanted to put Ovid through the experience of discovering that, so that in a way the book is an argument about Australia as well. I've noticed in the last few years the novel has come to be regarded here, too, as an Australian novel rather than an exotic prose poem about a Roman poet or a wild boy or something else.

RW: As a young man did you feel a sense of geographical exile?

DM: Yes. Perhaps my generation was the last to feel it as a problem, educated in what used to be called the "New Britannia." It was a problem of having all your sensory life very strongly in one place and your language coming from somewhere else or the literary or cultural world belonging somewhere else. It's a question of making that authentically yours rather than secondhand. That has always been the great problem of Australia.

RW: Would you talk about your concern with language in *An Imaginary Life,* the act of naming or the metaphysics of naming?

DM: Until I wrote *Johnno* I had written poetry, interested as poets always are by what magical kind of process it is that allows a purely arbitrary set of syllables or sounds to stand so powerfully in your mind for real objects, events of weather, or emotions. I supposed I had it impressed on me, the arbitrariness of that but also the magic of it, by having grandparents who did not speak English, who clearly had other incomprehensible words for objects, so there was something very personal in the magic of making a sound and making that object come into existence, not in the world because it was there all the while, but in your mind or on a page. That still seems to me to be something miraculous and inexplicable each time it happens. I think also the way in which we name things geographically to bring ourselves home to the world we live in is a very moving kind of thing. After all, naming is one of the earliest, most private things that defines us as human, the fact that we can name the objects of our world, the places that we live in.

RW: In metaphysical terms, I'm thinking of the divisiveness of naming. Once you have named something, you have separated yourself from that something through the name.

DM: Yes. In fact there's a passage in *An Imaginary Life* that makes this very clear when Ovid realizes that he is part of the phenomenon or that the phenomenon is part of him, so that if it is raining, he says to the boy, "I am raining" or "I am thundering," while what we say, given our language, is "It rains" or "It thunders." That kind of separation Ovid recognizes as a step forward, but also as a kind of loss. I think that the paradox of what language is is again very moving; the way in which we lose the world by gaining a certain kind of power over it is something we can't reject, but it is part of the situation which in religious terms has been referred to as the Fall. It is a state we can't go back to, but we can know what it is we have come away from. There's something quite moving in that human situation.

RW: We tend to describe our lives, ourselves, in terms of nouns rather than verbs, as though life or parts of it were a finished rather than a continuing process.

DM: Yes. A lot of *An Imaginary Life* is about a kind of mystical process in which you see everything as continually evolving and moving and yourself as part of a process rather than as an entity. I know people who find that very disturbing in the book. For example, the passage where Ovid imagines himself as a pool of water and the deer comes and drinks him up. It's a passage a number of people have told me they find disturbing enough to be almost revolting.

RW: Why is that?

DM: They find in it a kind of passivity that is alarming to them because it is destructive . . .

RW: To the ego?

DM: Yes. It scares them.

RW: In the end of the book, Ovid says, "I am entering the dimensions of myself . . ." He is pushing away the old self to "let the universe in." You write from what seems to me to be an Eastern perspective—the ego dissolves into the whole, the drop returns to the ocean. With merger, transcendence occurs. Is this correct?

DM: Yes. I think that when you are writing, if you are writing at a certain kind of depth in yourself, you have to let a lot of what you know already drop out of your head, if you are going to let a certain kind of writing happen. I think a lot of that book got written for me. A lot of ideas got into it that I didn't know I knew. There were certainly things I hadn't worked out beforehand. Things get said, and you say to yourself, "Oh, that's what I think." It's a process like being asleep in the most wakeful possible way.

RW: How are Ovid and the wild boy versions of the same self?

DM: There is a much more primitive and innocent and unconscious self that Ovid has rejected to become the rather smart-assed poet he is, and part of the process of the psychology of the book is his rediscovery of that child in himself. That's why there is the business of the secret child, the little companion he had when he was young. The return to that child is also a process for him of working out his own way of dying, so that child who is himself which he has come from and rejected also becomes a kind of psychopomp, the spirit that leads the soul to death. I wanted to do all that and at the same time have that child be an absolutely real and separate self of its own. Then at the very end of the book Ovid is able to let go, not to have control of or to keep part of himself.

RW: Would a Jungian reading of the novel be a good approach? Ovid is moving from his social consciousness to a deeper presocial awareness?

DM: I don't know as much about Jung as I would if I were a better-informed person. The Jungian interpretations of the novel I've seen usually take me to task for not being more mature, not saving my soul. The novel has a lot to do with reconciling yourself to death. If I had gone through the Jungian process and made myself a more mature person, I wouldn't have had to write it.

RW: Patrick White uses a quotation from *An Imaginary Life* as an inscription for *The Twyborn Affair.* I'd like to read it and have you comment. Ovid says, "What else should our lives be but a continual series of beginnings, of painful settings out into the unknown, pushing off from the edges of consciousness into the mystery of what we have not yet become."

DM: I'm always, I think, impatient of things that get closed off and finished and only believe in things that are still open and moving in some kind of way. A couple of examples—I hate all those notions about Australia that tell us what Australians are like, that this is our national character, that this is what is central to the Australian mind. I feel comfortable with the notion of Australia as a place that is still in the process of being made. Things are changing all the time. I feel comfortable, as obviously some people don't, with things that are not yet settled and things that are not determined and things that are going to go ways we haven't predicted. That's one thing. I also like in ending books to try to keep the tense of the book open at the end and the ending in some ways suspended. I hate nice, neat, closed things. I want the book at the last moment to be open and going on in time in some way that I am no longer in control of. That's a habit of mind. That's all I can say about it.

RW: The open ending is for you an illustration of the fluid nature of time . . .

DM: Yes. I am quite interested in tense in writing, even the way the narrative places itself in the reader's time, some kind of continuous present. I find myself wanting to reject the continuous past tense even in narrative. I don't really like the form of the novel to be utterly chronological. I like shifting the chronology around.

RW: Well, some shifting then. You've won the Patrick White Prize. He quotes from *An Imaginary Life.* I know you are friends. Would you talk about your friendship or ways in which he has influenced your work?

DM: I don't think anyone could be writing in Australia without negotiating that great presence. It's really difficult to know. You can say, "Well I would never have even dreamed of doing these things or thought they were possible if he hadn't been there to show that they could be done," or you could say to yourself, "I would have done all sorts of things if he hadn't already done them." There are several things about Patrick's writing which attract me very much. One is something which he shares with other novelists that I admire very much in this century, like Faulkner, for example, or Lawrence; that is, a belief that what is going on inside people who would appear to be very ordinary and completely inarticulate is in fact very rich and it is part of the writer's business to express that richness. Even if the people themselves are quite inarticulate, the writer does not have to accept that inarticulateness. He can be articulate on their behalf. I think Patrick does that wonderfully. As a writer he is very like Faulkner and Lawrence. That is what I would like to do. The extent to which that puts you in debt to each of those people or even finding your way in the interstices of their work, trying not to repeat them, is a risk you have to take as a writer.

The other thing Patrick did which is immensely liberating to any Australian is to deal with another kind of Australian, Australians who are literate and interested in the world of culture and the world of spirit, and he simply places them as naturally in his books as they in fact do exist in the society, although a lot of literature until that point would lead you to believe that there were no such people about. So in both of those things one owes to him and one wants to follow. Also, he saw that the continent is a great subject, that there was a matter of Australia as there was for Shakespeare a matter of England, and he took that on in big symbolical or metaphysical or problematic terms, and again I think if you want to write at any size here you have to do that, too, always at the risk that he has been there before you.

RW: You both share spiritual awe at the commonplace, the parings of a carrot, the migratory pattern of birds, the oneness of the spirit and the flesh, body and mind. Would you comment on your own spiritual sense of the connectedness of things?

DM: I don't know where that comes from, but I feel it quite strongly, and I think if I have any sort of notion of what the sacred is, it's in that area. I think the issue I would take with Patrick and his work is a disconnectedness which I feel. He has a very strong Manichean reading of the world, of Evil against Good, Darkness against Light. I don't think I have any feeling for that at all. He has a very strong sense that the spirit is only attainable at the expense of the body or that the body has to be rejected in some sort of way, and I don't think there is any sense of that in my work. I would hope that body and spirit are not oppositions in my work as they are in his, so I would want that kind of connectedness to be as central as any other, that is that the spirit doesn't exist apart from the body and that the body is in some ways what the spirit works through and thinks through and lives through. I think this is very different from Patrick's view.

RW: Again, this seems an Eastern idea, a kind of yin-yang, where the good and evil and light and dark are gradations of each other and are participating in each other and are both necessary.

DM: Yes. They aren't always in conflict. I think one of Patrick's qualities is that he feels able to be a great judge. There is something very judgmental at the center of his work. That is a great strength; I also think it is a great weakness. It's something I don't want to have, and I think there is no judging spirit that I want to work over the novels. I'm sure people see that, too, as a weakness; but it also seems to me a possible strength. I don't have that strong moral stance that can separate the sheep from the goats. I actually like goats. This seems a useful way you have offered to me of explaining what I feel I stand for.

RW: Have you done a lot of Eastern reading?

DM: No. It comes out of temperament. I believe people are their temperament.

RW: You have published books of poetry as well as novellas. Is there a lyrical connectedness in style, or a thematic similarity in your work?

DM: I wrote poetry for a long time before I wrote prose that I thought publishable, and I think that you learn habits of working as a poet which I've used in making the fictions, so I think they are in their structures very poetic. I hope the writing is as tough as prose ought to be, but also as tough as poetry ought to be. I think I've always structured the novels as I would have structured a poem, that is to find something that interested me and then let the novel create itself by association around that idea, by its oppositions, by the metaphorical extensions rather than its necessarily logical ones, and so the structure of the novel is often clearer around certain images or idea images than it is in terms of plot or chronology, and I think that's probably a habit that I learned from poetry. I tried to write many times what eventually became *Johnno.* You know, it's that first novel that you write out of some quite painful, particularly autobiographical experience you need to deal with, and I could never find the tone for doing it. It was always all wrong. It was only really when I looked at poems I had written, a poem like "The Year of the Foxes," which is a straightforward autobiographical poem, that I realized that if I went to the tone of the poem that I'd written some ten years before and simply picked that up and wrote the novel using that, there would be no problem, and there was no problem and I could write the novel from beginning to end because all I had to do was hit the tone I had hit years ago. It takes you a really long time to learn something.

RW: Do you go back to poems now as you are writing?

DM: No. I don't necessarily now. But it's very important with autobiographical material that you find out what the convincing and heavily scented voice is for making it happen naturally. I think once I had written that novel I thought now I could write another. I think what you discover—no one ever tells you this—is that having written one novel doesn't help you to write the next one. Having written five doesn't help you write number six. Every time there is an essential problem that has to be solved and nothing you've learned before is any help in doing it. But nevertheless the first one got written that way.

RW: If I had to suggest one novel to illustrate the beauty of your writing, the duality of light and dark, it would be *Fly Away Peter.* Would you talk about your concept in this novel, how you paralleled the lives of the young men, the flight of the birds, the death of the soldiers . . .

DM: I think *Fly Away Peter* is a good example of what I was talking about in terms of the poetic way of structuring the novel. I began with the young man with the birds. I was interested in the birds because here was a marvelous symbol but actual fact of the kind of world that Australians live in. There are the birds that do go back and forth across the world, who do belong to both hemispheres and that have no doubt about what the wholeness of their life is, and it is contained in their heads in the way of a map so that they do see the world as a whole as we who live on opposite sides of it don't necessarily. I then wanted the young man to go to the other side of the world in some way. Given the sort of person that he was, it seemed more likely that he would be sent there rather than choose to go like a Henry James character. He had to be taken against his will, and a war seemed to be the way that this would happen. And World War I seemed more useful than World War II. You can't really talk about these as conscious choices. All this choosing might have taken place in twenty seconds. I can't remember. In a way it all fits itself together for you. But the war became useful in terms of the theme, and you can explore that, the way the war is the right thing to push the book into the direction you want to go.

RW: You fly the reader up through the heavens in the first part of the book, then drop him unsuspectingly into the butchery of combat in the second half. How did you learn to write the kind of realism you get in the war sequence? I've never read anything stronger.

DM: It's quite strange. I wrote the book in Italy, and I wrote the whole draft of it with not much material at hand. I knew what was going to happen and I did all that. When I came back to Australia I realized I was going to have to find particular dates and days and battles for Jim Saddler to be involved in. I worked out what regiment he ought to have been in, the 41st or 42nd, and I went to the RSA, the Returned Service Association, and asked if they had a battalion history for that regiment. Some very interesting material came out of that. Going past the lunatic asylum and the glue factory came straight out of that regimental history. But everything that makes the emotional impact would have existed in the first draft. It's interesting the way you understand at some point the sentence or the paragraph to which the whole book has been leading. It's as if it has always been up there and that's what you're working toward, except at no point did you know that that's necessarily the way the book was going. This came to me toward the end. It is in a very long sentence where Jim Saddler is running along in the battle and kind of everything he is and knows gets into that sentence and that's what the book has been leading up to. I liked, myself, the things which move away from this at the end of the book, the scene where he meets Clancy in the potato field and the last scene where the woman who is the photographer sees the figure in the surf.

RW: The ending of this novel is similar to the ending of *Johnno* and *An Imaginary Life*. All three end with a character's death and his transition from one level of consciousness to another. Would you speak about these endings, perhaps how a personal philosophy might be reflected?

DM: Again, you go back and back to what it is you want to know about yourself. Without being consciously aware of it, I think I am obsessed with the moment of death and trying to work that out through the writing. I don't necessarily mean how one might face death, you never know how you might face it, or what it might be, but so you can see death in some kind of way so that it, too, is not just an abrupt event that ends something, but death becomes part of a whole process of being, a whole process of the world which might be separate from you while you are a part of it. I think why that is a point I keep pushing the novels to and why I need to keep facing that situation and keep writing about it in what I hope are different ways I don't really know. But that's what I do.

RW: You always show death as a transition, never as an abrupt end . . .

DM: I think that's part of what I was talking about earlier. Simply not seeing the world as separate events in that way but seeing the world as an evolving, fluid process. Again, I think I probably don't have a very strong notion of what ego is. I don't mean in my personal life; I may be as egotistical as anyone is. I don't seem to have a very strong idea of how you separate self off from everything else. That probably works stronger in writing than in living. I can't guarantee people won't say of me, "He's the most egotistical person I know."

RW: In *Child's Play,* you write about a terrorist in Italy and in *Harland's Half Acre,* about an Australian artist. In these novels you continue with a kind of character who has absorbed you again and again, the man who is abstracted from life. Is this preoccupation autobiographical?

DM: I don't know. You write from a point from which you feel comfortable, from which you can move into a world. I suppose that the character who is abstracted and isolated in some kind of way without necessarily feeling outcast is where I honestly feel quite comfortable for watching the world. None of those characters feel themselves to be alienated, they are not outcast characters. They feel themselves as absolutely involved in the world and that the world is important to them while being isolated from it. I don't think the modern sense of alienation is an important factor in my work.

RW: What I have in mind is detachment. Do you live with a sort of detachment in the midst of social or creative activity?

DM: I suppose I do. It's difficult to look at it from outside. You live any way you can live.

RW: You've written for the stage twice, the libretto for *Voss* and more recently your first drama, *Blood Relations.* What was it like to go public with your imagination through the medium of drama?

DM: I really don't like any of that. I felt it was the sort of thing I ought to try. You don't know what you might discover about yourself by going out and doing something you've never done, but that whole public world I really find painful. I worked with good people who were very helpful, but I found it an uncomfortable way to be working. I like to be in the book and behind the book. I don't want to come out from behind the writing at all. That becomes increasingly difficult these days. People are always wanting to push you forward, but I hate that whole process. I wish I had started off calling myself Joe Bloke and not admitting who I was. I want to write, but I don't want to be a Writer. But there is no way out of that problem. It's too late.

RW: Would you do another play?

DM: Yes. I might, if the subject came along that was very clear to me, but writing a play for the sake of writing a play doesn't interest me.

RW: Your most recent novel is *The Great World.* Is the title ironical?

DM: Yes. One of the things fiction does is give a life to people who are living inside what comes to be called history but who don't appear on the page of any history. The new book takes a couple of characters who live through a very painful part of Australian history, the defeat in Malaya and the years those people lived in camps and on the Burma railway under the Japs. It puts them in an extreme situation and then attempts to show that life is always extreme, that ordinary life is extreme. The title *The Great World* is in some ways ironical; in some ways it goes back to the question of where Australia is and where it belongs. It covers a period from World War I until 1987.

RW: Your work celebrates the mystery of existence. Do you take comfort from any sense of pattern, or is the dance chaotic?

DM: I'm pausing because I find this a difficult question to answer. I don't think I take comfort from any sense of pattern. Yet it doesn't necessarily seem chaotic.

RW: Your work is metaphysical, you push the reader so often from the physical into the spiritual and then pull him back again. Do you see any cause working through all this or is it simply life endlessly replicating itself?

DM: I think I genuinely don't know still. I suppose I think an awful lot of what happens to people is pretty accidental and random. That's the only way I can cope with the extraordinary injustice of things. What we have to keep doing all the time is rejecting readings of life that make us believe that we deserve our good fortunes. As an Australian it seems to me that the fact that you are born in Australia at all rather than Calcutta or Central Africa is such an extraordinary good fortune; no one could possibly deserve that, not in my reading of things. Nothing that I've ever done in this life or the last could ever make it a matter of deserving to be born here rather than there. In the same way the accident of being born in 1934 rather than in 1924 means that I didn't fight in World War II; I didn't go through what the men went through in *Fly Away Peter.* That is the purest accident; I did nothing to deserve any of that, but then neither do people deserve the terrible things which happen to them. I can't believe that this is anything but accident. It is the way you act after that point that matters. I don't believe there is any pattern in what happens to people. I believe in some kind of moral or spiritual consequences of the random things, but I can't believe that the other things are not in some way random.

FRANK MOORHOUSE

was born in 1938 in Nowra, a town one hundred miles down the coast south of Sydney. Coming to Sydney as a journalist in the 1960s, Moorhouse lived a bohemian life, sharing flats, people, and Libertarian ideas. Considered the chronicler of his generation, Moorhouse has preserved experiences from these and later years in Sydney, as well as from his travel experiences as a journalist, in essays, in newspaper and magazine columns, and in short stories. His fiction is characterized by wit and close observation of modern neurosis, Australian style. The following conversation occurred in a boat house/office on a Balmain waterfront in Sydney.

Futility and Other Animals, 1969
The Americans, Baby, 1972
The Electrical Experience, 1974
Conference-ville, 1976
Tales of Mystery and Romance, 1977
The Everlasting Secret Family and Other Secrets, 1980
Room Service, 1987
Forty-Seventeen, 1988

INTERVIEW

RW: A biography of Frank Moorhouse would read like a romantic's notion of what a writer's life might be. You began with frantic days of newspaper reporting, early marriage, early physical and marital collapse. You tried your hand with little magazines, with experimental writing, with experimental living, combative politics. You delighted and outraged the Australian public with sex-specific documentation, both heterosexual and homosexual. You battled censorship, parliamentary attack, poverty, reversals. Throughout this you've published ten books, movie scripts, essays, edited anthologies. At mid-life you've been made a Member of the Order of Australia for service to literature, and recently the Literature Board has awarded you a $50,000 fellowship yearly for four years. Critics call you the voice of your generation. Would you talk about your life and work in Sydney in the sixties and early seventies?

FM: The sixties is the hardest decade for me to reconstruct. The seventies I've documented. The sixties coincides with my twenties, and I didn't keep a diary or take many photographs, nor had I developed my filing system for saving information. I was forever losing whatever notebooks I had. I changed residence almost every six months and I lost something every time; jetsam and flotsam occurs out of the back of your life; you look out the back of your life and you see it receding. You lose friends, sell books, and you are careless with time and personal history. Life is too urgent. I also feel that I was drunk a lot of the time and waking up in houses that I hadn't been in before with women, sometimes men, I hadn't seen before or didn't remember from the night before. I learned to lean out of bed and take a book off a shelf and look for the name of the person who owned the book as a clue to the person beside me. It was a time of intense promiscuity in Sydney. I was part of a political sect called the Libertarians, which was an intellectual group from the University of Sydney, but it had a downtown bohemian chapter, and this was essentially romantic bohemia with a special Sydney flavor. The Libertarian ideology was very much a part of my 1960s. Among other things, Libertarianism involved the suppression of jealousy and the involvement in experimental sexual behavior. I think it was tribal. Everyone belonged sexually to everyone. Looking back, some might see it as a male-dominated tribe sharing the women, but I remember the women as being strong, equal, and some of them sexually predatory. I was sexually recruited by a young woman. At its strongest, it was a group that involved three to four hundred people of all ages. It had a newsletter, a high-quality magazine; it had its bars and restaurants where one went. I remember it as endless conversation and drinking and partying. It was a total life and for me, as a country boy up from Nowra, it was extraordinarily heady. I owe a lot to it intellectually for my development. It believed that the intellectuals lived in the crevices of the society and any involvement in orthodox politics could only corrupt you intellectually, that the world was governed by unintended consequence, that any endeavor undertaken politically ended in disaster, that all one could do as an honorable intellectual was to maintain permanent protest, though it didn't actually believe in social change. It drew into itself and created a tribe.

RW: You wrote a column called "Around the Laundromat." What was this about?

FM: Some of us came out of Libertarianism into a form of social interaction. We started an underground newspaper called *Thor.* My column was a dialogue between me and my cat, Ward. Most people didn't know that Ward was a cat. The rationale of the column was that the laundromat had become the village stream where the village came and washed its clothes and gossip was exchanged. It was a point of meeting where people were not dressed to go out. We were our natural selves and were displaying our soiled selves together. It was a place of exposure. I would make comments on the mores of the laundromat. I would take a perverse position on issues and Ward would unseat that position by taking a rational opposing argument. The column became satirical of Libertarian behavior; it was then picked up by the *Bulletin,* our national magazine, and became a part of the mainstream, which of course disqualified me forever from being a part of the Libertarian society.

RW: Your first two books of stories, *Futility and Other Animals* and *The Americans, Baby,* were published around the turn of the decade and caused a furor. Why was that?

FM: Australia was just facing up to the rebellion of words. The young were sick of censorship. The Libertarian maxim that we were living by was that you are only free if you can act free, if you can live free. We decided to publish and did publish for the first time in Australian history an uncensored magazine. I'm talking about sexual censorship, but in Australian history everything has been censored at one time or another. Some of us were reading work in public because we hadn't been able to get it published. That created the Balmain Readings of Prose and Verse. This grew until there were hundreds and hundreds of people at the readings. We eventually put that material into magazines. The police prosecuted us and a couple of editors were jailed. We were raising money and fighting cases in the courts. It became exhausting.

RW: Give me an example of the kinds of stories that you published in your book *The Americans, Baby.*

FM: The most eye-opening book we read in those days from the United States was *Portnoy's Complaint.* It was banned here, but I read a section in *Paris Review.* We stood around in clusters reading the masturbation story; we wrote stories like that too, but here something of this nature was published in a respectable magazine. In *The Americans, Baby,* the story that caused a furor was "Letters to Twiggy." These were letters written by an aroused academic male who had become sexually obsessed with Twiggy, the androgynous English model. As the story progresses the letters become more obsessive and obscene and there is an outburst of a sexual torrent which reveals the confused sexuality of the academic writer. This could have never been printed except in an underground publication, but by 1972 the censorship laws had been abolished. Up until 1972 Australia could be compared with Ireland as the most censored country in the free world.

RW: Why did you give the collection of stories this title?

FM: A lot of the stories are about contact with Americans in Australia. We had from World War II and through my childhood forward various waves of American contacts in Australia, and Australia had begun growing closer to America. In the sixties we had what we called nuclear refugees, Americans from the Peace Movement who thought World War III was about to break out and that the United States was about to become devastated. They thought Australia could come through, and they came here with their families to set up a bastion of civilized liberalism. These people were very important in stimulating the Peace Movement here; they represented the best in leftist thought. There are also some American businessmen in the stories, a Coca Cola salesman from Atlanta, a journalist from the States. The book is mainly the chronicle of my encounters with and friendliness to Americans in Australia.

RW: At the beginning of *Futility and Other Animals,* the reader finds a description of the form of the stories and your offering of an original term to describe the form. The term "discontinuous narrative" describes a process of organization you've used throughout your writing career. Would you talk about this term, "discontinuous narrative"?

FM: It was an intuitive sort of stumbling toward finding structures and a form which would work for me and which I could work with. I seemed to be uninterested in the novel form. I loved the short story, but I wanted to do more than the short story and I was doing more; I was assembling the stories. These assemblages were a bit worrying because we had been taught that the short story was an autonomous form which should not rely on any other story outside itself. At first, I tried to conceal the related characters in the stories and tried to make them autonomous. I knew the same characters were in story one and ten and seven, but I would change their names. Ultimately, I decided to identify them and to come clean. I thought I had a failure because the stories were leaning on each other, or at least holding hands. When I eventually got an assembly of the stories together, I was worried about them. I gave them to a new publisher who read them and became excited about them. He said, "Moorhouse, you're doing something here and I'm worried, because I don't think I can call this a novel. What are you doing?" This was over a long lunch and I was feeling defensive and frightened that he wasn't going to publish the book, and I said, "I call this a discontinuous narrative." This was an act of bravado on my part. I invented the term in an attempt to give legitimacy to something I felt in my heart illegitimate. He was bowled over and said, "Fantastic! Of course that's what it is." I can now identify all of my narratives as discontinuous; all the books are related to each other in some way or other. Looking back now, I can see some of the work I've done as novellas. I see *Everlasting Secret Family and Other Secrets* as four distinct novellas on a common theme.

RW: I believe you've said you've found this form legitimized in Sherwood Anderson's *Winesburg, Ohio* and in works of J. D. Salinger.

FM: I was excited by Salinger. I read his Glass stories at different times in magazines and saw how they were related and realized that I was allowed to do that. He was breaking rules that I had been taught in school. People have since pointed out to me that Henry Lawson has stories with the same characters. I had studied Lawson in school but hadn't been aware he was doing this. I'd turned my back on Australian writers for awhile in my twenties. We just didn't want to know anything about the bush. Over the years I've experimented a lot with moving the stories around, making different juxtapositions. By moving them around, recombining them, you can get a different effect. The French got very excited about this when I did a new assemblage for them.

RW: What would you say to critics who might accuse you of simply recycling old material?

FM: Some critics get annoyed by it and some enjoy it. I see it as a coupling from book to book. I see it also as accretion, in geological terms, the books combining on top of each other. I've always found it fascinating to see a story in a new context. I feel that it is revivified in a new position. I am not a theoretician, I'm an intuitive writer, but I'm aware now that I am playing with the gap, in physics the distance that the spark can jump between two poles and the spark that is created by bringing the poles closer together or farther apart. I'm playing with gap and accretion and reverberation.

RW: It sounds similar to T. S. Eliot's idea that a new work of literature affects both the literature that has come before as well as that which comes after. What does "discontinuous narrative" say about your view of the nature of life itself?

FM: I suspect that it has to do with the fact that we live with the illusion that there is a continuity of sensory data and continuity of personal history and a continuity of memory and so on, but, in fact, we know that the memory is faulty, that the historical picture presented to us is partial, that our own knowledge of ourselves is very limited, that our knowledge of people with whom we are most intimate is very limited, but also the very physical experience of our children or our lovers is remarkably fragmented. They are out of our lives so much of the time. We see them 12 percent of the time and the rest of the time they are not in our vision, and in fact we do not know what they are doing. We are often devastated to find out what they have been doing. In some ways my structures are an attempt to break through that illusory sense of a continuous and harmonious view of the world and to work with the fragment. The paradox is that all my work is continuous.

RW: Your constant regrouping creates a new gestalt.

FM: That's right. It is also related to the notion in physics that ultimately there is no pattern. Once you get to a certain point with matter, we can't discern the pattern. Certainly, through our senses we impose pattern. The comfort of the form of the traditional novel is that it produces a great harmony.

RW: Although you have dodged bullets in Beirut and lived for periods in many parts of the world, I think of you as a Sydney writer, a chronicler of Sydney life. We are sitting here even now on the deck of a boat house in the Sydney Harbor suburb of Balmain, where you live. Would you talk about Balmain, the part of Sydney where so many writers live?

FM: In the nineteenth century Balmain was a place with beautiful houses where high-income people lived. Because of its proximity to the working harbor, it eventually became proletariat. The rich left and the old houses became rooming houses. In the sixties Balmain was cheap and beautiful and amazing. We held the Balmain Readings in Prose and Verse. We fiction writers forced ourselves onto the platform with the poets, and it was the first time we realized that reading short stories could work in public; it was a little like the oral tradition of telling stories around a campfire. The readings now take place in Glebe, often at the Harold Park Hotel. Glebe is a low-rent student suburb in which the University of Sydney is located. The current real estate transformation has made Balmain again an upper income place for young professionals. Economically successful writers have bought houses here—Peter Carey, David Williamson, Kate

Grenville, Bruce Petty, the cartoonist. For a long time Murray Bail lived here, as did Michael Wilding and Nigel Roberts. There are quite a few musicians and actors here.

RW: Since you so often write in the first person, your recent book *Forty-Seventeen*, for example, readers often assume that the narrator is Frank Moorhouse himself, or some version of him. Does this assumption bother you? Are you an autobiographical writer?

FM: I have not written autobiographical work in that *Forty-Seventeen* represents a chronologically accurate picture of my life or that it is a record of actual events or people that I've met or people I've interacted with or lived with. Sometimes I do draw directly, but I think I follow the same process that most fiction writers do. I don't think my own story is particularly interesting. The story has to have a social dimension and it has to be enlarged by collage and combination and it has to become a vehicle for the times, or it has to embrace more of the world than my own particular life, so in that sense my writing is very much a use of the imagination for processing data and for using it in an enlarging way. My books are consistently from one point of view. I use the first person. They often make use of selves that I have passed by, selves that I've discarded, or selves that could have been.

RW: You once said that you regard a person's insistence on privacy as pathological and unhealthy. Would you speak of this in terms of your using yourself in your fiction?

FM: It's a messy position. I think it's Descartes who says, "I am a human being and all things that concern humans concern me." I also feel extending from this is that anything one wants to know of me as a human being he is entitled to ask and get an honest answer. I try to follow this in my fiction, my interview work, and in my journalism, because I've always failed to understand what it is we are frightened to tell other people. I know that in the real world things can be held against you and that as a writer I am licensed to tell the truth, whereas most of us have reasons to conceal things because we are in dangerously competitive work situations or dangerous political situations. I've also had the privilege of growing up in a nation with no civil unrest, but generally I think we are on the right track, that it was very civilizing in the late sixties and in the seventies when we started to create an ethos of candor and, to use the hippie expression, when we "put everything up front." It was liberating that we acknowledged our frailties and hang-ups and fears. There was a lot to be gained. In my fiction and in my direct autobiographical writing I've tried to adhere to candor.

RW: *Tales of Mystery and Romance* caused a scandal when it was published, particularly because of the intimate sexual revelations in the relationships of the characters. Are these stories in part autobiographical?

FM: They are not autobiographical in the strict chronological reporting of events or people in my life, but the stories are a report of my spiritual or sexual chaos, or interpersonal chaos. The two central male characters describe themselves as failed homosexuals. They were caught up in the swirl of the liberation of that period where anything could happen and we were encouraged to do everything that crossed our minds, so the book is somewhat a satire of that. It was before AIDS and a very special time in human history.

RW: You don't regret any of the revelations that might be construed as autobiographical?

FM: No. When the book was first published, I feared that I had broken taboos and that there were untold punishments waiting. Especially the erotic memoir in *Everlasting Secret Family.* I thought it would tread on nervous boundaries. Some of my friends found it hard to read. I was filled with trepidations about what would happen in my life after I published it. Nothing happened and, of course, a lot of these taboos and trepidations in retrospect seem primitive.

RW: I understand that Australia, Sydney in particular, has a large homosexual population. I read in the newspaper about a recent gay party with 16,000 people attending. Yet *Everlasting Secret Family,* published in 1980, was considered scandalous. I've read it described as one of the most sensational books dealing with sexuality in Australia. Does Australia deny its decadence?

FM: Definitely. That's why it's not hard to write the most sexually sensational book in Australia. That's very easy to do. Our erotic work would fit on one corner of a bookshelf. We are not great erotic writers. We suffered all the bad things of English repression and reserve and lack of candor, plus all the repressive things of Irish culture. When the society became bourgeois and started to stabilize and build its family structure after the first settlement, its middle class tried to be even more Victorian than the English middle class. We had all the sexual imbalances that pioneering countries had so that by the time the family structure started to set in there was an attempt to suppress and forget all the pioneering days, not only the convict decadence, but poverty, the fact that we lived off rabbits and kangaroos. We denied the decadent relationships with the aboriginal population; we denied the inescapable pioneering homosexual bonding which occurred in the scarcity of, or absence of, women. The party you read about was the Gay Mardi Gras. The international, basically American movement for gay rights has had an effect in Australia, as has AIDS. The devastation of AIDS has in many ways driven the gay population back into a concealment of sexuality and self. The Gay Mardi Gras in Sydney is an assertion of a celebratory kind, and there is nothing like it anywhere else in Australia. It's a magnificent assertion, given the great pressures inherent in Australia against homosexuals.

RW: Still?

FM: Still, though it was looking good until AIDS stirred very primitive superstitions and prejudices. Homosexuals are being persecuted now in Tasmania and in Queensland.

RW: Has homosexuality been important in your life?

FM: I've had homosexual relationships, especially in my youth, in my twenties, diminishing in my thirties and since then. Some were very important relationships. But throughout my life I've lived with women, basically. The most longtime cohabiting relationships have been with women. I've had three very important relationships with women in my life.

RW: Someone once asked D. H. Lawrence about himself. He wondered which self the person was asking about or how many of the selves. A writer creates many observable selves. Are some versions of Frank Moorhouse more true than others?

FM: That's a fascinating question. I've been very suspicious of the practice of artist therapy because I don't feel that one writes himself out of personal problems, but that in fact the writing is a symptom of them, of personal conflicts and anxieties. They may be discharged temporarily, but in my experience in observing other writers, I don't see any evidence that the practice of writing is necessarily therapeutic. It may be stabilizing; it may make one's neurosis into a socially useful product which allows you to negotiate your existence, but I don't think writing equals psychotherapy as an instrument for dislodging or understanding destructive tensions.

RW: Do you learn from the versions you create of yourself?

FM: Yes. I think you learn in looking back on your own fiction; you can see something of yourself, but I'm not sure how much one acts on what he sees. I am not an alcoholic but I have an alcohol dependency; alcohol has played a part in the management of my anxieties and I've written about this, but I don't think my writing has helped me to come to terms with alcohol.

RW: More than coming to terms with an aspect of self, I simply meant that one might recognize with a kind of fascination that here is a part of myself, here's another fragment, and still another. With all of these different versions of who I am, perhaps there is no central version.

FM: There is something very encapsulating and healing about fiction writing. It seals off things into shapes like stories and books and goes back into latent memory. I've never talked about this, and it's hard for me to even begin to objectively observe it—the relationship between one's self and the created fiction. Something might be alive in the active consciousness during the time of writing and then it goes out to the other end into a capsule and is lost to you again. That's why reading early writing is sometimes quite amazing.

RW: Since you are re-using and making new shapes from the juxtaposition of your stories, I would think you'd see a part of your captured self that you don't remember.

FM: Yes. Having written fiction for thirty years, I can still see the spiritual self that I've left behind. Writing may also accelerate the process of discarding that I was talking about. One grows out of certain postures from decade to decade.

RW: Which of your works have been turned into films?

FM: There have been a couple of television movies which have been adaptations of short stories. I did the screen adaptations. One was based on *Conference-ville;* one was called "Time's Raging," based on *Futility and Other Animals.* I've done three feature films—*Between Wars,* an original screenplay; *The Coca-Cola Kid,* with Makavejev, and I did *Everlasting Secret Family,* which the Australian critics hated. *The Coca-Cola Kid* was the most successful international movie. I don't enjoy the movie at all. The story was distorted and reorganized by the director. He does not come from Australia and there was a lot of cultural misunderstanding. The project took nine years or more. There were eleven drafts of the script.

RW: The best known of your books in the U.S. are *Room Service* and *Forty-Seventeen.* I'd like to talk about these books as examples of the Moorhouse world. First *Room Service.* Who is François Blase?

FM: He's a persona; he's how I see myself as either the world's worst traveler or the world's most cunning traveler. I've always thought of myself as a bad traveler. I can't seem to get the right things out of monuments and I can't find the *Mona Lisa* in the gallery; I get back to the pool at the hotel or I'm sitting in the bar having a martini and someone will say, "Did you go to the north face of the pyramid? That's the side to see," and I will not have been to the north side. In the end, François Blase thinks there is more to be learned sitting in a bar and watching the barman making martinis in Cairo than there is going out looking at monuments. Consequently, Blase stays more and more in his room, arguing that there is more to be learned talking to the maid than going out on the street.

RW: How is *Room Service* organized?

FM: There is an assembly of Blase pieces done over the years, mainly out of my travels, some from local travels in Australia. The pieces were brought together and joined with a section called "The Oral History of Childhood," recollections of how we use language in the playground and the school, incantations and various bits of primitive behavior of children in the use of language. In a way, this is a history of my childhood. The last section is a collection of miscellaneous comic pieces from over the last ten years.

RW: Let me give you a few chapter titles, and you give me a quick response. "The New York Bell Captain."

FM: That's a terrified-tourist-in-New-York story, which must be a subgenre of travel stories. It's about an Australian dealing with the American idea of tipping and the tyranny of the hotel management and staff against the helpless traveler coming from a non-tipping, non-service-oriented country.

RW: "The Indian Bell Captain."

FM: This comes close to actual reporting. It's about the other kind of bell captain where you are over-serviced and there are too many people doing too many things for you. In this situation it is the tyranny of excessive attention which one cannot escape.

RW: "Hiltonia."

FM: This is a recognition that there is another country called Hiltonia, which is the country created by the Hilton hotel and, by extension, airlines, American Express, group tours, and so forth. These all join together to form a unified culture and terrain with its common practices and mores. François Blase finds he is very much at home in Hiltonia. He grows to love this country where you can travel pretending to be in France or Egypt or Africa, but in fact you are in Hiltonia. François can book into the Hilton hotel in Sydney and never hear an Australian voice and have club sandwiches and get a martini mixed the right way and read the *New Yorker* and have a holiday without ever leaving the city.

RW: *Forty-Seventeen* is your most recent book. In form is it closer to novel than any of your other works?

FM: I suspect so. It seems to be giving the reader the gratifications that he expects from the novel. It's a fairly cohesive narrative. From the way I assemble things there is obviously little planning of fictional destinations. I work with one story suggesting the next. Where I arrive is as much a surprise for me as it will be for the reader. I set out on a narrative journey to follow my characters.

RW: Consistent with your discontinuous narrative in *Forty-Seventeen,* there are many fragments, moments, detours in the life of the narrator. Let me mention some of the subjects which you cover, sometimes dramatically, sometimes as a short story, sometimes as a tongue-in-cheek essay. First, the forty-seventeen love affair.

FM: I think what I was doing, linking a forty-year-old with a seventeen-year-old, was setting up age perspectives, because I also bring in a seventy-year-old woman who plays an increasing role in the narrative as it goes on. The forty-year-old narrator also returns to his own experiences at seventeen through a childhood sweetheart and her letters. There is an attempt to relate what the world is at seventeen and what it is at forty and at seventy. I'm looking at how age perspective alters reality perspective.

RW: Are there different codes appropriate for the different decades of one's life?

FM: I now think so. The young think there are single fixed codes by which you judge your elders, and they are forever putting the older generations on trial for ideological crimes. We punish our parents for their failures. Looking back, one realizes that one adopts different codes and that life involves adaptation and modification and refinement and sculpturing of one's self. The book is very much about sculpturing, shaping a life.

RW: Another topic you cover in *Forty-Seventeen* is middle age. You are over fifty now. Is it all right to be that old?

FM: Yes. Things shape up. Your expectations change, your pleasures change, your drives change. The important thing is to make sure that you get your due pleasures and live your passions when they are appropriate. It is probably the living of inappropriate passions that brings us undone.

RW: You begin the book with "The Slut." Why is this in the book?

FM: It's an exploration of a personality type and a code of sexual behavior which I think harks back to the days of promiscuity that I lived through in the sixties. Belle, the female narrator who lays down the rules for sluttishness, describes it as a personal sexual rebellion of the highest order. She defines it as a temporary loss of the inhibited and the respectable self. One has to return to a degree of the respectable self so as to maintain a stabilized life. The male, the central narrator, is leaving sluttishness behind.

RW: You have a chapter on drinking. You write, "Alcohol was like a campfire they huddled around." Is this a national campfire?

FM: Yes. I think social drinking is a centerpiece that allows people to escape from solitude, and at its best, alcohol allows one to escape from the all-enclosing darkness. This chapter is the nearest to autobiography in the book. The narrator has a bout with hepatitis and this puts him off alcohol for the first time since childhood and he records his experiences for six months. This was my experience and

I was interested to see how it changed my life, or didn't change it. I think this chapter is the definitive piece on alcohol that has been written in Australia. Lots of men have commented to me what an important part drinking plays in the Australian male's life and how little has been recorded or observed about it in an anthropological sense. We have folklore about it, but no one in my generation has actually looked at what we are doing and how it affects us.

RW: Your writing has been described as having a "compassionate absurdist tone." In addition to the wit and humor in *Forty-Seventeen,* there is a lot of melancholy. Again, some lines for your comment. About middle age, you write, "You realize that no person with a system of knowledge is going to release you from intellectual dilemma. No book will come along to seriously alter your life."

FM: The narrator is recalling that in your twenties books do come along to change your life and systems of thinking do come along and cause upheavals and change your direction. At some time in your life you realize that this is not going to happen again, that you are either writing the books that change people's lives or that you have critically refined and sophisticated yourself to being at a point beyond that type of excitement. The narrator has reached a point of maturity; he knows he will now have to do for himself. But the narrator also has days of hoping that a letter will arrive that will change his life.

RW: Your work is a reflection of life in Sydney, in Australia, and of Western angst in general. After decades of observation and documentation, what remains important to you?

FM: I think inquiry is still important to me. The life of inquiry is still gratifying and stabilizing and marvelous. Even though one knows that inquiry is not going to reach a coherent single philosophical approach to all questions at all times, it's still a fascinating way to spend time. It produces temporary positions which allow us to act and behave with some competence. The thing which is growing stronger in me is the belief in the pleasures and terribly complex and wondrous nature of storytelling. I think storytelling is what we do best as a culture and as a species. All of us go on endlessly telling stories, whether it is in the oral tradition of the campfire yarn or at the bar, or the personal telling of our own story to each other. I find it more and more marvelous that we do this. It is what makes life bearable and whole for me. Storytelling is a way of holding the incomprehensible at bay, of holding panic at bay. It is a way of avoiding having to make answers, because we suspect that there aren't any permanent answers. Storytelling is a wonderful way of being civilized and holding ourselves together.

DAVID WILLIAMSON

The Removalists, 1972
Don's Party, 1973
The Coming of Stork, 1974
Jugglers Three, 1974
What if You Died Tomorrow, 1974
The Department, 1975
A Handful of Friends, 1976
The Club, 1978
Travelling North, 1980
The Perfectionist, 1983
Sons of Cain, 1985
Emerald City, 1987
Siren, 1989
Top Silk, 1989

was born in 1942 in Melbourne. He studied mechanical engineering at Monash University and went on to teach thermodynamics at the Swinburne Institute of Technology. Interested in writing from an early age, Williamson had his first play, *The Coming of Stork,* produced at the experimental La Mama Theater in Melbourne in 1970. His second play, *The Removalist,* was performed in London, and later worldwide. This play established him as an international playwright and gave him enough income to establish himself as a full-time writer. Since that time Williamson has written prolifically for the stage. His plays are satirical, sometimes darkly comic explorations of the Australian character. He has also written for television, as well as a number of screenplays, among them *Don's Party, Gallipoli, The Year of Living Dangerously, Phar Lap.* His latest screenplay for Paramount Pictures is based on the life of Martin Luther King, Jr. David Williamson is Australia's leading dramatist.

INTERVIEW

RW: Would you say a few words about your childhood?

DW: I grew up in lower-middle-class suburban Melbourne. My father worked in a bank. My mother worked in various cake shops, things like that. I suppose it was a typical Australian childhood.

RW: Were you pretty much at one with your family and friends or were you an outsider?

DW: I was always a bit precocious in the sense that I wrote very early and was an avid reader. Perhaps I was lacking a little in the sporting direction at a time when in Australia it was important to be obsessed with sport. I always felt slightly out of kilter in those years. Not drastically to the point that I was miserable, because I did like sport, but because I did read and could put words together I felt a sense of difference.

RW: You took your university degrees in mechanical engineering and social psychology?

DW: The engineering degree was a very theoretical and mathematical degree, very close to a physics degree. While I was teaching thermodynamics and fluid mechanics at Swinburne, I went back to Melbourne University and studied psychology. When I was appointed to the general studies department at Swinburne to teach psychology, I had to make a choice between further academic work and writing.

RW: What stimulated you toward the keen satirical observations that you've brought to your writing?

DW: I honestly don't know. In the sixties I found satire and black satire in American fiction very appealing, writers like Barth, Pynchon, Heller, and James Purdy. I was reading them as an undergraduate when I should have been studying engineering.

RW: Any American playwrights?

DW: No. At that age I mainly read American prose, contemporary satirical American prose.

RW: What about after you started writing plays?

DW: I think my appreciation of the American theater has been in retrospect. I did see a production when I was in my early twenties of Edward Albee's *Who's Afraid of Virginia Woolf?* I thought that was terrific. In terms of English drama, I'd seen some student productions of Pinter and Osborne, typical things you would see in the late sixties. But it wasn't until later that I became acquainted with Tennessee Williams, Arthur Miller, Eugene O'Neill.

RW: Is there an American dramatist writing now that you feel a kinship with?

DW: I like the work of David Mamet. I think he's the best I can name off the top of my head. I've seen some very good work on my trips to New York. Some things of Sam Shepard.

RW: What about Neil Simon?

DW: I find his work very skilled technically, but he's a little too sunny for my taste. I think there's a heart of gold in all his characters. I think Mamet has a more realistic level of pessimism about the human species.

RW: Have any members of your family or any friends become models for characters in your plays?

DW: I've been accused of that very often. I've been accused of grabbing from life and holding people up to ridicule on stage. My defense is that everyone draws from life, but literary or dramatic characters do become composite characters. They may have their genesis in an observed character, but they take on elements of your own character, your imagination, of other characters, so they become amalgamations, and in certain ways I shape them to fit dramatic purpose within the structure of a play. Although someone might go to one of my plays and recognize an action that he or she can remember having done, in the construction of a play it's never an attempt to photograph a particular person. The thematic concerns of the play take over and I shape the character to suit that.

RW: Is any one of your plays particularly autobiographical?

DW: Yes. I think an early play called *What if You Died Tomorrow* was pretty close. It upset, or half upset, my parents. They didn't know whether to be angry or pleased. I remember my mother going up to the actress and saying, "You took me off very well." "Taking off" is an Australian term for acting. In some ways, obviously, *Emerald City* had a strong element of autobiography. It's about a screenwriter who comes from Melbourne to Sydney as I did. But there were all sorts of distortions from the real-life situation that were there to suit the thematic concerns: greed, avarice, and lust. Again, there was a subtle shaping away from life, although I used the natural research I had done to advantage. I knew the differences between Melbourne and Sydney, but it was less a play about the two cities than it was about those dark and Freudian desires that humans have to cope with.

RW: Some critics insist that you are a very autobiographical writer and as a record of your experiences, your plays draw a social map of the mores and concerns of Australia in the 1970s and 1980s. Do you think this is an accurate description?

DW: Some plays such as *Emerald City, The Perfectionist,* and *Top Silk* do have elements of autobiography. Others, less so. *Sons of Cain, The Club, The Removalists, Travelling North* were not autobiographical, so they vary. In terms of charting a social map of the times, I hope that's partly true. I'd like to think that the writing is based on the society I observe around me. Critics have said that it is a select area of Australian society—middle-class, white, Anglo-Celtic. I say, "So what?" But in some circles it is a crime to write about this segment of society. One always feels a moral pressure to be writing about black or migrant ethnic experience, but not having been black or ethnic, it's something that would be to some extent forced if I wrote it. I would get brownie points if I tried to write a play about the difficulties of ethnic adjustment to the Australian society. I don't try to write such a play because I think people most suited to do it are those who have undergone that experience.

RW: I think also implicit in the critical statement is that as you personally have moved upward, from the working-class background to the house on the harbor, your plays can be read in terms of a similar metamorphosis in character concern. Is this true?

DW: It's partly accurate if you take an autobiographical line from *What if You Died Tomorrow, Handful of Friends, The Perfectionist,* and *Emerald City.* If you take those plays, they do describe these sorts of changes, but they are only four out of fourteen plays. My latest play, *Siren,* has nothing to do with my personal experiences. There is no thread within the whole body of work.

RW: What was your first big success?

DW: I suppose it would be *The Removalists* and *Don's Party* together, when they were produced in Sydney. They were both written very close to each other and produced very close to each other in 1972, early 1973. That was when my career took off.

RW: What did the Australian audience see in those two plays that surprised, or delighted, or shocked them?

DW: There was a lot of shock. They weren't greeted euphorically by all sections of the public. I remember a taxi driver taking me somewhere and telling me that he had just been enormously embarrassed because he had heard that this play called *Don's Party* was good and he had taken his wife to see it, and he was extremely embarrassed at the bad language and wondered how anyone could put that sort of play on stage. There was certainly an ambivalence because people realized that I was satirizing some of the worst aspects of Australian society in those two plays as well as celebrating them. In *Don's Party,* in particular, some in the audience chose to ignore the criticism and embrace the celebration—the energy and the humor. They chose to minimize the sexism, materialism, and anti-intellectualism. I suppose in actuality the audiences came for mixed reasons, some to celebrate, others to see themselves criticized.

RW: That seems from the Australian critics' point of view to be one of the ongoing problems they find in your work. Some want you to be either celebratory or satirical, but not both at the same time. Do you see any conflict in the combination?

DW: I think I personally have a deep ambivalence toward this country. If I am writing truthfully, that has to be reflected in my work. I do find a lot of aspects of this society distasteful, but I also find a lot of elements refreshing. I can only write how I feel. I don't loathe the society beyond belief as some Australian writers do. Some writers gain their creative energy out of a deep detestation of everything that is Australian. It is a very common attitude among the older generation of Australian writers. They really fuel themselves up on hatred. That can give a certain kind of energy. But I don't have that deep hatred; I have a deep ambivalence. I think in some ways it makes for more interesting writing because it has no clear line, no easy moral charm underlying the structure. It might confuse people more, but it's probably closer to the truth about whatever this country is.

RW: Is there such a thing as a typical David Williamson play?

DW: Though they do vary, there is always a satirical element in the plays. I used to describe my plays as inhabiting the borderland between naturalism and satire, somewhere in that area. Some go closer toward realism and some closer toward satire and I think they vary round about in that area. They generally do focus on power manipulations of one form or another, be it within marriage between the marriage partners, or within institutions as in plays like *The Club* and *The Department*. People use language as a mask, sometimes consciously, sometimes unconsciously for their true motivations. In plays like *The Department* and *The Club*, the players are frantically manipulating for their own personal ends and pretending that they are working for the common good, some more blatantly than others.

RW: From the very beginning of your career and all along the way you've moved back and forth between writing for the stage and writing film scripts. Would you talk about the difference in writing for the two?

DW: I started out as a playwright. I always wanted to write plays, and the first full-length play I wrote way back in 1970 was called *The Coming of Stork*. It was quickly turned into a movie. It was one of the first, if not the first, of the new wave Australian films. It was made on a budget of about sixty thousand dollars. It was really crudely made, and I had to write the screenplay, so suddenly I had to learn the difference between stage and screen. I had to have a crash course in screenwriting. There are substantial differences. You can see it if you look at the scripts. The play is a mass of dialogue, whereas the screenplay typically has more of the words spent describing actions and scenes and events than are spent writing dialogue, so immediately you are in an area of visual language where things visually are happening on that big screen and the story has to be told through visuals, facial close-ups and body language, scenery, mood, atmosphere. All these things are more important than they are on stage, so you find yourself writing those visual events, close-ups, and describing them and cutting back very substantially on the dialogue. While on the stage, a three-dimensional person standing there actually delivering dialogue, as a violinist might deliver an aria, still has a captivating and magnetic effect that isn't there once he's reduced to a two-dimensional person on the screen. I do still think theater can deal with subtleties and complexities of human interaction processes better than any other medium because it can accommodate more language and more interaction than the screen. On the screen you are always getting the feeling that there must not be "talking heads"; there must be action. "Cinema is action," one of my characters says in *Emerald City,* and you always feel guilty if you just have two people talking, while that is the very essence of the stage.

RW: I have heard you say that you put television between drama and film as being a more satisfying medium than film. Why do you think that?

DW: Because the screen is so much smaller, it is somewhat more permissible to have so-called talking heads. You can use people speaking to each other, relating to each other quite powerfully on television, so you don't feel you are being rapped over the knuckles if you write a dialogue line longer than five words. You get that feeling in film. "Oh, Christ, too much dialogue. How do we show this visually?" Or with some directors you go to absurd lengths. You can't even have two people sitting talking; they've got to be talking on the move. They've got to be on horseback, or diving off high boards simultaneously and talking, or anything to put some movement into the scene, whereas in television you don't feel that you have to do that.

RW: Of your screenplays, do you have a favorite?

DW: I'm always influenced by the last one I see. At the moment my favorite is *Emerald City.* The film was directed by Michael Jenkins using a strong local cast. In some ways it's punchier than the play because Michael injects a lot of vitality into his work. We made a conscious decision there because we thought we'd play around with the ironies a bit. In the play there's a scene where the screenwriter is working on this visual Australian *Miami Vice;* they've written twenty minutes of the episode and only twelve words have been spoken and the writer is getting agitated and pleading with his collaborator for more dialogue, so we thought we'd play with that irony a littlc bit, and we actually have made the dialogue with film just to see if it can be done. As our models, we went back to the films of the thirties and forties, films like *The Philadelphia Story* and other great articulate movies of that era when people actually spoke to each other wittily and intelligently at a rapid rate. Cary Grant actually used to spit out the lines of dialogue. So Michael Jenkins said, "Let's do it. Let's not do a *Reader's Digest* version of your play and condense the long speeches," which is the usual tactic. "Let's just cut sections out of the play, but leave the other sections intact and let the actors really do their stuff." And it seems to have worked very well. We have two highly articulate leads who are belting out the dialogue in the old Cary Grant–Katherine Hepburn manner. I'll be interested to see how it works because the film has a lot of vitality in it and some of the vitality comes from the energetic way the actors have done the dialogue. I hope I'm not wrong. I think it works.

RW: In the States, *Gallipoli* is perhaps your best-known screenplay. Would you discuss the writing of it?

DW: It was Peter Weir's idea to make a film about Gallipoli. He had a rough storyline worked out and we started with that. The original story line involved many characters and was much grander. When we had written the first draft, the budget restrictions were such that we had to keep paring the story down and finally make it a simple story about the relationship between two young men. That process went on and off for four years. I'd write the draft; we'd get criticism; I'd go away and write the next draft, and we finally arrived at the screenplay.

RW: What was it like to work with Peter Weir?

DW: In *Gallipoli* we were both passionate about the project and we had a very good collaboration. He would leave me to write but he would certainly have a lot of input between the drafts. We had a trickier collaboration on *The Year of Living Dangerously* because Peter had already written a draft with the novelist Chris Koch. Their relationship had broken down because they are both strong-minded gentlemen and Chris thought it should be a film *of* the book and Peter thought it should be a film *based on* the book and this sort of brought them to an impasse. That's when I came in. It was a tricky adaptation and there was a little more friction on that one. I did the next five drafts, but Chris still got a credit on the screenplay because he started the process with Peter.

RW: When you write dramas, do you project your work outside Australia? Do you see yourself writing for a world market?

DW: I have never seen myself as writing for a world market. From the very earliest days I was writing Australian plays for Australian people. Australian playwrights before me who were consciously writing for a world market would not put in any local references or place-names. They would either locate their plays in hypothetical lands that didn't have place-names or in other countries. We've had a tradition of that sort of writing, but I've always seen myself as an observer of the life around me and reflecting that life. If the writing is good enough and does travel to other cultures I am delighted, but the writing is not predicated with that ambition. Someone said, of all the art forms, drama is the most parochial. It really is rooted in its particular tribe. The very best of that tribal writing transcends the boundaries of that tribe. I mean, what could be more provincial than Chekhov's plays about Russia and aristocracy in the late nineteenth century? It so happens that he is a very good dramatist as well. When I've been working on a script for Home Box Office the extent of the cultural imperialism is not often recognized by the perpetrators. For example, our scripts have to go out with American spelling, even though the producers are Australian. We've got to spell asshole the American way, not "arsehole," and all of that. When we've queried why, the final answer is, "We're bigger than you." It's only a tiny point, and, after all, culture does travel from the larger to the smaller. For example, there is good writing in New Zealand, but we Australians know very little about it because we are always looking to the U.K. or the U.S.

RW: Perhaps that's changing in the United States. Australian literature and film have had a strong showing in the United States in the last few years. Americans are interested in Australia.

DW: I do think there is more openness toward what's happening here in Australia in the States than there is in England. I'm absolutely sure of that.

RW: Why is there more interest from America than from England?

DW: The English don't want to know that we have any literature or any culture because it's comfortable for them to think of us as being barbarous. In the Simon Gray play *The Common Pursuit,* which I saw recently in London, the biggest laugh of the night was when the drunken ex-Cambridge character staggers on stage and announces that he thinks he has spent the last night in Earl's Court, but he's not certain; he's had so much to drink. He woke up beside someone in a bed. He thinks it was a woman, its back looked like a woman, but it snored—so it was either an hermaphrodite or an Australian. That line got at least a two-minute laugh.

RW: Why is Australia the butt of British humor?

DW: There is a deep racist feeling about Australians in England. I don't quite know why it is as intense as it is, but it certainly is there. And it goes right back to their literature. In Oscar Wilde's *The Importance of Being Earnest* the aunt threatens to send a young bounder to Australia. It's the worst possible threat she can think of. I don't know where they get their information. I mean, I'm sitting here in shirt sleeves in the sun in the middle of winter. I've spent a lot of time in England and it is a thoroughly miserable country. It is so structured and the class system is still so rigid. The political system is appalling and I wonder how they can still feel so superior. They've obviously never been here, never want to come here. Let them stay in their gray little land and drink their tea and feel superior. The reality is somewhat different. I think America will accept this reality a lot more easily than the English ever will.

RW: The British critics have liked your work. Wasn't it in 1973 that the *London Evening Standard* nominated you most promising playwright for the British production of *The Removalists*?

RW: Yes. But here's an example of what I'm talking about. And it's recent. The most offensive line of criticism I've ever got from the British was in the first paragraph of a review in *The Independent* or some other fairly respectable newspaper commenting on *Emerald City*. The critic said, "I could not believe my ears when I heard Miss Niven" (who is the actress) "describe Sydney as sophisticated, until I realized that she had probably never been outside Australia in her life." I really don't think such comments have any place at the head of a review. It typifies in a way the worst of the British attitude toward Australia. Not all the critics were like that. *The Times, The Guardian,* the ones I would have wanted were all fair and terrific. But the down-market press in particular still think it a joke that any Australian can pretend to be sophisticated, let alone erudite.

RW: Why is that?

DW: I think part of the reason is that the only theatrical representations of Australians they ever see are from Barry Humphries or Paul Hogan. Paul Hogan plays a rather amiable but rather unsophisticated backwoodsman, and Barry Humphries in his very successful stageshows, which are actually more successful in London than they are in Australia, plays a nightmare tradition of Australian gaucheness. Barry Humphries has abstracted the very worst of the Australian psyche and presented it as a gross Hogarthian stereotype for the amusement of the Londoners, so that any other theatrical representation of someone articulate and intelligent is beyond their belief or comprehension.

RW: Tell me about your writing habits.

DW: I write at home, primarily during the daylight hours. It's a practical necessity because of the children and school. I write reasonably long hours if I have a big project on.

RW: Do you hear a play, hear the dialogue before you put it down?

DW: Yes. Very much so. I hear it in my head. I run through it to see if it sounds right. Sometimes I've tape-recorded the dialogue to test it out to see if it sounds right, but not very often. I usually trust what I hear in my head. My daughter Rebecca heard me acting out *Emerald City,* and I heard great gales of laughter coming from next door. My theory is that if the play can survive my acting, it can survive any acting.

RW: How much of a play would you have in your head at any one time?

DW: Only three or four lines at a time. I can usually hear what is coming up.

RW: You live in a jasmine-fenced, rose-covered nineteenth-century house which backs up to the sparkling water in Balmain, a harbor suburb of Sydney, a kind of Australian Greenwich village. Would you say a few words about where you live?

DW: The white roses are my wife, Kristin's, pride and joy. She is a keen gardener. The roses bloom five times a year. Sydney is subtropical. The climate is warm and the growth is lush. It's a lovely place to live on two counts. It is near the water. Louisa Road is a peninsula that is cut off from heavy traffic. One can go by private boat or public ferry at the end of the street into downtown Sydney. Balmain has a community-like feel to it. There are a lot of writers, artists, filmmakers who live in the area within a couple of square kilometers. Peter Carey lives down the street, Frank Moorhouse across the bit of water. Murray Bail used to live nearby.

RW: You've recently finished *Siren.* How long did it take you to write the play?

DW: Four to six weeks for a first draft.

RW: You write very fast.

DW: I'd been thinking around the subject for quite awhile, so it's not as though I just sat down with nothing there.

RW: Is writing easy for you?

DW: Once I've a decent idea—well, it's hard work, but it's exciting work. When a play is being generated there is a lot of momentum. I like to get it out in a hurry even if it's imperfect. I go back and do it again. I like to write while the momentum is there. Drama has to have the momentum, so it helps me to write it in a burst of activity.

RW: How do those wonderful comic lines come in?

DW: I don't always see it. I'm often surprised when the audience laughs. I just think as I write that they are accurate lines. This is what this character would say. A lot of the laughs come out of character. People realize they've heard that type of character say that sort of thing. They are not wisecracks or shaped lines; they are just accurate.

RW: You don't say, "Three minutes have gone by and I need a laugh here . . ."

DW: Very much, no. I'm not a gag writer as such. I've never seen myself setting up laughs. I've seen myself as setting up characters and situations. The writing has to be absolutely true to that character. If you start distorting a character in order to get a laugh, then you are veering toward the facile, where a cheap laugh will destroy the integrity of the scene or of the character. I have honestly never been looking for laughs as I've been writing. I've been looking for truth of characterization. I do like to observe adult characters behaving as though they are not adults, which a lot of us do a lot of the time. Laughs often come from that area.

RW: How much of an audience is there for theater in Australia?

DW: A large audience, per capita. We are a very active theater-going people. I was surprised to read that Australians are the greatest opera-goers per capita in the world. That rather alarmed me. I didn't find much solace in that. But we also go to the theaters in large numbers. Of course, more people go to film than drama.

RW: Would a company tour around Australia with one of your plays, or would the play be staged differently in different cities?

DW: The play might be staged differently in Sydney and Melbourne and a touring company launched from either of those cities. *Siren* will be playing in Melbourne and Sydney simultaneously, and the Melbourne production will go on tour.

RW: What is *Siren* about?

DW: *Siren* is a fairly tough war-of-the-sexes comedy. It is about an interesting but reasonably bad woman. I think it's time for male playwrights to stop feeling that they have to write women who are forthright, intelligent, assertive, independent, suffering under the yoke of male oppression, but fighting back valiantly. There are a number of male playwrights who have made a lot of money writing such characters. I felt a sense of rebellion, so I've written a different character. She is a young, attractive woman who enjoys having men fall in love with her, the more powerful and influential the better. She doesn't do it in a malevolent sense; she genuinely believes she is falling in love with them, but once they have fallen in love with her she is less interested than she was and moves on to someone else. Her purpose in life is to be good at something; she wants to find a skill that she is admired for, but she is not above using men to get into a position where she can start to exercise that skill. There are women out there like that. I've met them, and for hard-line feminists to pretend that the revolution has been so complete that there aren't such women is foolish, so I thought if they are there and I've observed them, than I'm allowed to write about them. There will no doubt be picket lines of angry feminists throwing eggs at the opening-night performance but I like to be able to write the truth.

RW: Is this an external or an internal observation of the woman? Liz is her name?

DW: Yes, Liz. We get both. We see how she behaves and we see her rationalizations for her behavior. We see that she doesn't really believe that she's acting malevolently. I've developed the line from *The Perfectionist* through *Emerald City* of a lot of direct address to the audience. I've taken it a step further this time in that the actors who are playing the characters make no pretense that they are not involved in an artifice. The device gives us a lot of information about the internal thought process of the main characters as well as their external actions.

RW: Is it difficult to get into the head of a woman?

DW: No. I don't think so. I've lived with a couple of women and I've known others quite well over the years. I think my portrait is pretty accurate.

RW: Is there a difference between a female mind and a male mind?

DW: I think there tend to be average differences. I think, talking averages, that the male mind spends more of its time thinking about politics in a broader sense, that it is more concerned with power, advancement, and status and more finely attuned to power gradations than the female mind, which is perhaps more finely tuned to aesthetic considerations, to human communications, to relationships. I think the male mind is a *thing*-oriented mind and the female mind still is a *people*-oriented mind. All the studies these days tend to be showing that there is a biological difference between males and females that affect the mind. For example, male testosterone levels are greater, and the male does have a greater interest in power and status. Females have more verbal ability and more accurate personal perception. Every psychological study seems to show this. That is probably why there are so many fine women novelists, but not so many female playwrights, because plays are still about drama, which is about power and conflict. This statement should cause yelps of outrage from feminists who'll say there is absolutely no biological difference whatsoever, but increasingly, the evidence is coming in that you can't just explain everything by environmental differences.

RW: Do you always have a piece of writing going? Are you ever without an idea or a project?

DW: I wish I was. The film scripts I'm doing for Hollywood at the moment are very involving and interesting, but I'll try after these next couple of films to take a slight rest.

RW: What is happening with the Australian film industry now? Is there still the excitement of the seventies and early eighties?

DW: In the seventies there was a bursting out of creative energy that had been potentially there for a long time but that hadn't been able to surface because financial and government encouragement just wasn't there. Then suddenly the state and commonwealth government started to find money for film and investing in film. The floodgates burst and there was such a desire to make film that in the mid- and late seventies and early eighties there was an enormous flurry of activity and some very good films were made. What has happened now is that a lot of the talent has gone to California. The basis of the funding, which was a tax funding scheme, attracted the attention of some people who were not so much interested in making films as they were in making money quickly because of the tax breaks. Therefore, in the later eighties a lot of bad films were made and people started caring less about films than about deals. A lot of films simply weren't released they were so bad, so the government has abolished the tax incentive scheme and gone back to a direct funding concept where a certain amount of money is set aside each year to fund Australian films, and we are awaiting the results of this change, which I think will lead to a different sort of film, a lower-budget, human-relationship, instead of a science fiction or a genre film. It's a wait-and-see period at the moment after a considerable trough.

RW: Do you think it is possible to again get films like *My Brilliant Career* or *The Year of Living Dangerously* or *Gallipoli?*

DW: I hope so. There is no reason why it couldn't happen, but the signs aren't great right at the moment.

RW: I would like to do a quick rundown of your major plays for the person unfamiliar with your work. If I give you the title would you give me a couple of sentences of what the play is about?

DW: Yes.

RW: *Don's Party?*

DW: An election-night party where student left-wingers who have become more conservative meet to hopefully watch a left liberal government be elected. It is based on the real election of 1969. Their hopes are disappointed, and personal recriminations with small dramas break out as the night wears on. Permissive sexual behavior had hit Australia like a bombshell in the late sixties, and there is rampant sexual behavior during the evening.

RW: Were you Don?

DW: There was an element of biography in that, yeah.

RW: *The Removalists?*

DW: *The Removalists* is about a sergeant and a new recruit who become involved in a domestic dispute and the situation escalates. It is a black comedy. It's meant to show that the Freudian is never far below the surface and in the wrong circumstances can emerge and cause devastating damage.

RW: *What if You Died Tomorrow?*

DW: It is about how a young, newly successful novelist copes with his broken marriage, his new wife, his de facto children, and his parents returning from abroad.

RW: *The Club?*

DW: It is about the political intrigue and backstabbing that happens as a football club slides toward the bottom of the competition.

RW: On Broadway this was called *Players?*

DW: Yes. It had to be changed because there was already a play called *The Club* running.

RW: *Travelling North?*

DW: It is about the relationship between a crusty, authoritarian old socialist who falls in love with a middle-aged woman called Frances. They decide to leave Frances's demanding daughters in Melbourne and travel north to find a peaceful paradise in which to let their love blossom. Unfortunately, it doesn't work out that way.

RW: *The Department?*

DW: It's about the bureaucratic and interpersonal backstabbing that occurs during a two-hour departmental meeting in a college of technology. Its theme is to suggest that the reason why institutions are founded, i.e., to educate students, tends to be forgotten by the staff hired to do this institutional task. Their own personal concerns tend to predominate at the staff meeting.

RW: *The Perfectionist?*

DW: It is about a marriage in which the husband is nominally the perfectionist. He has been doing a Ph.D. thesis for nine years and is unable to finish it because he doesn't feel that it is right. His wife is expected to subjugate her development in the interest of this thesis but finally gets fed up and has an affair with a Danish babysitter, which causes certain disruptions in the marriage.

RW: *Emerald City?*

DW: It is about greed, power, and lust, the temptations that a husband and wife succumb to when they travel from the moral city of Melbourne to the hedonistic city of Sydney.

RW: You are writing at the moment two screenplays for Paramount. What has this experience been like?

DW: Very revivifying. I've become tired of working in an Australian film industry where producers are trying to make American films. It's much more exciting to be working for American producers directly. I'm writing about real-life situations, a film script which is a black comedy with a serious subtext about two defense attorneys during the McCarthy era, and a film about Martin Luther King, Jr. during the desegregation period in the late fifties and sixties. I was very glad to get the King project. There were quite a few American writers who wanted it.

RW: How did an Australian get such an American subject?

DW: The producers liked the work I had done on the McCarthy script.

RW: Do you see yourself doing more screenplays and fewer stage plays?

DW: I hope to keep doing both. I really love being a dramatist because that's where I can use my love of dialogue most fully.

RW: You are unquestionably Australia's most successful dramatist, her most popular dramatist, and I would guess her most successful screenwriter, yet critics are often scornful of you as if your success were a personal affront. Is this simply the Tall Poppy syndrome, Australian self-flagellation, or something more?

DW: I think the tone turned nasty as soon as I got a waterfront place. In Australia, there is the notion that if you are a true artist you are meant to be in a garret starving; you are certainly not meant to have a pleasant house with roses on the water. There is a lot of negativity about the fact that I earn a good living at a trade that is peculiar to Australia because it simply hasn't happened before. But more seriously, I think there is a studied blindness to the darkness in my work. Because it is popular, my most trenchant critics would like to say that I write only comedy. I know I don't. There is a lot of darkness in the subtext about the human condition that people choose not to see.

RW: That would suggest you have some depth, wouldn't it?

DW: Yes. They wouldn't like to admit that. I also think there is a genuine Tall Poppy syndrome here. American society was started by idealists who were fleeing oppression and trying to construct a society that did justice to man's potential. Our society started as a dumping ground for convicts. Therefore, there has been a deep degree of pessimism about human potential. As a consequence, American society has tended to regard success as being an indicator of inner qualities, whereas Australian society has always tended to suspect that success was due to negative inner qualities, such as thievery, sucking up to one's superiors, dumping on one's mates. Success is equated with nastiness in Australia; I think less so in America.

RW: If you wrote less, would you write better?

DW: No. I am a compulsive writer and I actually like writing, so I've come to accept that my work will not be all of even quality. But I don't really work until I am sitting at the word processor. Until I am sitting there, nothing much happens. All my plays that are now regarded as my best plays were, if anything, written at a faster rate than the ones that aren't regarded as my best. *The Removalists* I wrote in two weeks, and *Don's Party* took only a bit longer. I don't think there is any correlation between the time taken and the quality of work. I do quite a few drafts, but often that rush of momentum can lead to something exciting.

TIM WINTON

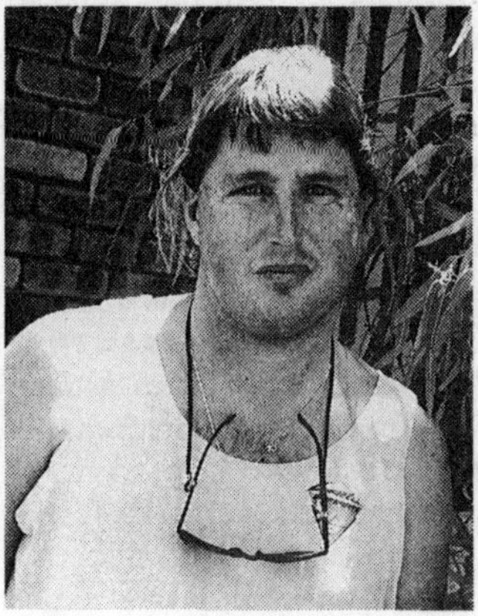

is the most prolific and most successful of Australia's young writers. He was born in 1960 and educated in Perth and Albany, Western Australia. Written when he was twenty, his first novel, *An Open Swimmer,* was the joint winner of the 1981 *Australian*/Vogel award. In 1984 *Shallows* won the Miles Franklin Award. After living two years in France, Ireland, and Greece, Tim Winton returned to Western Australia in 1989 and lives with his wife and two children in a small coastal town north of Perth. Although Winton's fiction covers a variety of subjects, he enjoys using Australia's West Coast as his setting and the adolescent or young adult male as his protagonist. The following interview occurred in Perth.

An Open Swimmer, 1981
Shallows, 1984
Scission (stories), 1985
That Eye, the Sky, 1987
Minimum of Two (stories), 1988
In the Winter Dark, 1988
Cloudstreet, 1991

INTERVIEW

RW: As a writer, you have the coast of Western Australia pretty much to yourself, don't you?

TW: At present. Robert Drewe has used it in the past and he comes and goes from it, mostly out of nostalgia I think, but he's based in Sydney now. Some of the stories in *The Bodysurfers* were set here. A part of *Fortune* was set in Perth and on the coast.

RW: Has Robert Drewe's writing had an influence on you?

TW: Yes. He's someone I've always admired. Actually, I won my first literary prize when he was one of the judges. For me the money was great and the prize was great, but getting it from someone I admire so much was especially great. I admire Robert Drewe because he's the kind of writer who straddles all worlds in terms of readership. Anybody can read Robert Drewe and take from it what he will. He's not an academic writer, which is something that I'm happy about.

RW: You want a broad readership for yourself?

TW: Yes. It took me a while to realize that. My first couple of books were more literary than the rest. Discovering that all kinds of people could enjoy my writing was a shock to me because when I came out of the university I thought fiction was written by professors for professors because Australian writing for the better half of this century has been deeply entrenched in the academic tradition. Discovering almost by accident that people were interested broadly in what I was doing was a tremendous pleasure. I started getting letters from people who did all kinds of things for work, or didn't have work, or who had never read much. I felt potent. It was really weird. I felt like I understood what I was doing for the first time.

RW: Do you think your writing has got more commercial since your earlier work?

TW: Certainly it's more accessible. People have told me that I'm an up-and-coming middlebrow. I don't mind this judgment at all because all the old male pop heroes were all middlebrows. Hemingway was a middlebrow; Dickens was a middlebrow. That's fine by me.

RW: You don't want to be a Henry James?

TW: No. I can't think of many things that would displease me more than being a Henry James, but I like the fact that people who are educated and in the educational elite can occasionally find things that will satisfy them in my work. People who don't usually read books also read me, and people who don't read literary books at all read me, and I find that's nice. I'm not in the millions of sellers; I sell very modestly. But I have kind of a faithful audience that I've picked up along the way, and that's great. I may make a living out of this, and that's also a shock.

RW: You *are* making a living.

TW: Yes, I've been doing it. I've never done anything else. I'm lucky that way.

RW: Would you talk about the importance of the coast in your writing?

TW: It has turned out to be my saving, I guess. Almost all writers are writing about themselves in disguise. Book after book, the same kind of story and usually about themselves for want of something else to write about. You haven't got the time to experience all things.

You write what you know and make up the rest. Pinch it from other peoples' books and just borrow from the collective unconscious, or whatever is out there. The coast just seemed to be where I spent most of my time, and where, I suppose in terms of my literary world inside of my head, that's where I go when I'm writing. I don't know if there's anything deeply meaningful in the setting itself, but yes, it's an area I know about; there are people in that area that I know about. I'm a coastal person.

RW: You've had a lot of lessons observing the interaction between people and the sea, haven't you?

TW: Yes. I've never lived beyond sight of the sea, so for me to be living inland—I'm talking about a couple of miles inland, not the desert—is kind of uncomfortable.

RW: Are you living on the ocean now?

TW: Yes. I live in a little fishing town ninety miles north of Perth.

RW: What's the population?

TW: About six hundred. It's lobster fishing, and it just exists during the season. When the season finishes, it shrinks down to a kind of a skeleton crew of a few hundred. It's a flat, ugly, tough, redneck town.

RW: Why do you choose to live there?

TW: Because it's right on the sea. It's quiet. It's the kind of place that interests me. It's cheap, which was important to us because we came back from Europe with no prospect of being able to buy a house in the city, so we bought a fish deco kind of place. If you can afford to put a bore down to get water, you can live any kind of life.

RW: Do you have children?

TW: Two boys, one five, one seven months. We live a nice life. We have a boat; we fish, and dive a lot, and surf.

RW: What's the West Coast of Australia like?

TW: It's incredibly varied and incredibly long. In the south it's granite cliffs and a really impressive, dramatic coastline, which is what I wrote about in *Shallows* and *An Open Swimmer* and some of the stories. On the west it's more flat and jagged with shelving reefs that go out. It's harsh; but it's mean in a nice way. It's uncompromising and spare. It's the kind of place we should be building Algerian villas on, little white joints with courtyards. I really like it. It reminds me of Greece, too, which is why I like Greece so much and why I came back from Greece to be here. The water's clean too. There's no shit in the water, which is always a great advantage. This is a place in the world where I can live by the sea and where the sea still has bounty; everything is alive and it's not polluted and I don't have to pay to use it. I get up at 5:30 and pull my pots, and maybe if I'm not working—I tend not to work so much in the summer—I can dive later in the day. I can take the kids out to the islands; I can do whatever. It's a good life; the only trouble is in not getting skin cancer. The ozone layer has a big hole right above us. We are where the biggest concentration is. We have to wear hats, baste on sunblocker. We put out only a minuscule of fluorocarbons in West Australia, but we get the ozone hole.

RW: Is a firm sense of place important to you as a writer?

TW: Yes. If I know where I am, I usually know what I am. I write about small places; about people in small situations. If I get a grip on the geography, I can get a grip on the people. A friend of mine once cracked a joke that whenever he got his characters outside of the house or outside of a city, he had major trouble getting them around on the page. When I get them into the room, I have the same problem; once I get them out in landscape I'm okay. It would be useless for me to try to be a Henry James because if I had characters in a drawing room, I'd be stuck forever. So the people I responded to the most when I was discovering literature were the people who had their characters out in landscape. I could see them. There's Twain and Stow and Hemingway. There's that outdoorsy tradition, not so much the Jim Harrison shooting and bruising kind of tradition, but the tradition of having a life that involves being outside. That's the kind of people I know, and that's the kind of life that I've had.

RW: You're twenty-nine now?

TW: Yes.

RW: And you've published six books and finished seven?

TW: Eight. I have four novels published and two books of stories. I have a children's picture book published and I have two books coming out next year that are getting typeset. So that's nine, I guess.

RW: One London critic in the *Times Literary Supplement* calls you the *Wunderkind* of Australian literature. You've won the Vogel Prize and Australia's most prestigious literary prize, the Miles Franklin Award. Do you think all this critical attention has been good for you? Has it stimulated you or has it made demands on you?

TW: It has stimulated me, but probably not in the sense that you might think. It's been a worry, but it's nice to be approved, even though it's a pretty loaded kind of approval. I'm always of two minds about it. Maybe it keeps me honest a little bit, but the big thing is that it has made me self-conscious, and I was never a very self-conscious writer. I resent that. Whereas once I would have traded solely on instinct, now I'm sometimes double-thinking myself; that annoys me because almost always what I do first is what I should have done. When I get on it for the third time and I'm doing what I did the first time, I think, I wouldn't have done this if I didn't have those people, those unknown literary experts sitting on a panel waiting to see what tradition my work fits into, how it compares with what I've done before. Everyone's got an agenda and a theory. Winning the awards has been a stimulus for me, but the best stimulus, I find, is having to pay the rent.

RW: Do you have any fear of burn-out?

TW: People asked me that question often enough that I started to think about it. I was young and I was using up heaps and heaps of ideas. I tended to waste a lot of ideas; I think as you get older you get meaner with what comes along to you. It's hard to know what makes a burn-out.

RW: You've said that Randolph Stow is your idol. He had published a lot when he was young, too. But nine books at thirty . . .

TW: Stow had written a lot, and he had written bigger books, too. He said at thirty that he'd had enough and it was all over. But he had a very different disposition to me; he was a very nervous man, a very sensitive man with a fragile personality, and he was very reclusive. He's a person who would have been self-conscious from the moment that he was born. You can see it in him. I feel I've had literary self-consciousness implanted in me, almost surgically. I'm not naturally very self-conscious. But burn-out—it's something to think about. Can you publish too much? Can you hurry too much?

RW: Do you feel hurried?

TW: Occasionally. If you don't work as a teacher and write, or if you don't write part time and have a separate job, or if you don't have an independent income like Patrick White, then you don't always get to publish when the time is right. Patrick White took about seven years for every book. It's more that he had seven years, rather than that he took seven years. I feel a lot of pressure to publish to make money. That's the problem which comes from deciding to be a professional writer.

RW: It's amazing in a country this size that you make a living as a writer.

TW: It's only because I have written so many books. I was lucky to start when I was a teenager; I was nineteen and publishing in national magazines. I was twenty when *An Open Swimmer* was done, so I had a huge head start. To tell you the truth, the way in which I write is the result of a conscious decision. I thought, if I'm going to live from writing, I'm either going to write one book that's going to make me a fortune, or I'm going to have to write a lot of books. I knew that if I used my ideas I could succeed. I have spent my twenties in a writing room laboring in a way that now makes me feel tired and a little self-conscious, but it was the only way it was possible to live from writing in a country like this.

RW: A protagonist common to most of your fiction is the sensitive young man seen at various ages and at various passage points. Would you talk about your use of this kind of protagonist?

TW: Are you talking about my character Jarra, or just about my characters in general?

RW: Yes, Jarra, but you otherwise use the sensitive young man as a common character in your novels and stories.

TW: When you're writing books before you are thirty you have to be authoritative on one subject, and I guess I've got some authority on being a young man. I'm always interested in and I've probably never outgrown my childhood in the sense that I had a happy childhood and a very comfortable one, emotionally. I realized by the time I was a teenager that I'd seen a lot of things as a very young boy that I'd never really understood. My father was a policeman and still is. I used to hear a lot of things that I wasn't supposed to hear. I was an insomniac, so I used to listen in on what my father told my mother in confidence at night, after they were in bed. I guess there was a lot of that stuff coming my way, and I was able to draw on it when I was a teenager and beginning to write. From a narrative perspective, having a young boy is helpful because a writer can do a lot with naïveté. I also find it nostalgic to put myself into that situation again, being twelve, being seven, being fourteen. But in the stories I've written with children undergoing pain and suffering and confusion, very little of it is genuine in the sense that it comes from my own life. I am just guessing about other people's lives.

RW: What about your young adult stories, the Jarra stories?

TW: Yes, I guess I get a little closer to the bone. They're not what I'd call autobiographical, but there are certainly things there, the stories of birth for example. The story "Blood and Water" is not fiction; it's a piece of journalism.

RW: The story reminds me of the hospital scene in *A Farewell to Arms.*

TW: That's probably right, although I haven't read that novel in ten years.

RW: In fact, when I read it, I thought, "Humm, this is awfully close."

TW: That's terrible isn't it, especially since it's my least favorite of Hemingway's books.

RW: "Forest Winter," the first story in *Minimum of Two,* is a good story to illustrate what you do. Would you talk about this story?

TW: It's the story of a young guy who's got a wife and a very young child, a baby only a couple of months old. He's been in rock-and-roll bands and fails. She's had one baby and is pregnant again. He is not working and has left the city and gone to the country to look for some means of survival. It hasn't worked out and it has kind of become a disaster, and at the last minute they come across a little ex-forestry town where he gets a job sawing wood. He's at the end of his emotional tether and he seems to survive one crisis just to climb into another. He comes home and finds his wife in a bad way with an asthma attack. He rushes her to town to buy medicine, knowing he doesn't have the money to pay for it. He tries to get into a pharmacy and he almost has to bash the door down because they think he is a junkie trying to rob them. He gets hold of some Ventolin for his wife and drives back home. The next morning he has another catastrophe. The old Ventolin cylinder that his wife has previously had finds its way into the wastepaper basket. He lights the wood stove the next morning and the cylinder explodes in his face. He thinks he's been blinded and he panics. His wife shows her very sensible nature. I think she says, "Don't be wet."

RW: How did that story come to you? Was it your experience?

TW: No, not at all. I like any story that has an excuse for chopping or sawing wood in it. When I was a young boy my father used to have to go out of Albany, the town where we lived, to relieve at other police stations in very small country towns, and in his absence I was the man looking after the family. My idea of looking after the family was to chop six or seven tons of wood. I quite like chopping wood. It's a weird thing. I've always enjoyed the whole ritualistic process. But in terms of the story, once I went down South for awhile. I stayed overnight in a little house in a small forest town. For some reason the setting, the geography of the place got to me and I had to find an excuse to get it into a story.

RW: Why do you think chopping wood has remained important to you?

TW: I don't know what it is in later times. When I chopped wood as a young boy, it wasn't just a matter of pride; it was also a matter of rage and hurt. I used to miss my father a lot, so I would go out and beat the hell out of the woodpile. In later years, as a young father or as a young husband, I used to go out and do the same thing. Chopping wood in summer is always a good sign that someone is not doing too well. You know, we don't even have to burn fires here. Where I live now, a fire is just an aesthetic event.

RW: You have that closeness of the boy to his father in your fiction; that's a lovely thing in your writing.

TW: Well, it's something some people have become impatient with, and maybe I've earned that impatience. I don't know.
RW: Are you thinking that people are becoming impatient with reading it?
TW: Yes. I think they think it's just more of this kind of father-and-son stuff, the old Hemingway thing.
RW: But Hemingway didn't quite get along with his father. You do a lot of loving from the boy's point of view in *That Eye, the Sky.*
TW: I suppose I'm thinking of those early Nick Adams stories; they're nice in their own way. It's something that I've always been interested in. There isn't much in literature between fathers and sons and mothers and sons within families that's positive, that doesn't see the family as anything but a wire that binds the foot. My life hasn't been like that and I suppose that's the only excuse I have for having all these people who are trying to get along in their own way, and whose travails don't stem from each other so much as from what surrounds them.
RW: One of the things you deal with so well is the complexity of family relationships: *Scissions, Shallows, That Eye, the Sky.*
TW: You probably couldn't accuse me of complexity; that's one of the things critics complain about. I am called a literalist because I've gone beyond realism into literalism.
RW: Again, I'm thinking of *That Eye, the Sky*—the mother and the son; the daughter and the preacher. The mother/daughter relationship is very complex.
TW: I suppose it becomes complex from their not saying anything.
RW: From your leaving out?
TW: Yes. There's the wonderful American/Australian movie, *Tender Mercies,* which is my favorite movie. What I love about it is that no one ever says anything and no one can say anything. When the woman asks the man what's the matter, he says, "I can't." He just can't tell her, that's all. What I like about it is that's what people usually are like. People can't. They don't have the words; they can't say what they mean. They know what they feel, but they don't have the words for it. That old theory—"language is meaning"; I believe that. People have terrible yearnings and feelings. They know what they think and they know what they want to say, but they just don't have the words. It's not so much the vocabulary; the words are in their throat, but they're not on their tongue. That's what I like. I like that in *Tender Mercies* and I like that in my favorite books. My favorite books are the ones in which people are not articulate; they're not stupid, but they're not articulate, and they battle with it, with their silence. I guess in my stories people can't really articulate what

they're feeling. Also, my narrators never say anything; there's very little in my stories or novels of a narrator commenting on the action, or judging the action. I suppose I have an impatience with books whose narrators are voluble. Unless they're extremely funny, I don't want to hear them. I want to get it from the characters and not from the narrator. I don't know what that is. Perhaps it's my feeling, as I do feel, a little inarticulate in a business of words. I'm still going more on instinct than a critical outlook.

RW: Your instincts are serving you well.

TW: I hope so. I'd like not to have to change; I mean, maybe I will, but I'm certainly not going to buy any bill of goods from anybody else.

RW: In *That Eye, the Sky* and *In the Winter Dark*, I'm reminded of Flannery O'Connor. Has she been an influence?

TW: She's my favorite writer. She's my hero. I think that America still hasn't come to terms with how significant she was. She was taken up by the women's movement who, I think, just completely misunderstood what she was about. But at least in England and Australia they got her read again. She was a stylist and she had an amazing understanding of the human soul.

RW: She is usually on the curriculum at American universities.

TW: She's often taught, but she's rarely ever read by the general reader. She's not an easy writer, I suppose. She is totally uncompromising. What she was on about offends the world. She's fabulous. She gets to the end of the story and she sticks a spike up your ass. She's great. She doesn't go for any kind of lowdown, cheap gothic. There seems to be a big difference between her and Carson McCullers. There's no tat there, it's all authentic and straight to the gut. If she has some evangelist slaying a goat on the front of a Dodge in the main street singing, hallelujah, you believe it; it's not there for effect and it's not there as a kind of scenery and it's not there to say, let's get grotesque. She's wincing every time, every word.

RW: I was thinking of your evangelist in *That Eye, the Sky.* Being the age that you are, with so many writers having gone before you, is it difficult not to be influenced, not to be derivative?

TW: I'm sure I've been derivative and I'm sure I've been influenced. Yeah, I think it's pretty difficult. If you have an evangelist come into your story, everyone's going to jump up and say, Flannery O'Connor. She's made that her own. She's been there before with a kind of integrity. You can't help but make the comparison, I suppose, so, I'm just stuck with that. I think the worse thing for me to do would be to shy off it because Flannery O'Connor has done it. That's what I call surrendering to self-consciousness.

RW: Tell me about your interest in the supernatural.

TW: Well, I come from nonconformist protestant stock. I was baptized in a little corrugated iron tank like the guy in *Tender Mercies.* I grew up in the Church of Christ. It's a little different here than in the States, but still fundamental and conservative. While I outgrew that kind of sect, part of it and the limitations of it, the fundamental belief is still there. Outgrowing a Church of Christ culture didn't mean outgrowing faith and it didn't mean outgrowing interests in the big questions. All the interest in life and death and evil and good is still there.

RW: In fundamentalism, one certainly deals with the big questions.

TW: That's right. Living with a huge swatch of doubt now and again kind of gets you off. So, it's not just writing that I've felt like I've had in common with Flannery O'Connor. It's faith. That goes in a kind of a different wave from Walker Percy and most of my favorite American writers. Some of the others I like are Thomas McGuane, Larry Woiwode, Cormac McCarthy, Barry Hannah.

RW: In *That Eye, the Sky,* the young boy sees something protective, a benevolent light hovering over the house; do you have any belief in a benevolent protector?

TW: Yes. I suppose when it comes down to it, I'm still an orthodox Christian. I'm not sure which heresy I fit into best, but I'm a believer in the God of the Old and New Testament. I'm stuck with that. If I didn't have faith, I don't know what I would have. I guess I'm asking, what does the rest of Australia have? In America being part of a church is a respectable thing, but in Australia, faith has never been a respectable thing. It is not part of the Australian character. I feel well behind the eight ball anyway, on the outside of the outside. I'm twenty years too young; I live on the wrong coast; I write the wrong kind of things. Having religious faith on top of this is a real aberration that in the literary culture people will, at best, kind of put up with. I am middlebrow and out of the mainstream.

RW: Australians aren't particularly concerned with spiritual questions, are they?

TW: No. A critic of my first book said that I was obviously showing my youth in presupposing that meaning could be quested for, sought for and found. I thought that I was just showing my different world view.

RW: You use the supernatural in creating a sense of menace or horror. Are you interested in evil?

TW: I'm actually not as interested in evil as I should be, I guess, never having had to deal with it in any raw way, I mean, not in terms of Auschwitz and having suffered terrible things, but when I was writing my first books a lot of catastrophes happened to friends and family. I think I went to five funerals in four months. There was a murder, a cancer job, a car accident; someone died of old age. I ran the gambit the year when I was writing *Shallows.* I think the feeling of impending menace probably rubbed off and stuck with me. My early stories are pretty dark; *Scission* is a dark collection of stories. When it comes to *In the Winter Dark,* the sense of menace and evil, it's a kind of a different thing. It's an interior business. What I've done in that book with the darkness is to set up a Thing. I run a few red herrings around the valley and I watch people shit themselves. I suppose the book is about fear and guilt and how they become the progenitor of evil. The four people living in the valley each have a past. Something out there is eating their animals and prowling around at night. None of them really have any idea what it is, but each of them has worked up a whole pile of memories and guilt and personal fears that seem to grow until it almost becomes irrelevant what's truly out there; it's what's in them that is working itself up into a frenzy. They're running scared, getting panicky, and the thing builds out of a communal fear.

RW: What is out there?

TW: It works on the old story of the Nawnup tiger, which is still reported to be seen. It's either a cougar, which is obviously an import because we don't have any carnivores . . .

RW: What tiger did you say?

TW: The Nawnup tiger, there's a little town called Nawnup. It is a real deep South hick farming town where the hippies went in the seventies. In Nawnup there have been constant sightings of something, some carnivore that's too big for anything that's native. This sort of thing happens in small communities. It's alternatively ridiculous and plausible. It's either the return of a thought-to-be-extinct animal, a crocodile with a pouch like a kangaroo, the Tasmanian tiger, or it's a wild dog or a wild cat. We have a terrible cat problem here because we don't have any natural carnivores except for the dingo, which is much further inland now. Nothing eats birds and other things. Nothing has fangs. And there is fear of the feral cat, as it has been growing and adapting for a hundred years.

RW: You have both ideas working at the same time, the psychological and the possible.

TW: Yes. There are about four psychological possibilities. In the end of the book a catastrophe happens and two men collude to cover up what they did in panic. The critics hated it. In Australia the critics have a hard time even granting you your subject matter, let alone how you do it.

RW: You use panic, a sense of entrapment, claustrophobia, aspects of living so seemingly at variance with the wide, blue Western Australian sky. When Elizabeth Jolley uses the same sorts of things, I sense an English imagination working with her, but there's no such background for you. Where do you think this interest comes from?

TW: Well, hell. You've got to write about something, don't you? I've never really had to face panic and entrapment that much. I've had it in small doses, but none of these things have ever happened to me. I suppose, really the only thing I can put it down to is what I said before. Being introduced to the adult world as an insomniac and hearing some of the terrible things my father had saved up all during dinner to tell to my mother in order to be able to sleep himself that night. I was listening to what happened to a child in a car accident or what somebody had been found doing to somebody else. And also, I was affected by the spirit I heard in his voice. He was daily confronted by only the very worst in people, and he couldn't change the nature of people. I think he felt the shit was rubbing off, in the sense that it begins to affect your outlook. After awhile, you begin to fear for yourself, wondering if it can rub off. Can I become one of these people? So, I was absorbing the powerlessness and despair of someone who was essentially, and still is, an honorable, good, kind man, a man faced with depravity all the time. Perhaps I can trace what is dark in my writing back to this. A lot of my material has been stolen from conversations. I'm definitely not an urban writer. Urban writing, unless it's very funny, often doesn't hold my attention. I like reading adventure stories, young boys finding out about themselves. I like it when someone is wringing his hands and something dramatic is happening. I was brought up on adventure stories. That's what I read. I read Stevenson and I read all those boy stories, *The Coral Island* and *The Swiss Family Robinson,* which are all coastal as well, and to do with islands and young boys making their way and finding out about themselves. So, I like a story that gets along with a narrative pace which generally you don't get in urban introspective novels. And that's what I like about Cormac McCarthy and Thomas McGuane, the more mature bits of Jim Harrison and Barry Hannah. They kind of get along. There's a whole stack of those people that I read.

RW: You've just recently returned to West Australia after two years in Europe; tell me where you were and something about your time there.

TW: I was in Paris for about six months. I was staying in the studio the Australian Council makes available for artists and writers. It was my first experience living in a city bigger than a million people and the first time I'd lived in an apartment. Those walls—I just suffered. The three of us were packed in, but it was a good life lesson. It was a good place to have it; Paris is the most beautiful city in the world. In the summer I worked in the studio and Denise and Jesse walked the streets and hung out in the parks. In the winter, they had the studio and I actually did that old thing of working in a café. There was a café where they didn't mind me working. Every couple of hours I'd have a coffee or a Perrier. I wrote a hundred pages of the novel that I've got now and I rewrote a good part of *In the Winter Dark*. I wrote stories and travel pieces. It was great, but the weather got us down. For someone who comes from a good climate like this, it was hard. About the time that winter got down in Paris, it was time to go. The little boy got sick and we got depressed and it was time to move on.

RW: Hemingway wrote, "Paris in the winter is wet, dripping, depressing, gray."

TW: Well, you know, you get the language frustrations as well, and Parisians are complete pigs. We put up with that for a while and after a while we realized that it wasn't just that they just misunderstood; they were really nasty. A friend of a friend had called before we left Australia and offered us the gatehouse of his medieval castle in Tipperary. We decided to leave Paris and go to Ireland. Again, the weather was putrid; it rained every day and was damp and depressing, but the people were fabulous, the landscape was strongly interesting, although almost featureless because it's been stripped of its trees. To someone like me, the land was tamed to the point of being impotent, but it's not impotent at all. It's a very strong place. I'm not a romantic person, but I was very deeply affected by it. The place seemed to stink of time. The gatehouse where we lived was filled with books about historic Australia, and I had a little gardener's cottage up on a hill about four hundred yards away called Spender's Cottage where I used to work beside a coal fire. I used to burn anything just to keep the water off the paper. I wrote quite a bit of my new novel, *Cloudstreet*. We stayed until the weather ground us down again. After that we went to Greece and lived on the island of Hydra for six months. George Johnston, who wrote *My Brother Jack* and *Clean Straw for Nothing*, once lived there. He's an author I've always been fascinated by. When I got to Greece I realized why I live in Australia and why I always want to stay in Australia. It's what the landscape and the weather does to you. I'd never believed that weather and landscape and geography affected people so deeply, but I found on Hydra that the people lived very differently to the people who lived further north, and they lived in approximation to how I live in Australia. Hydra is an island of fishermen; they are connected to the physical world in a way that Western urban people aren't. I lived in a village of thirty-five people. There were no cars. I couldn't communicate with the people, but I was very happy. I realized that there were a lot of things I didn't need and that when I went back to Australia I would try to carry this over. It's difficult not to be changed by these things. In terms of what I learned for my work, I guess my life is my work. I saw things, met people, heard stories. I lived with people who were very different from me in a more extended way than I'd ever had to before. I lived among expatriates who were a-bottle-of-vodka-a-day people. I discovered that I was never going to be an expatriate, that this kind of romance is destructive, soul-destroying, unless the person is strong enough, productive enough to overcome total displacement. I did realize that I could probably live anywhere, as long as I was connected to my family and my work.

RW: How long were you away?

TW: Almost two years. I was prostrate with homesickness.

RW: What made you stay so long?

TW: Maybe it was a matter of pride. I did want to see some things, and it cost so much to get there. I thought I might never have the chance again; you don't have many choices. You have to be realistic. Next year I might not have a readership. In the nineties my books might be out of print and I might be working as a clerk somewhere.

B. WONGAR

Aboriginal Myths (with Alan Marshall), 1972
The Sinners, 1972
The Track to Bralgu, 1978
The Trackers, 1978
Babaru, 1982
Bilma (poems), 1984
Nuclear Trilogy:
Walg, 1983
Karan, 1985
Gabo Djara, 1987

was born in 1936 of a Yugoslavian father. He is certain neither where he was born nor who his mother was. He grew up in a small village in Yugoslavia. In 1960 he immigrated to Australia and spent ten years living with aboriginal tribes in the Northern Territory. Wongar learned a large aboriginal vocabulary, immersed himself in aboriginal myth as well as in daily tribal life, and set about to raise Australian and international consciousness concerning the wealth of the aboriginal culture, the importance of oral tradition, and the pernicious effect of the whites' subjugation of the blacks in Australia, particularly as it has been expressed through nuclear testing and the relocation and fragmentation of aboriginal tribes. These last issues are the subject of three novels which Wongar calls his Nuclear Trilogy. More highly regarded for his fiction abroad than in Australia, Wongar has won the praise of such important writers as Alan Paton, and the resentment of some white Australians who accuse him of speaking as an Aborigine when he is not one. Regardless of this issue, Wongar is a highly imaginative and poetically skillful writer. He recreates the haunting aboriginal world with beauty, compassion, and humor.

INTERVIEW

RW: Do you prefer to be called by your birth name, Sreten Bozic, or by your Australian name, B. Wongar?

BW: B. Wongar. It's a name that was given to me by the aboriginal people. It was a name used by my late tribal wife; therefore, I still like to be known as Wongar.

RW: What does Wongar mean?

BW: Once I was sunburned and had a dark bushy beard. I was often on an aboriginal reserve in the North without permit. I was living with the Aborigines. I was lying down; I had some pain in my chest. A tribal medicine man was chanting over my chest and trying to do a bit of healing. A government supervisor came over. He saw me and realized that I did not belong to that group of people. He asked where I came from, and the medicine man said, "He comes from Wongar." What he was telling the supervisor was that I came from the spirit world, but the supervisor did not understand. He thought I came from a subtribe called Wongar. He said, "When he gets well, tell him to go back to his mob." The Aborigines died laughing because they knew he had told me to go back to the spirit world. My wife started calling me that and so did the rest of them.

RW: Where does the "B" come from?

BW: It comes from my own original name, Bozic, and from the tribal name given me, Banumbir, which means "morning star" and "messenger from the spirit world."

RW: You were born in Yugoslavia in 1936. Is that correct?

BW: I'm not sure I was born in Yugoslavia. I never knew my mother. In the 1930s my father went to Australia as an illegal immigrant to prospect for gold. He spent a lot of time in the bush prospecting at old mining sites and was often among the aboriginal people. He returned to Yugoslavia sometime in the thirties. The only thing to show that I was born was that my name was put in a christening book when I was three years of age. The woman who raised me wasn't my mother. She told me that my father brought me with him when he came back to the village. I don't know whether he brought me back from Australia or where he brought me from. He was to go back to Australia again, but the war caught him up. He was put in jail. When I was a child he used to tell me that we were going back to Australia.

RW: But he never told you who your mother was?

BW: No, but the woman who raised me was a dear woman. She had seven children of her own, but she never made a difference between us. The people in the village called me "Gara," which means someone who differs in color. In English you might say "darkie."

RW: But you are not really dark.

BW: To the village I was a different color. I was from outside. I don't know where. There wasn't much possibility for a school education during the war years, but the oral tradition was very strong in the village and I learned from that. When I was about eight, soldiers came to ask for information about my father; this was before he was in jail, and they put a gun to my mouth and told me to put it between my teeth. They started discussing who they should kill, me, or my sister, while I held the gun between my teeth. They didn't kill either of us; it was just to scare us, but that's what a hell it was. After the war, things didn't change much. My father was still in jail. He died in jail. I left the village when I was about thirteen. I lived in a nearby town, but I couldn't get worthwhile work because I didn't have Party papers and I couldn't get them because of my father's name. I did my national service and then I fled the country. I went to Italy and was forced to go on to France. I worked in an automobile factory in Paris.

RW: Why did you come to Australia?

BW: Partly because of my father's stories. I landed in Sydney without a word of English. I had no identification papers. The only thing I had was a paper issued by the French police. On it was written, "This man claims that he is called so and so." That is all I had. I had a little money and I made my way from Sydney to Central Australia. I was headed for the West Kimberleys because my father had told me about a place called Halls Creek where he had done some prospecting. I didn't want to prospect; I just thought it might be a good place because he had told me about it. I didn't know it was just a dot in the desert. I got to Alice Springs and asked around to see if anyone was going to Halls Creek by car. Later, I realized that of course no one was going to this place. There wasn't even a road there. I asked a man how to get to Halls Creek and he told me the cheapest way was by camel, and he sold me a camel. I had never ridden a horse before, let alone a camel. I'm not even sure I'd ever seen a camel before.

RW: Is this a true story you're telling me?

BW: It is true. My concept of Australia was a European concept. You see the places on the map and you think you are traveling as you would from Frankfort to Munich. I was in Central Australia, but I knew nothing of the desert. If the man told me to buy a camel it was no different than if he had told me to buy a horse. I didn't know. I rode the camel for about three weeks. I had a map and I knew the direction of Halls Creek. After about three weeks the camel didn't want to move anymore. I didn't know then, but I learned later that the camel was sick. He'd been eating salt bush. He just didn't want to get up. There was nothing I could do. I started to look for water without knowing how foolish this was. You don't look for water on the desert. I did see a windmill in the far distance and walked to it, but it was derelict. It was without a pump and was rattling in the wind. On my way back I lost my way; I couldn't find the camel. I lost what moisture was in my body and began to hallucinate. I thought I was passing. Then I saw a black face looming over me. I thought I had already gone to heaven; Saint Peter was black. The man squeezed something liquid in my mouth, a few drops from a plant. The Aborigine then brought a frog which had a bellyful of water. He squeezed the water from the frog into my throat. I know it sounds like a joke, but it happened. He buried me in a pit of sand so that I wouldn't lose more moisture. He stayed with me and brought more roots for water until I recovered. Eventually, he found the camel and I started riding him again. The camel had been eating salt bush and he had needed to lie down. If I had just waited with him it would have been all right. Anyway, I was on the right track and the Aborigine accompanied me to Halls Creek, then later on beyond toward Wyndham, which is in the direction of the sea. It took about three months.

RW: What did you eat?

BW: Bush food. He found roots and whatever was there and took care to share.

RW: The experience with the man who saved you was your first experience with an Aborigine?

BW: Yes. I met other Aborigines at Wyndham and got into a close friendship. Afterwards, I moved on to the Northern Territory and stayed with the people there. A good many tribal communities were still living there in the 1960s. I was slipping away from the white communities and spending more and more time with the tribal people.

RW: How were you supporting yourself?

BW: I worked a day here and there for necessities. In a tribal society you don't need much. You sleep under the stars. If you get cold, someone maybe gives you a dog or dingo for a blanket; sometimes there was a windbreak of corrugated iron.

RW: Were you writing in those days?

BW: Not very much. Sometimes I took notes. I was interested in the oral tradition and the art because of the oral tradition I came from. I had written poetry since I was a little child and had memorized poetry. I was interested in collecting myths. I have published a book of tribal myths. I was also interested in the different languages, in the different art. I spent ten years looking into that and I wrote a manuscript called *Forty Thousand Years of Aboriginal Creativity.*

RW: I was curious how you were learning language. Were you learning English and an aboriginal dialect at much the same time?

BW: Living in that land you could recognize one dialect from another. I wasn't fully aware of all dialects, but I could distinguish one dialect from another. I would ask questions.

RW: Did you live with different tribes?

BW: I moved from area to area. The tribes were breaking down. The disruption of the Aborigines had been going on since a uranium mine was opened in the Northern Territory in the early fifties. The Aborigines were shifted from the tribal ground and placed in camps.

RW: In your stories and in your novels your sentences are marked with aboriginal words. How do you authenticate these words? Are they part of your own vocabulary?

BW: If I use a word I take it from my memory or from somewhere where I have it written or from some source that I can check. But each word I use is chosen because I feel it is the correct word.

RW: Is there a general aboriginal dictionary?

BW: It is sad, but there is no such. Sometimes I do research.

RW: And how would you do that?

BW: By asking another person, looking in a letter. If I remain uncertain, I have to use a different word.

RW: In the story you published in *Antipodes*, "Walpadja, the Stormmaker," did you know the word *walpadja*? Is that a common enough word?

BW: It appears in one form or another in lots of Central tribes. There are variations of sounds. If you do a phonetic spelling you will find a slight deviation here and there, but the concept of the word will remain the same. I try to place the spelling of the word from where my character is set. I try to get his dialect right. These days because the people travel so much the dialects are becoming mixed.

RW: Other than your father's interest in oral tradition, what caused you to identify so closely with the Aborigines when you came to Australia, or as you continued to live among them? Why didn't you come back into a more traditional European situation?

BW: I'm not sure. At the time I left Europe I was more or less fed up with everything that was there. The aboriginal world was something to move into. It came almost as a relief. Aboriginal life in the bush is far from comfortable. It's a life of hardship and misery and sadness and unhappiness and disaster. It was not happy, but somehow for me at that time, since I had left such a disaster in Europe, the new life felt more comfortable. Besides, I grew up in a village in the time of war. The people were forced to resort to their own production of everything. The Aborigines have this same pattern of life. I was familiar with it; it was an independent existence that attracted me.

RW: How long did you live in the bush or in an aboriginal setting?

BW: About ten years. I broke it a few times to come down to Melbourne to see Alan Marshall with whom I published *Aboriginal Myths.*

RW: You married a tribal woman?

BW: Yes. In the bush. We lived in the tribal areas west of Darwin.

RW: Did you have children?

BW: Two children. We moved about to avoid the authorities. I didn't want to be charged with anything. We joined wandering bands. Part of the family is always on the move; and we moved about also for economic and for social reasons. We formed relationships, brotherhood relationships for mutual protection in case of hardships or in case something happened to the family.

RW: What made you decide to separate from a tribal life?

BW: Things were becoming harder. Aboriginal tribal land was being taken over by mining concerns. People were being forcibly moved about. Politically, things were getting bad. It wasn't good for me as a white to be in the area, to be on a reservation. I had started writing and protesting locally and I was getting known. I had published *Aboriginal Myths.* I thought I should go down South, find a piece of land and move my family. I went down to Victoria and found some land, and about the time these things were taken care of I learned that my family had been wiped out. They had disappeared in the bush.

RW: Wiped out?

BW: The news that I got, not from the authorities, but from the tribal people who lived in the area, was that they drank from a water hole which was poisoned, or in some way polluted. The water wasn't fit to drink, and they died. The authorities kept no records at that time in the seventies. If an aboriginal disappeared in the bush, he disappeared.

RW: How were you affected by their deaths?

BW: I felt guilty because I was down South. Although there was nothing I could have done, I felt that I should have been there. For years I kept dreaming and dreaming of it. It was one of the reasons I've had to write.

RW: Did you have the close emotional tie with your aboriginal family that one would expect in any family relationship?

BW: Oh, yes. I still feel the strong tie. According to aboriginal beliefs the dogs, the dingoes, are your reincarnated relatives. I have three dingoes here in the house. If I go to bed they all sleep on the bed with me. I would rather go to the floor than kick them out.

RW: Do you think your dingoes specifically carry the souls of your wife and children?

BW: Put it this way. I will believe what my wife would believe. And she would believe that, so I will believe what the aboriginal people tell me. They have a different insight into the soul. In their mythology such things happen. Dingoes turn into people; people turn into dingoes.

RW: You use dingoes a lot in your fiction as the carrier of the soul. Is the dingo the only animal which does this?

BW: In most cases, not all. They are the closest animal to the human. They are the only domesticated animal, the animal which comes close when you call. In some cases a soul might be recognized in a bird following you, or a lizard, or a kangaroo.

RW: This is not just a mental belief with you, is it? You believe it from the heart?

BW: If you go into science and analyze you might come to a conclusion that this is not possible. I am not a man of science. I am a man of oral literature. These things happen in oral literature and for me it is something which is logical and comforting. If I tell myself this is not possible, I am telling myself that I don't believe in oral literature, in all that I have been taught. For me, a book of physics doesn't have much meaning, for even though I live in a house, wear bought clothing, drive a car, my mind stays different. I don't ask how these things work, but they happen to me. If I start divorcing myself from my beliefs, then I have the feeling that the whole structure will crumble, because if you divorce yourself from family and from what you believe, then there is nothing else. My world is there. If I couldn't believe myself related to the grass and to the trees and other living things I would probably be dead by now. I would be stripped of everything. You build a cocoon that keeps you safe so that you carry on. One of the reasons I write is to find out what would happen if the world falls in. I question that and write it out and get caught up in the story.

RW: One of the charges that has been made against you by some white Australians is that you don't speak for the Aborigines because you are not an Aborigine. How would you deal with this charge? Do you feel that you have the authority to write the aboriginal stories and books that you write?

BW: I am not in the political field; I'm not standing for election. I have the right, my own soul duty to tell what I feel. I have gone through experiences; I have had to tell about my wife, my children. My main reason for writing has been to look into my own life and at the lives of those affected by my own life. Once a man reviewed a book of mine in the *London Times Book Review* and he accused me of exploiting Aborigines. Now, when I came to Australia the aboriginal society was disintegrating and I witnessed my own tragedy. By sheer luck, I was saved. Am I not entitled to look and to try to understand why these things have happened? Whatever has happened to Aborigines, it has happened because of British and European colonization of this land. To read this remark about me in a London paper is very distressing. Here in Australia, I am accused, I think, because of a guilt complex that is in the mind of many white Australians. It is very clear that something wrong has been done to the Aborigines, and people confuse me with the evil that has been done. If you look at what I have taken out of my aboriginal experience, you will see that I have taken nothing but tragedy. I write books which are sad, which are depressing, which are not comforting to read. I've had to persuade publishers to publish the material. It's not as if I were writing best-sellers about sharks or something like that. I've had letters from American editors saying that they've had enough tragedy from Africa, from at home; that people don't want to read about such tragic things as have happened to the Aborigines. And, too, oral literature is not popular.

RW: You feel that your books are recordings of oral history?

BW: I have taken them from that background. It is part of my own experience as well. I could not write about cricket or racehorses or that sort of thing.

RW: Your own experience of being a tribal member gives you authority to write about aboriginal experience, doesn't it?

BW: I entered into a tribal relationship, where if a family calls, you go. You realize that your own family has six new members because one of your relatives has died, maybe someone whom you met along the way. You feel a new responsibility for the new larger family because you are bound to that tradition. How I can be in this situation and be deprived of having the right to write about it, I don't know. Even if I did not have these ties to the Aborigines, there is something called creative freedom. I am allowed to write about Hellenics, Vikings—why am I not allowed to write about Aborigines? Surely I am allowed to write stories about anything.

RW: Do you identify at all with Colin Johnson or Sally Morgan or Archie Weller, the best known of the contemporary aboriginal writers?

BW: Each Aborigine has his own area. The older-generation Aborigines who were writing were to me closer to their own culture. The younger writers seem more divorced from their culture, as if it were not worthwhile. When he first began to publish, it seemed that Colin Johnson was writing as a white man. You couldn't tell that he was an Aborigine. Now he seems to be looking more to his aboriginal background and this is a positive change. Archie Weller seems to me to be the most promising; given the time and opportunity, he will probably be a great writer. He has maintained close ties to his aboriginal background.

RW: Have you had any association with any of the aboriginal writers?

BW: Of the ones you mentioned, I know Archie Weller. I was writer in residence at the Koorie Aboriginal Research Center at Monash University. Dr. Eve Fesl, the director, invited me there to help inspire the young Aborigines to become interested in writing.

RW: Would you say that the Aborigines who might know about your work would not be offended that you are doing this writing?

BW: Let me say this, Dr. Fesl, who is the head of the whole aboriginal community in Victoria, launched all three of my books jointly with the Aboriginal Advancement League.

RW: So, as far as you know, any Australian complaints about your interpretation of aboriginal culture have come from whites?

BW: Yes. A lot of trouble began for me after I mounted an exhibition of photographs which I took in the bush showing the condition of the Aborigines displaced by uranium mining and British nuclear testing. The pictures show how the Aborigines suffered from nuclear testing and from the mining which disturbed the tribal life. When the first Land Rights Bill came up, it was to be debated in Parliament in Canberra. An officer from the library had seen my collection of photographs at the Australian National University and wrote asking if he could have the collection on loan for Parliamentarians to see the impact of the industrial development on tribal life. I mounted the exhibit thinking naïvely that the Parliamentarians could learn something. Of course, they knew everything they wanted to know. The same day the exhibition was mounted, it was ordered taken down. The man who was the chief librarian in the Parliament Library attacked me in the press, saying that my pictures distorted the facts.

RW: How were the Aborigines affected by the nuclear testing?

BW: The authorities cleared a huge area, probably bigger than England. Many tribes were shipped from their tribal place to the far end of the country, thousands of miles away. Then they had to make their way back. The Aborigines were mixed in camps; they spoke different languages, had different customs. The only way many of them could communicate with each other was through some kind of broken English. This was the first time the people were taken from the land in such large numbers.

RW: Were Aborigines contaminated by nuclear fallout?

BW: Yes. Supposedly the land was cleared, but it wasn't completely. Aborigines were found camping in nuclear bomb craters. No one really knows how many Aborigines have died from the testing. No accurate records were kept.

RW: How long did the nuclear testing take place?

BW: It stretched over about ten years. They decided to call it something other than nuclear testing. They called it nuclear trials, something like this. Strangely, not much was written about this at the time. I feel that I have paid a price for writing about it, but in my chest I feel that I have coughed out something that was clotting for so long. I don't regret writing about it, because it would have been on my conscience if I had not.

RW: Your outspokenness wouldn't have anything to do with the attitude of the literary establishment toward you, would it? You've had grants from the Literature Board.

BW: No, nothing personal, not from other writers. But I still have books that have not been published here. I do think the publishers are aware of the politics of what I've done and have taken it into consideration in their attitude toward publishing my work.

RW: Do you think your wife and children might have died from drinking water contaminated by nuclear testing?

BW: Uranium was mined in that area, but I cannot say.

RW: You call your three novels your Nuclear Trilogy. This explains the very personal interest you have in the stories you tell, doesn't it?

BW: Yes.

RW: Your style of writing has been compared to both Rousseau and Kafka, in some stories poetic and romantic, in others surreal. Would you talk about the way you write?

BW: Both of those writers the critics have spoken of are European writers; they are products of Europe. I don't regard myself as a European writer. My roots are in oral literature. I don't think I write in any genre; whatever style develops comes as I explore the relationship between man and the ancient culture, the preindustrial culture. The aboriginal culture kept regenerating for forty thousand years; it always looked fresh; it never entered a creative crisis because the telling of stories was a part of the necessary process of educating the young: hunting, saving the water hole, explaining the essence of life. While in Europe one could be a businessman and never read a single book, the aboriginal literature was spoken and a part of daily life. In my style, I try to re-create the texture of the aboriginal view of the world. In *Walg,* for example, I am trying to picture a world with a balance between man and nature and I am showing the world as changed by the white man. I try also to show the mystical, or the mystical possibilities. When Alan Paton read *Walg,* he wrote me that through the whole book he was prepared for some great tragedy, which would have been logical, but he was very happy to find out that it didn't end that way. In my work I move away from Western reality, and the more I move away from that reality the more creative and comfortable I feel. Reality in my experience is a dreadful thing; it is a policeman coming into my house and seizing my manuscript and destroying it. That happened to me at my place in the bush not very long ago. If you can move yourself in your writing from this kind of reality into the mystical, you leave yourself a hope. It is a place in which it is possible to live; otherwise, you just close in on yourself. Writing is for me a part of survival.

RW: If someone asked you to say in a sentence or two what your books are about, what would you say?

BW: I would say the searching for the essence of life, searching for a cause for the things that happen on the earth, for a way to go on living.

RW: Why do you insert so many aboriginal words in your writing?

BW: Somehow they come; I feel that they should be there. Culture is setting the character. The aboriginal words take you from your accustomed world. Most of the stories I tell, I would like to tell orally, but I must work with print. The few aboriginal words that I use remind the reader that the story comes from elsewhere.

RW: Seeing the aboriginal word on the page does something to our eyesight and to our hearing as well.

BW: Yes. The sheer presence of the word is a reminder. I often start a story from one aboriginal word or from a few of them. It says to the reader that I am going to tell a story from a far, troubled land and that I am going to tell it from the heart. The aboriginal culture in modern times has been reduced to almost nothing; here at least a few words are kept. It's a small contribution, but at least the words are there.

RW: You were first published in Europe, with the help of Simone de Beauvoir. Alan Paton in his foreword to your first book, *The Track to Bralgu,* wrote, "These stories are harsh, bitter, magical . . . they open up a new world." Would you say a few words about this first collection of stories?

BW: The stories are about the collapse of tribal culture. They illustrate how it would be for an old man from the bush to pass his culture on. The only escape route in this disintegrating world is the path, or the track from this world to the next, which is the track to Bralgu. The teller of each story follows this track. When an Aborigine dies, his spirit divides into three parts. One goes to Bralgu to join the ancestors; one sits on the bottom of the totemic water hole and waits to be reborn; the third, the Mogwori, wanders around the tribal country. *Marhgit* is another book following the collapse of a family; it has been written, but not published. Marhgit is trying to heal the soul of the departed people.

RW: Let's talk about your Nuclear Trilogy: the three novels *Walg, Karan,* and *Gabo Djara. Walg* is set in the Northern Territory. When the book opens, the nuclear holocaust is already in the past, isn't it?

BW: Yes, we are already in the age of genetic engineering. *Walg* is about a tribal woman who hopes to regenerate her tribe, which has been decimated by the mining of uranium. She sets out on an epic journey to travel back to her country because, according to the tribal belief, a child should only be born in the mother's own country. By the time she reaches her land she is to bear a child, but she finds that her country has been wiped out by mining.

RW: This first novel is dedicated to your wife.

BW: Yes, the beliefs of her tribe are shown more in this book than in the others. Also, there is more tribal poetry; it was my first novel and probably it is more lyrical than my other books. The female character thinks about initiation, the beauty of the country; she wants to start the tribe again. Compared to *Karan,* even the setting is more lyrical. *Karan* deals with the second phase of the nuclear tragedy: nuclear testing. Most of the people in the novel didn't know anything about the white civilization before the testing occurred.

RW: *Karan* is the story of the displacement of the tribes through nuclear testing. In this story, white men are trying to put tribal culture into a computer. What does the computer symbolize?

BW: The computer is more symbolic than real; it represents the whole apparatus of white administration, from the Parliament who passed all the laws controlling the aboriginal culture to the individuals who implemented the laws. It all appears quite democratic as debated and decided in Parliament, but it comes down to something very cruel, because one culture is eating another.

RW: The protagonist in the first novel is a female, and the protagonist in the second is an aboriginal male who has himself been almost consumed by the white culture. He is an aboriginal acting as if he were a white man as the novel begins, but as the novel ends he regains a part of his original identity. Is this right?

BW: He serves his white masters, but there is a boundary, a limit as to how far he will go. He steps back. With some Aborigines it happens early; with others it happens later; but it is a real occurrence among the Aborigines. In the beginning of *Karan,* the man awakens one morning and finds his chest covered with tribal initiation markings. This turns him toward his interior life. His conscience starts troubling him and he starts questioning the system within which he is working.

RW: What does "Karan" mean?

BW: Soul, or spirit.

RW: In your most recent novel, *Gabo Djara,* you write, "The tribal man exists no longer and the white world has descended into chaos . . . this creates the need for fantasy." Would you talk about the novel and its fantasy?

BW: *Gabo Djara* is about the world that comes after the mining and the dropping of the bombs. It is the period of radioactive pollution. Gabo Djara is a product of the radiation that has spread all over the world.

RW: Gabo Djara is a huge green ant who goes all over the world spreading radioactivity. He has breakfast with the Queen; he visits the President of the United States; he goes to Parliament House in Canberra. Where did you get the idea to make him a comic figure?

BW: These people are all in some sense evil. They've all in some direct or passive way had something to do with atomic fallout. Gabo Djara is their conscience. If this green ant from the tribal bush knocks on their door and troubles their yellow cake, then they have to think about what has happened. I decided on a bit of a comic treatment, but at Gabo Djara's time in history nothing can be changed. He is comic because this is the way the European would see him, but he is a tribal spiritual figure and to the tribe his status as a spiritual leader is recognizable. Because they recognize him, they would never disturb his sacred sites; they would never mine. But the book is supposed to be seen from the white man's angle, not from the ant's, because it represents the white man's conscience. All is done; the mining is completed.

RW: You call this work a nuclear trilogy, but in fact you are writing another book which will move beyond the trilogy. What is the next step?

BW: Originally, I meant to have a nuclear cycle. There is a physical nuclear cycle which would occur in nature and there is in aboriginal literature the tribal cycle. The poetry comes in cycles—birth, growth, death. I don't yet have the concept for this next novel clearly in mind, but the story might actually come in time before *Gabo Djara,* rather than after it. I might have in it some autobiographical material.

RW: Do you think you will continue in your writing to express yourself from an Aborigine's point of view, or might your fictional stance become that of a European-Australian?

BW: I write because I have to answer certain things for myself. I am interested in the spiritual in the aboriginal culture. I don't think that there's anything in the white society that I am really passionate about.

FAY ZWICKY

Isaac Babel's Fiddle (poems), 1975
Quarry: A Selection of Western Australian Poetry (ed.), 1981
Journeys: Four Australian Women Poets, (ed.), 1982
Kaddish and Other Poems, 1982
Hostages (short stories), 1983
The Lyre in the Pawnshop (essays), 1986
Ask Me (poems), 1990

was born in Melbourne in 1933 and educated at the University of Melbourne. Trained as a professional pianist, she played the concert circuit in Australia and abroad before turning to writing and teaching. She was a Senior Lecturer in English at the University of Western Australia for a number of years until her retirement in 1988. Noted for her sharp, frank literary criticism, Fay Zwicky has done critical work for the Australian Broadcasting Company and has been writer in residence at numerous universities in Australia and in the United States. Her publications include criticism, fiction, poetry, and two anthologies of Australian poetry, which she edited. The following interview occurred in her apartment in Melbourne in 1987 and in her home in Perth in 1989.

INTERVIEW

RW: What is it like to be a writer in Australia?

FZ: Australia is a very unfriendly society for writers.

RW: More unfriendly than America?

FZ: In Australia there is a vast difference between people who want to live in a sort of natural spontaneous way and people who want to keep in step. It really goes back to the individual versus the collective. The bureaucratic state mechanisms that are now coming into play sort of squelch people together. I think this is getting worse. The writer, particularly the poet, is a very threatened species in Australia. In America the history of the poet isn't too good either; just look at the degree of self-destruction, alcoholism, suicide among American poets. Pretty bad.

RW: Why does the writer in Australia have to bother with what society or the government thinks?

FZ: You are a member of society. You have to exist in it. In a country of only 16 million you are aware of other people. You have to be. In America there is such a huge population that I don't think people are affected in the same sort of way at all. If you have 250 million people and you have writers all over, in different places, different regions, with different forums for their work, they know that at least somewhere along the line is a supporting group. But here, the terrible thing is that it comes down to an incestuous collective of a very small nature, simply because of the numbers. Everybody knows everybody. You can never read a piece by an Australian writer without knowing who wrote it. You know the person, so consequently your reading is always going to be colored to some extent by knowing the person. I don't care what anyone says; it's impossible to be a dispassionate reader of the work of someone you know. You can't, you just can't. I've tried and it doesn't work. So, in effect, it means that the writers who are reading each other are in fact living like a family, absorbing the family gossip. That's why it's imperative to keep out of it. Now, if you keep out of it, you are condemned to a double loneliness. You are kept right out of it. I know a lot of writers who enjoy each other's company simply because it makes them feel good to know that other people are doing the same thing. Now, once upon a time that would have meant something to me. It doesn't now, because I don't care anymore.

RW: It seems to me that in America it's not just the writer, it's anyone who is different from the norm who is cut off. Isn't alienation non-national?

FZ: There are a lot of norms in America to which you may or may not conform. It's hard to explain the difference here, but there is a difference and I think it has something to do with the fact that we pretend to a unity in this country that we don't have. Regionally we're terribly different. Each city stowed around the coast is very different from the others.

RW: You grew up and were educated in Melbourne, but you've lived much of your life in Perth. Perth is 2,500 miles across the desert from the centers of population—Melbourne and Sydney. The experience of living in Western Australia is very different from living on the more populated East Coast. Would you talk about what it is like for you as a writer living in such an isolated spot?

FZ: I've lived thirty years in Western Australia. It's a very resourceful place in its way. Because it is so isolated from everywhere else it tends to lean inward, and people are self-generating to a degree, which means that they each within their own little confines have established their own particular world which is not exclusively linked to the Australia that an Eastern States writer knows as a kind of coherent unit. It's interesting that Western Australia has produced a lot of individualistic writers, and I don't think they tell you about the place so much as about the isolation of the place. Starting with Randolph Stow, for example, one can see the silence in his novels and in his poetry. The leaning toward Taoism in his work is a very natural inclination in a place where silence is a natural state. If you live in a pressured city like Melbourne or Sydney, silence is a different component altogether. But silence here is a reality; it's a positive entity. It's not something that is a break between noise; it is a condition that you live with.

RW: You came, then, to the theme of silence in your work from your experience?

FZ: Yes. Living here has kept me out of touch with a kind of dialogue that keeps you checked and balanced against the general cultural patterns. Western Australia gives you an enormous, limitless freedom to speculate. Very often you are the only point of reference, which can be dangerous; it encourages grandiosity. It can give you illusions that what you are thinking is shared by everybody. Elizabeth Jolley's work illustrates something else about living in Western Australia. Elizabeth is writing about her experience, but it is amazing how the setting of that experience is peculiarly English. There is a kind of retention of the past possible to a migrant in Western Australia which I don't think would stay so firmly embedded in a state which would dissipate that experience. If you lived in Melbourne or Sydney you'd have the past pretty well diffused because the present is so immediate. Here, because of this quietness, this stillness, this possibility of meditative contemplation, you are invaded by past voices, past experience, to a degree that you might not be in a more stimulating place, and I don't mean stimulating in a positive sense. You are not knocked about by external circumstance in the same way. You make your life here; it doesn't make you to the same extent.

RW: Is this one of the reasons that your work draws more from the Western literary heritage for allusion or reference than it draws from your Australian experiences or inherited Australian experiences?

FZ: Let me put it this way, when you come to a strange place you often cling to what matters to your identity most. You hang on to it urgently. In looking back over my thirty years here, I have clung with great urgency to what I have felt was my inheritance. At the same time, in later years I have become more aware of the aboriginal experience and of how ill placed we are here to maintain with such passion the Western tradition. Also, our closeness to Asia has always impressed me as a way of breaking down those rigid adherences to the West. This place has offered me the chance to be rash or to be wise, and I can't tell whether I've ended up on one side or the other. You can call it defeat or you can call it acceptance, but I appreciate silence now more than I ever did.

RW: Most of the Australian literature of the nineteenth and early twentieth century was dominated by males writing for males. How has that pattern affected women writers in Australia?

FZ: It depends on when you were born. My generation was born to feel that Australian literature didn't exist at all. We didn't read it. We knew a few isolated writers; they were nearly all men. I didn't meet an Australian woman writer in book form until I was nineteen. I met Henry Handel Richardson in my second year at the university, and I read *Maurice Guest* and was astonished that an Australian woman, even though she had to call herself Henry, was writing this wonderful book. I thought it was one of the most fantastic, romantic books I'd ever read. It also spelled out the conditions of expatriation; it spelled out the longing I had to go to Europe, to be in some place where people seemed alive to music, to art, which was in fact denying what was actually present in my own childhood, because those things were there. But I wanted a bigger community.

RW: Men no longer dominate fiction writing in Australia, do they?

FZ: There are a number of women writing; whether in fact their experience is meaningful to men, I couldn't tell you. It's not meaningful to me. I call it the whinge novel.

RW: What do you mean?

FZ: Whine, gripe, carp, misery, poor me. Victim literature. I can't stand it, and there's a lot of it. There are plenty of women saying, "My experience is so wretched, I want to be heard. Listen to me." You could call it the upsurge of the first waves of oppression.

RW: Are you suggesting that most white female writing in Australia today is whinge writing?

FZ: A lot of it is.

RW: Do you include yourself in that?
FZ: No.
RW: Who are some writers you would not include?
FZ: I would not include Jessica Anderson. I would not include Beverley Farmer. I would not include those who are skillful enough to keep the whinge out, even though you know it is there somewhere. I don't want to read about people's gropings in bed with the end of it being that the woman is the victim. I get tired of the stuff.
RW: Are you saying that in the woman writer's movement from silence into articulation there is an initial stage that must be passed through?
FZ: I am suggesting that it is possible that everyone moves at different paces and that I really don't want to be bothered with stuff that once used to be put in a bottom drawer, but now because of the publication subsidies, it is permissible to publish. Also, not only because of subsidy, but because of a climate that encourages this self-revelation. There is a fine line between self-dramatization and self-examination, and what I find disappointing is that self-examination which can lead to great insight, enlightenment, illumination, say in the work of Jessica Anderson or Beverley Farmer, when she is writing about Greece, can lead to exhibitionism which you get in something like Germaine Greer's recent book, *Daddy, I Hardly Knew You*. I think there is a time in every country's literary development when a recording has to take place of certain features of identity. Now, Australia is taking a very long time to find its identity, which means that at several points there is going to be an upsurge to define what we are, how we come across to each other, to the rest of the world. It's no accident a playwright like David Williamson, who is in fact depicting some very basic rituals in our society, is very popular. People love to go to see what they look like. When I went to see *The Club*, whole football clubs were filling the theaters. This has little to do with literature or art. It has to do with a people in transition trying to find out who they are. Their writers will naturally define them for them. They are turning to their writers for that, but they are not turning to them for the reason I will turn to Tolstoy or Melville. There is a difference in how you read and what you are reading for. I am not saying that everyone should read the same way I do; I am saying that what I am missing in the cultural dialogue about writing is some kind of deep philosophical insight into what makes people tick, why do they exist, why are they here. I don't really want to go over surface rituals again and again. That's just a private stage I'm at; that's not to say writers are not correct to write in this way, because many people haven't been through those dig-

gings and forays that I have already made. Perhaps I am too impatient; perhaps I want our writers to jump ahead too fast.

RW: National identity is a big issue in Australia. Why are Australians still so concerned with their convict past, the Aborigines, with their own place in the world?

FZ: Australia is very late repairing the damage to Aborigines. We are as late proportionately as America was in dealing with its Indians. It's a question of all the unseen and unspoken things that are hanging around our history. People are trying to define something because it has never really been spoken. Don't forget we're still an appendage of Britain. We still have a Governor-General approved by Britain. It's all very well to talk about freedom and independence, but America has it, and Australia hasn't. That's something that has always rankled in the national mind. To an American it looks funny to be clamoring about our identity, but it's still an issue when you're not independent, you're still not a republic. And then again you realize that, stuck out here, in the middle of nowhere, we are still identity-less in the sense that we're not sure how close we should be to Asia, which is our neighbor, or how we should relate to European powers. That's where the trouble really lies in Australia, in not knowing where we belong. This landmass that's stuck right out in the middle of nowhere. In my view, Australia has every reason in looking to Asia. It's a much more viable interest. On the other hand, I can see equally our cultural roots with Europe. We're stuck in this dilemma. You find writers trying to use an Asian setting. I'm thinking of Christopher Koch and Robert Drewe. They drop their characters down in Asia. It's clear they're feeling some need to link Australian experience with what is geographically closer.

RW: In your own work you've looked outside Australia, particularly in your poetic expressions of an interest in classical myths. You have interpreted your characters by playing them through versions of myth. Is this right?

FZ: Yes. But it has been an unconscious choice; characters in myth have been the figures of my imagination since I was a very young child. To me the notion of myth is not something separate from my life. I grew up reading Greek myths and legends as though their figures were people next door. There was drama in them and this was what I felt I was missing. I liked the idea of interaction and conflict and people developing out of conflict, the notion of the interactions of opposites and how this produces the most interesting tensions and what grows out of it and what you learn from these tensions. In Australia this seemed to be what was missing to me when I was growing up; there was too much of the bland surface of life. I think many young people see this as the case now. But each generation responds differently. My generation has gone through periods of intense withdrawal from what is going on at the moment and for good reason. We feel that what we learned and struggled for and hoped for has gone for nothing.

RW: Because of what?

FZ: Because this country is rather given to the unexamined life. People are content to fix their attention on getting richer, getting more of everything, publishing more, reading more. But what are they doing with what they publish and read? I still look for that magic moment when somebody's published words come out at me and say, "This is how it is," and I say, "Yes, this is how it is." I don't want art as entertainment. I am looking for someone who introduces me to an idea and lets the idea develop and grow, be it through character or philosophical speculation, something that tells me that we are not just here as hedonistic climbers on the beach. I don't want to know about it. I've had that. I've seen it.

RW: Because of grants to writers from the Literature Board and subsidies to publishers, it has been said that almost anyone in Australia can get into print. As a critic, would you talk about the truth of this statement and its implications?

FZ: I believe there is a lot of truth in it. The Literature Board has done a very good job in helping to stimulate interest in Australian writing; there is no doubt that this had to be done. It's been valuable for many reasons; it's made people aware that there are writers, that books don't just spring from nothing, that there are people behind it who have to live. I also think that because of the lack of critical premise established in our intellectual life it's very hard to get some sort of critical assessment of what really is worth publishing and reading. I would personally like to see the Board put more money into good editorial work in publishing houses; by that I mean people who would actually give the writers the kind of creative help which would enable them to become better writers. We need editors with vision. I don't see this in the publishing houses; I think this often accounts for material coming out very poorly edited, too prolix. It often comes out as if no editing has been done at all. Good editors can do marvels for writers.

RW: Does the problem of conformity that you spoke of carry over into publishing? You mentioned "joining the pack." What did you mean?

FZ: If you join the pack you write about what people are currently seeming to want to know about. What they want to know about isn't necessarily what you want to write about. You find publishers showing little enthusiasm for anything that isn't Anglo-Saxon, Celtic traditional pre-war social realism. You would never know, reading the canon of Australian literature, that there was any migrant literature at all. The vast influx of multicultural voices isn't being accommodated in what is called Australian literature. I don't believe that's right. There are a few exceptions, the Greek writers Angelo Loukakis, Antigone Kefala, George Papaellinas, for example, but there are so many others who don't even get looked at by publishers.

RW: If you look at a literary history of Australia it will cite the fifties, the early sixties as a period of movement away from social realism. The writers cited are, of course, White and Stow, perhaps a few others. What you are telling me is that . . .

FZ: Well, it's true that there are Australians trying to write in other directions. I'm not saying it's entirely one-way traffic, but it has still remained a limited sphere of experience, in other words, this landscape untainted by the coming of post-war displaced persons. This is what we have in large numbers, and very little accommodation to that fact is registered. They don't register the fact that we have in Melbourne a huge Greek community, the second-biggest Greek community of any place in the world. Fortunately, there are some Greek writers beginning to emerge. But they are not considered part of the mainstream. They are always "Greek writers." Yet they are Australians. In America, because its school system indoctrinates its newcomers very quickly into being Americans, you never feel that sense of difference. Everyone is American from the word go. They get the flag up; you learn the loyalty oath. People know from the moment they touch those shores that they are Americans. America sees to it that they are accommodated, whereas Australia still makes very little accommodation to the migrant. I think it's in spite of, rather than because of, that these people are accepted at all. It makes no sense the way people live here. If you go on public transport, every face you see registers another continent. There are a lot of Asian faces, a tremendous number of Southern European faces, Middle Eastern faces. Where are they represented? You can't tell me they haven't something to say about their experience here. The pace of change has been very rapid, perhaps too fast. People haven't been able to accommodate it. They can't cope with it. What they do is block it off and say, "Hang on, we want to define ourselves first; then we'll deal with you later." Well, how much later? Already the students within the university are students with Greek and Italian names. They are not just the Anglo-Saxon kids any longer.

RW: Counting yourself, this book contains interviews with sixteen Australian writers who have achieved various measures of national and international acclaim, yet in your book of collected essays, *The Lyre in the Pawnshop,* you lament that Australia has produced "no unashamed ego such as a Whitman, a Melville, a Faulkner." Why do you believe Australia has not produced such a writer?

FZ: This is a complicated issue. I think it goes back to our beginnings, that the diffidence, the uncertainty, the tenuous connection that European Australians have had with this land has inhibited us to a degree. Either writers become overly strident in their proclamation of a national identity or they withdraw and look inside and turn to more quietistic cultures for a confirmation of identity. It has to do with time. We have been here two hundred years, which is a very short time in terms of growing a national identity. People have been transported away from their roots so far that they naturally will have trouble assigning themselves some sort of mythological place in a creation which, as one grows more and more conscious, belongs to someone else. It is the feeling of displacing someone. Fundamentally, I think Australians are very tenuously based in this country, even though they cling, and rightly so, to their Western traditions. At the same time, one is conscious all the while that there are the aboriginal traditions that have been displaced in order to keep a dominance. The conflict is there all the time. Where is the great upsurge of a literary consciousness which is complex enough to tell us that we are presumptuous and to say that this presumptuousness and self-destruction is at the root of the national heart? There are upsurges of activism in this country, but no one is transmitting this in literature. Writers are not telling us this. They are telling us how wonderful this country is, sometimes with irony, I know. But generally if this sort of truth comes out in literature at all, it comes out in a way that I feel preached at. I don't see the tragic vision coming out as it did with the great American writers. This is what I feel we are missing, particularly in fiction. We need a writer with a prophetic vision.

RW: In this part of the twentieth century, so does America. Perhaps this lack in both countries has to do with the complexities of the times.

FZ: Perhaps, but let's go back to myth, our Gallipoli myth which tells of a golden period of youth who went to war and rolled on the beaches of Gallipoli. It's amazing the way we perpetrate that golden glow around these episodes which were in fact horrendous; they destroyed our best young men. Why is it that we don't see the dark underbelly, or we won't show it? This is what I am trying to say. It's not that it doesn't exist, but the general way of placing it in the cultural canon is to place it in a romantic fantasy of some golden time. We insist on the notion that we are a kindly, decent people. Surely there is enough we've done that tells us we are not that all the time. We have had lessons, but they have not gone home. The lesson has not registered. We've been party to power while pretending we were doves. All this good humor, this camaraderie, this macho drinking is an evasion of the fact that we are capable of evil. Australians believe that everything evil happens elsewhere. Nothing evil ever happens here. But we, too, participate in the evil of the human heart. That is what Melville was trying to tell the Americans. This is the kind of writer I'm looking for. We should be chastened. People do tell us about our darkness from time to time in works of history, Robert Hughes' *The Fatal Shore,* for example, but they do not tell us this in drama or in fiction.

RW: Australia does not now, nor has it ever considered itself a religious nation, so the spiritual quest has never been a part of the national identity, has it?

FZ: No. Again it has to do with our beginnings. America started as a theocratic state; our lot was dumped. The brutality of our beginning was not conducive to religion. With the start the convicts had here you'd give up on God quickly. I think of it as our having wandered out of the earshot of God. In Western Australia there are no seasons. Only wet and dry. Seldom are there clouds. The sky is an endless, relentless electric blue. The sun will knock a spiritual awareness right out of you. If you have a cloudless blue sky where there is no drama in it, it colors your inner responses. How could you write a *Wuthering Heights*? What contrasts are possible here when there are no contrasts? Who thinks of evil when the sky is blue?

RW: What about the need for a writer to leave Australia? I don't find expatriation as common a theme in contemporary Australian literature as it once was.

FZ: Put it this way. The people who have chosen to expatriate themselves clearly have done so because of some difference they felt from the rest of their community. I can only suggest that the people that are currently writing within Australia are people who have agreed, unconsciously if you like, to fit in with what Australia seems to expect them to be, to record what Australia wants them to record. In other words, there are still some people living here who are not a part of that ethos but who stay here in spite of, not because of. You can say that they are people who are psychic expatriates even though they live here.

RW: Is now the longing to go home more a psychological longing for an internal home than a physical longing for somewhere else?

FZ: I don't think it has anything to do with longing to go home physically. I don't think anyone knows where home is anymore.

RW: In the nineteenth century and in the early part of this century, Australians knew home as another place: England.

FZ: Well, maybe that's why some wanted to go. There's Henry Handel Richardson who went abroad because she was sent abroad to study music, and it just so happened that, in line with her interest with European literature, she found living abroad obviously congenial to her temperament. In Australia she was always the square peg in the round hole. She clearly felt, just as I do when I go abroad, more at home. It's something to do with a kind of embarrassment. Being visible in a country that you are not comfortable in. Henry Handel Richardson had a marvelous description of her embarrassment at playing the piano in front of people. It was not that she feared that she couldn't play, it was the censure of all those eyes boring in on her. In other words, her shyness of temperament—I think that goes for Randolph Stow and a lot of other people—was better accommodated in anonymity elsewhere, whereas here differences in temperament are not publicly accommodated. Some writers need to belong to the pack and others need to have privacy, and the only way to get privacy is to go away from the country that presses in on you because it is demanding something from you. It's like living with a family. You've got to get out of it.

RW: I am still asking whether Australian artists have grown out of the notion that home is geographically somewhere else?

FZ: I think a lot of Australians now don't think like that. The younger ones. Don't forget that it's a generational thing. For example, my generation and Stow's generation came of a very deprived environment. It's hard to explain. *Now* it's all right to be a painter, it's all right to be a writer, a musician. You're not paid well, but at least society says you have a place. It's not a very comfortable place, and the more critical you are of society, the less comfortable the place will get. But at least there is an opening for you. But when we were growing up—well, even then there were a few places where you were encouraged; there was the odd teacher who encouraged you, and if you were lucky you had a parent who encouraged you, but it was not an encouraging environment for the creative mind. It was a flat, gray, puritanical, extremely repressive environment. It was protestantism at its worst. I've written about it in my book of essays (*The Lyre in the Pawnshop*). I thought growing up here was an exercise in repression. I never felt I existed as myself here. I was always flattened into the ground, from teachers, for example, who cut out all your adjectives. That kind of pre-war repression affected everything. A little example: color. Do you see how colorful clothes are today? I don't think I ever saw people in bright-colored clothes when I was younger. Women, when they hit what was regarded as maturity, which could have been thirty-five, turned into matrons. My mother at thirty-five would have been regarded as a staid woman. Not that she was, but women had to dress accordingly, to behave accordingly. I think my mother when she was seventy enjoyed more freedom than she ever did when she was a young woman. My memory of Melbourne as a young person was gray. I saw it as all gray. When I was in the American Midwest I saw it the same way. I wrote a narrative poem, "Mid Western Wife." The woman is coming toward the end of her life and suddenly she sees everything in gray. What does it all mean? Where's the color? Where's the life? This was why English people were always going to Italy, because that was where they found life. Not at home. Not in the Anglo-Saxon culture. I love looking at color on others. But my temperament doesn't fit with that. In Melbourne I still don't feel like wearing color.

RW: There has been expressed in earlier literature a longing to go where culture is. Is the contemporary Australian writer still pulled by that need?

FZ: I don't think realistically that's true. I don't believe for a moment that so-called culture (if you are talking about art galleries, opera houses, etc.) is impoverished in that way for us. I think, on the contrary, we've a plethora of stuff. The people who say there is no culture here are simply talking through their hats. And all the great artists and orchestras eventually visit here, so you can't say we're deprived in that way. It might have been true before the war; it's not true now. It's not the deficiency of culture. You can't tell me that all these people rushing hither and yon in Europe are going to art galleries and theaters and concert halls. They're not. If they are writers, they are sitting in their room and writing and it doesn't matter where one is. But somehow or other anonymity is useful. I know, for instance, when I visited Sumner Lock Elliott in New York, he was living quite monastically in a little room and writing about his Australian boyhood. I remember thinking, isn't this fascinating that you can only see your own country when you're far from it. When you're in it you can't see it because you're pressured by everything you don't want to know about. To me, a country is simply the extension of a family; it's an embarrassment because of all the things that rile you. It means, in fact, that you have a deeper allegiance to it than you know. It doesn't mean you reject it. People are so naïve. They think you are rejecting your nationality. Look at James Joyce. He had to leave Ireland, but in Trieste he was writing about it all the time. What kind of nonsense is it to say that you've rejected your country? You see it clearer. Joyce talked about an old sow eating her farrow; well, that's the way I feel about Australia. I feel eaten up here. And I love this country. I love the physical landscapes here. When I go away, the thing I desperately miss is the coastline I live near. The Indian Ocean. I wouldn't trade that for anything, not all the beautiful beaches near San Francisco or St. Tropez. Nothing in exchange for this coastline. To me the physical nature of this country is the thing that is always in my mind; it nurtures me, keeps me. But the people, no. Because the people have done terrible things to this country. The coming of man has practically killed off what is good and beautiful. In Tasmania there is beautiful forest land and everywhere you go you hear the chain saw ringing in the forest. They're hacking down the forests as fast as they can. How can you like people who do that? How can you possibly claim any kinship with them? I know it's not the general rule. I know there are a lot of people living behind their walls that I know nothing about who have the same feelings, but they're not coming out and saying these things. They are not the people who make the decisions. To me, in many ways Australia is a dream gone sour. Economics has taken over. I sound like I'm proposing Noble Savagery; I'm not. But I am saying there are people like Stow and other sensitive people who have given up finally on trying to make some rapport with a place which is so alien. I mean, I'm sure that Stow's living in Constable country in England was important to him, because there was a country which looked relatively unchanged since Constable painted it. No matter how peculiar the English might be, they at least have a reverence for their heritage. They don't knock it over. At least when an Englishman goes home, he can say his mother's house is still standing. I go home and find my mother's house gone. And every tree on the block gone. How can you love a country in which people do this kind of thing? They don't respect age, the past, traditions. It's not a yearning for home. Artists are immediately displaced. There is no home. But they know damn well they had better find some place where they can make some peace with their environment. Stow has always been a sort of paradigm of the Australian who must leave. And I'm sure he deeply loves his country. The novels tell me that. You get the sort of naïve nationalists who say, "If you don't like it here, why don't you go somewhere else?" but they don't even read the message that is coming through. People have such high ideals for this country that they can't bear to see it ruined, and these days that is what you're watching. How do you live with people who have learned nothing? Stow is a writer who is a perfect example of someone who's had to make his peace with wherever he's been and so England suits him. Not, I think, because it's any sort of sentimental view of "home" in the old snobbish way.

RW: If I said "going home" to you, what would you say? Where would you go? Is there a home for you, or is it a psychological place where you reside wherever you are?

FZ: I don't think I have the fixed certainty of a home anymore. As far as I'm concerned, I left this country in the same spirit that James Joyce left Ireland. I will fly by those nets: family, religion, nationality. All had to go in order to be rediscovered. If you're going to be a writer, you have to be purged of allegiances to false ideals. After that, you get to the stage where you just look from a distance at everything and say, "Well, what's home?" Home is where you make it. It could be anywhere. It doesn't matter. I don't believe that I could be more or less unhappy anywhere. I'll be what I am wherever I am. I'll take with me whatever burdens or whatever lightness I carry with me.

RW: You are known in Australia for the quality of your poetry and your short stories and for your tough-minded criticism. You hold yourself and the Australian writer to the highest international standards. What positive thing can be said for contemporary Australian literature?

FZ: I am very impressed with the sheer energy of the quality of Australian writing. I don't set out to knock it. There is a lot in it that is very valuable in defining the present state of affairs in Australia. I am not saying that I personally get nourishment from it. But it has to exist, and I admire it at a distance for its energy, for its sheer impertinence, and for its attempt to carve out of very little substantial cultural underpinnings something that is unique and fresh.

INDEX